Naked Objects

Naked Objects

Richard Pawson

and

Robert Matthews

JOHN WILEY & SONS, LTD

© Copyright Richard Pawson and Robert Matthews 2002.

Published by
John Wiley & Sons Ltd, The Atrium, Southern Gate, Chichester,
West Sussex PO19 8SQ, England

Telephone (+44) 1243 779777

Email (for orders and customer service enquiries): cs-books@wiley.co.uk
Visit our Home Page on www.wileyeurope.com or www.wiley.com

An electronic version of this work is available at www.nakedobjects.org

This publication is designed to provide accurate and authoritative information in regard to
the subject matter covered. It is sold on the understanding that the Publisher is not engaged
in rendering professional services. If professional advice or other expert assistance is
required, the services of a competent professional should be sought.

Other Wiley Editorial Offices

John Wiley & Sons Inc., 111 River Street, Hoboken, NJ 07030, USA

Jossey-Bass, 989 Market Street, San Francisco, CA 94103-1741, USA

Wiley-VCH Verlag GmbH, Boschstr. 12, D-69469 Weinheim, Germany

John Wiley & Sons Australia Ltd, 33 Park Road, Milton, Queensland 4064, Australia

John Wiley & Sons (Asia) Pte Ltd, 2 Clementi Loop #02-01, Jin Xing Distripark, Singapore 129809

John Wiley & Sons Canada Ltd, 22 Worcester Road, Etobicoke, Ontario, Canada M9W 1L1

01-06-04

Library of Congress Cataloging-in-Publication Data

(applied for)

British Library Cataloguing in Publication Data

A catalogue record for this book is available from the British Library

ISBN 0-470-84420-5

Typeset in Maiandra by Laserwords Private Limited, Chennai, India
Printed and bound in Italy by Conti Tipocolor SpA, Firenze
This book is printed on acid-free paper responsibly manufactured from sustainable forestry
in which at least two trees are planted for each one used for paper production.

Contents

In anything at all, perfection is finally attained
not when there is no longer anything to add
but when there is no longer anything to take away,
when a body has been stripped down to its nakedness.

Antoine de Saint-Exupéry in *Wind, Sand and Stars*

Introduction

Most people who believe they are doing object-oriented design and development are doing no such thing, because they are ignoring the most important principle of object-orientation. We describe that principle as 'behavioural completeness': an object should completely model the behaviour of the thing that it represents. Instead, most people continue to design business systems that separate procedure from data, albeit dressed up in the language and technology of object-orientation.

Why is this distinction important? Because behavioural completeness is the key to realising the principal benefit of object-orientation: the ability to cope with unforeseen changes in requirements.

We suggest that even where there is a will to design behaviourally-complete objects, there are subtle forces that push back towards data and procedure. We have identified five such forces:

- Business process orientation
- Task-optimised user interfaces
- Use-case driven methodologies
- The Model-View-Controller pattern
- Component-based software development.

The problem is that not only are all five considered to be best practices, but they also have the status of sacred cows amongst the software development community. We are not suggesting that any of them is itself a bad thing, but we are suggesting that they hinder good object-oriented design.

Naked Objects is an open-source Java-based framework designed specifically to encourage the creation of business systems from behaviourally-complete business objects. In fact, with the Naked Objects framework you have no alternative but to make your business objects behaviourally-complete. The reason is that the framework exposes your core business objects, such as Customer, Product and Order, directly to the user. All user actions consist of invoking methods directly upon those business objects, or sometimes upon the object's class. There are no scripts, no controllers, nor even any dialog boxes in between the user and the 'naked' objects. (Note: Wherever 'Naked Objects' is capitalized we are referring to the Java framework itself, and the term is singular. Where it is uncapitalized we are referring to business objects (plural) that are designed to work with the framework, and so are exposed directly to the user.)

Systems built using the Naked Objects framework are agile, meaning that they can accommodate changing business requirements, because behaviourally-complete objects carve the functionality of the system at its natural joints. Moreover, the lack of additional constructs around the naked business objects means that there will be fewer things to change.

The resulting systems are also more empowering from the user perspective. Giving the users direct access to the naked objects, instead of constraining their interaction through scripted tasks, means they have a strong sense of direct engagement. This is reinforced by the extensive use of drag and drop gestures that the framework provides automatically. The net effect is that business systems designed this way feel more like using a spreadsheet or a drawing program than a conventional transactional system: they treat the user as a problem solver, not merely as a process follower. This can have significant benefits not only in terms of employee motivation, but in improved customer service and operational decision making.

Even more significant than the improvements to the resulting systems is the impact on the development process. The naked objects provide a common language between the developer and the user, which significantly improves communication during the process of exploring requirements. And because the user presentation is auto-generated from the business object definitions, the developer does not need to write a single line of code to do with the user interface. In fact the whole conventional notion of a user interface just disappears. This facilitates very rapid prototyping. But unlike other forms of rapid prototyping, you are not merely prototyping the user interface – you are simultaneously prototyping the core object model.

The aim of this book is to introduce you to the concept of designing business systems from naked objects, and to enable you to start building such systems using the Naked Objects framework. The book will appeal primarily to two kinds of reader: object modellers who have at least some knowledge of Java programming (or want to acquire it), and Java developers who have some knowledge of object modelling (or want to acquire it). Indeed one of the messages in this book is that the notions of business object modelling and object-oriented programming are much more synergistic than is conventionally realised.

Structure of the book

Section 1 of this book provides a brief history of object-orientation and an analysis of the practices that tend to force the separation of procedure from data in business systems design. It concludes with a set of new design principles that we might call the 'naked object manifesto'. You don't need to read this history and analysis in order to get the benefits of using Naked Objects – you can skip straight on to the practical sections if you prefer – but you may find that this background deepens your understanding of the nature of object orientation and why current practice deviates so far from the original intent.

Section 1 is followed by a **Case study** on the Irish government's Department of Social and Family Affairs (DSFA). This was our first opportunity to apply the design principles to a mission-critical business system, and it was a big success. The DSFA used a very early and crude version of our framework to prototype its system, but had to commission its own dedicated architecture to implement the resulting design. This was one of the things that spurred us into redeveloping Naked Objects to make it suitable for full-scale development.

Section 2 provides a high-level overview of the Naked Object framework and describes the main benefits that you can realise from using it, in terms of both the qualities of the resulting systems, and improvements to the design and development process. This section concludes with a collection of Frequently Asked Questions (perhaps we ought to call them Frequently Raised Objections) that we have encountered over the last couple of years.

The second **Case study** shows an early prototype for a reservations system for Executive Car Services. This case provides a visual explanation of the close correspondence between the user's view of the naked objects and the structure of the underlying application written in Java. If you want a very rapid introduction to what the framework does, this is a good place to start.

Section 3 provides an introduction to programming with the Naked Objects framework. This section is written for Java programmers. Where possible the programming techniques are illustrated using the system described in the previous case study, the complete code for which is provided with the Naked Objects framework.

The next **Case study** describes the experience of Safeway Stores, the fourth largest supermarket chain in the UK. Safeway initially started exploring Naked Objects as a means to strengthening the object-modelling skills of its Java developers, and has since gone on to use the framework both for application prototyping and for implementation. The case describes how Safeway interfaced Naked Objects to Enterprise Java Beans and has deployed this combination with performance levels approaching that of traditional mainframe-based transaction-processing systems.

Section 4 looks at the design and development process for a Naked Objects project. We recommend that you manage the project in three phases: exploration, specification, delivery. The last two can be managed within the context of an existing methodology, be it the Unified Process or Extreme Programming (though we highlight a number of specific synergies with the latter). However, our particular approach to Exploration is unique – and can deliver some extraordinary benefits in its own right.

This is followed by a **Case study** describing some experiences from such an exploration phase conducted at a large bank. In particular this case looks at how naked objects fare in a domain that traditionally has been dominated by a process-oriented view of the business.

Section 5 takes a brief look at what the future holds for Naked Objects. The framework is constantly being improved and new facilities added, driven by the needs of the user community and developed by interested open source developers. We explain where to look for more information, how to get involved in the development process, and various ways in which the framework might be extended.

The final **Case study** concerns a Norwegian conglomerate, Norsk Hydro, that used the Naked Objects framework to build a highly graphical prototype, in which all user actions were invoked on objects within a map representation of the European electricity network. This involved adding another viewing type to the framework, but once that was done the entire business application was written without a single line of code referring to the user interface.

At the back of the book are a number of useful **Appendices**, the first of which takes you through the process of installing the framework and building an ultra-simple application step by step.

You can download the Naked Objects framework and further documentation from our website (www.nakedobjects.org). The Naked Objects framework is evolving rapidly. We've restricted the contents of this book to the aspects of the framework that we believe are now reasonably stable. Any necessary updates will be provided on the website.

As an open source project we hope that you will not only make use of the framework and its associated techniques, but think about contributing in some way to its ongoing development. In the meantime: enjoy!

Acknowledgements

The ideas now embodied in Naked Objects are based on ten years' research into object-oriented techniques, architectures for business agility, and 'expressive systems', undertaken by Richard, and funded throughout by CSC's Research Services (www.cscresearchservices.com). We gratefully acknowledge their generosity in allowing the fruits of this research to now be made public, as well as the contribution made by Richard's colleagues within CSC during many discussions and debates. Three years ago, Richard teamed up with Robert Matthews, longstanding friend and former colleague, who set about designing a Java framework to embody the design principles arising from this research.

Although some have hailed Naked Objects as an important new idea, we prefer to see it as an attempt to get back to an old idea. What led to Naked Objects was our belief that the most powerful aspects of the original concept of object-orientation, now almost four decades old, are not understood by most people who claim to practice OO. We have tried to summarise the insights of some of pioneers in object-oriented software design in the first section of the book, but regret that this story is by no means comprehensive. We are deeply indebted to these great thinkers. Some of the folk whose work we have admired for years – Alan Kay, Rebecca Wirfs-Brock, Oliver Sims, Dave Thomas – have given us active encouragement on this project, have helped to get our ideas more widely known, and have made incisive criticism of early drafts. Many others provided useful feedback on later manuscripts, including James Cooper, Ian Graham, Kevlin Henney, Alan Griffiths, Dan Haywood, and Andrew Broughton. The rigorous demands of Richard's PhD supervisor, Vincent Wade at Trinity College Dublin, have indirectly led to many improvements in this book.

Equally important has been the contribution of those who have already put our ideas into practice. The Department of Social and Family Affairs in Ireland was the first organisation to take Richard's ideas seriously, and is now already into its second major phase of development, using the same design principles as Naked Objects, although with its own technology. The team at DSFA – Philip, Niall, Joan, JB, Helen, Peg and so many others – has been a joy to work with over the last three years. Their constant challenges mean that the design principles have truly been through a testing of fire!

At Norsk Hydro, Ragnar Blekeli saw the potential of Naked Objects and kept plugging away within his organisation until he could get together their first exploratory project. The folks at Safeway have done the most to turn Naked Objects into a viable tool for developing real business systems. Rick Smith has been a tireless champion for our work there. Dave Slaughter, a powerhouse developer, has become Robert's principal thought partner on the infrastructural side of the framework. His linking of Naked Objects to EJB, and implementation on a mainframe server, put paid to the sceptics' predictions that naked objects would not meet enterprise performance requirements. Many others there have applied our concepts, tested them, and made several suggestions for improvements. Special thanks to Suki, Alison, Pam, Ian, and Chris.

Prior to this book we have done little to publicize Naked Objects. Yet the community of developers has been growing steadily. Robert would like to thank those developers who have been involved in testing the framework or have made specific contributions and suggestions, specifically Frank Harper, Paul Hammant, Sylvian Liege, Paul M Bethe, Mark Crocker, Bjarte Walaker, Lindsay Laird and Per Lundholm.

The book itself was a team effort. We thank Karen Mosman for championing our cause within Wiley, and Robert Hambrook for being willing to innovate with the production technology despite a very short schedule. And thanks, too, for letting us work with our favourite editor, Anne Pappenheim, and designer, Ian Head, who was also responsible for the Naked Objects logo used on the cover.

Finally, we thank our respective families for putting up with the long hours and frustrations that any book seems to involve, and for patiently explaining to friends that our 'naked objects' project wasn't what they thought it was ;-)

Richard Pawson and Robert Matthews, August 2002

Version information

This is the first printing of the first edition of the book.

For any corrections to this printing or subsequent updates see www.nakedobjects.org.

This book is compatible with version 1 of the Naked Objects framework, which in turn is compatible with Java version 1.1.7a or any later version. (Current development of Naked Objects is being done with Java 2 SDK version 1.3.1).

Section 1:
A critical look at object-orientation

'New York, February 5, 2002... The Association for Computing Machinery (ACM) has presented the 2001 A.M. Turing Award, considered the 'Nobel Prize of Computing', to Ole-Johan Dahl and Kristen Nygaard of Norway for their role in the invention of object-oriented programming, the most widely used programming model today. Their work has led to a fundamental change in how software systems are designed and programmed, resulting in reusable, reliable, scalable applications that have streamlined the process of writing software code and facilitated software programming.'
(www.acm.org/announcements/turing_2001.html)

It's official: object-orientation has won. The argument is over; it's time to celebrate and move on.

We beg to differ.

More and more business systems are designed using an object-oriented methodology, and written in an object-oriented programming language such as Java. Their user interfaces are invariably designed with object tools such as Visual Basic. And except for a few mainframe-only systems, they are built on top of distributed object infrastructures such as COM+, EJB or CORBA. So how can we dispute the success of the object-orientated paradigm?

Because current practice demonstrates almost no commitment to the true essence of object-orientation. We define this essence as 'behavioural completeness'. To understand this concept and its significance, it is worth taking a brief look at the history of object-orientation.

1.1 A brief history of objects

The concept of object-oriented software is almost forty years old. Over that period the ideas have evolved considerably, and this evolution can be roughly split into four phases:

- Simula and the birth of object-oriented programming

- Smalltalk and the object-oriented user interface

- The emergence of object-oriented methodologies

- Distributed object infrastructures.

1.1.1 Simula and the birth of object-oriented programming

The idea of object-oriented software originated in Norway in the mid 1960s with Simula, an extension to the Algol programming language. Simula was designed to make it easier to write programs that simulated real-world phenomena such as industrial processes, engineering problems, or disease epidemics*.

*Dahl 1966

Previously, all programming languages and techniques explicitly separated a system into procedure and data. Their assumption was that a computer system repeatedly applies the same procedure to different data.

Simulation challenges that assumption. Sometimes the data is fixed and the programmer manipulates the functional characteristics of the system until the output meets the required criteria. For example, the data might represent the roughness of a typical road and the programmer might alter the design of a simulated truck suspension system until the desired quality of ride is achieved. Sometimes it is even difficult to tell data and functionality apart: when you add another axle to your simulated truck, for example, are you changing the data (the number of wheels) or the functionality (the way in which the truck translates road bumps into ride quality)?

The inventors of Simula had the idea of building systems out of 'objects', each of which represents some element within the simulated domain. A simulation typically involves several classes of object – a Wheel class, a Spring class, a Chassis class, and so forth. Each class forms a template from which individual instances are created as needed for the simulation.

Each software object not only knows the properties of the real-world entity that it represents, but also knows how to model the behaviour of that entity.

Thus each Wheel object knows not just the dimensions and mass of a wheel, but also how to turn, to bounce, to model friction, and to pass on forces to the Axle object. These behaviours may operate continuously, or they may be specifically invoked by sending a message to the object.

We call this principle 'behavioural completeness'. This does not mean that the object must implement every possible behaviour that could ever be needed. It means that all the behaviours associated with an object that are necessary to the application being developed should be properties of that object and not implemented somewhere else in the system.

The word 'encapsulation' is often used in this context. The word has two meanings in English. The first has to do with being sealed, as in a medicinal capsule or a time capsule. This is how many people use it in the context of object-orientation: an object is sealed by a message-interface, with the internal implementation hidden from view. This is an important property of objects, but it is not unique to them. The ideas of black-box operation and of 'information hiding' are common to many forms of component-based systems development. The second meaning of encapsulation is that something exemplifies the essential features of something else, as in 'this document encapsulates our marketing strategy'. This second meaning – which corresponds to the principle of behavioural completeness – is far more important in the context of object-oriented modelling.

encapsulate /ɪnˈkapsjʊleɪt, ɛn-/ *v.t.* Also **in-**/ɪn-/ L19. [f. EN-[1], IN-[2] + CAPSULE *n.* + -ATE[3].] 1 Enclose in or as in a capsule. L19. 2 *fig.* Exemplify the essential features of; epitomize, typify. M20.

The Shorter Oxford Dictionary reveals the two meanings of the word 'encapsulation'. In the context of object-orientation most people assume the first meaning, but it is the second meaning that is more important.

The value of behavioural completeness is that any required changes to the application map simply onto changes in the program code. For example, adding a valve between two pipes in a Simula model of an oil refinery simply involved creating a new instance of the Valve class, setting its operating parameters, and linking it to the appropriate Pipe objects. The new valve object brought with it the ability to be opened and closed, altering the flow of oil appropriately, as well as to model the impact on construction costs. If the same refinery were modelled using a conventional programming language, the various behaviours associated with the valve would likely be distributed around the program and therefore harder to find and change.

1.1.2 Smalltalk and the object-oriented user interface

Although the Norwegian work continued for many years, by the early 1970s a new stream of object-oriented thinking was emerging from Xerox's new Palo Alto Research Center (Parc). Alan Kay, who led the Learning Research Group at Parc, was attracted to object-orientation for several reasons. The first had to do with scalability. At that time, lots of people were worrying about software scalability, but what most of them meant was scaling up by one or two orders of complexity.

But in 1965, Gordon Moore, who later co-founded Intel, had written in Electronics magazine that the number of transistors on an integrated circuit would continue to double every year for at least 10 years. The actual trend has been closer to doubling every two years, but it has continued unabated to the present day. Kay was one of the few researchers to take the implications of the newly-coined Moore's Law seriously, and he was interested how software complexity could scale up by a factor of a billion to take advantage of this hardware. Kay's conception of the future of computing – of notebook-sized computers with wireless connections into a gigantic network of information – looked like pure science fiction back in the early 1970s.

Drawing an analogy from microbiology, Kay argued that the only way that software could scale up in complexity by a factor of a billion would be if the software was self-similar at all scales: that the most elementary software building blocks were, in effect, complete miniature computers – in other words, 'objects'.

The first real application of this potential complexity lay in the user interface. Graphical user interfaces were not a new idea: Ivan Sutherland had demonstrated many of the key ideas in both graphical output and

*Sutherland
1963

direct-manipulation input with his Sketchpad system in 1963* but his ideas were not easy to generalize into other applications. By the early 1970s the falling cost of processing power made it possible to create similar effects in pure software using bit-mapped displays. The team at Parc used object-oriented programming techniques to manage hundreds of graphical objects on a bit-mapped display simultaneously, each monitoring and reacting to changes in other objects it was associated with, or to user-initiated events such as mouse

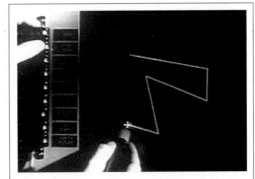

Ivan Sutherland's Sketchpad, developed in 1963, introduced the ideas of both graphical output and direct-manipulation input. In many ways, Sketchpad anticipated the ideas of object-oriented user interfaces, but it did not prove easy to generalize.

movements. Although there were hundreds not billions of objects, this was already way beyond the complexity that could be achieved using conventional programming approaches.

*Kay 1990

Kay also saw that the concept of objects had enormous potential as a cognitive tool: they corresponded well to the way people think about the world*. He noted that whereas an isolated noun conjures up a concrete image in people's minds (think of an apple), an isolated verb typically does not (try to visualise 'run'). This is because verbs are effectively properties of nouns: the boy runs, the dog runs, the water runs, the trains run. This gave rise to the object-oriented principle known as 'polymorphism': you can issue the same command (verb) to different objects, but it is up to the object to decide how to execute that verb.

*Kay 1996

One product of this way of thinking was the language Smalltalk*. Although it subsequently grew into a full-blown programming language, still revered by many as the purest form of object-oriented programming, the original idea of Smalltalk was a language that young children could use to instruct a computer to perform simple tasks and then build these into more complex tasks.

*Collins 1995

Another result was what we would today describe as an object-oriented user interface or OOUI. Unfortunately, this term has been diluted over the years. For example, one of the most popular references on OOUI design* uses the example of the simple calculator application, contrasting an old-style command-line version with the now-familiar accessory supplied with both the Windows and Mac user interfaces. Such a calculator has a graphical user interface (a picture on the screen), makes strong user of metaphor (it looks just like a real-world calculator), and uses direct-manipulation* (you point and click on the buttons). All these concepts have come to be associated with OOUIs, but they are merely by-products. The essence of an OOUI is that the user can refer to individual objects, and identify and invoke object behaviours directly upon those references. One effective implementation of this represents the objects as icons, and the behaviours as actions on a pop-up menu. However, it is perfectly possible to have an object-oriented user interface where the user's interaction is via a command-line, provided that the form of those commands is object-action (i.e. noun-verb). In fact some of the earliest examples of using Smalltalk for teaching purposes took this approach.

*Schneiderman 1982

The Xerox 8010 'Star' Workstation was the first commercial realisation of the ideas on object-oriented user interfaces developed at Xerox Parc in the early 1970s.

These concepts were first implemented in the Alto, an experimental machine that would become known as the first personal computer. The first commercial realization was in the Xerox 8010 or 'Star' workstation, which came with a fixed set of applications for word processing, drawing, and other document-related functions. The Alto and Star directly inspired the creation of the Apple Lisa and Macintosh*, and subsequently Microsoft Windows and Office, and a wide range of other systems.

*Levy 1994

Yet although the ideas of a desktop metaphor, icons, and overlapping windows are now pervasive, many of the most powerful ideas have been ignored, distorted, or diluted to the point where they have no value. Most of the applications now written to run within modern GUI environments show little evidence of object-oriented thinking. Consider two examples.

First, icons were conceived at Parc as representing instantiable nouns, yet today icons are mostly used on toolbars to represent actions or verbs. This may not be a bad idea in itself, but it distracts many developers from the more important concept of icons as nouns, where the icon indicates the properties and behaviours that can be invoked upon the item in question.

Second, in most cases there is a static menu-bar at the top of the screen instead of pop-up menus, which means the verbs and the nouns are physically separated. Both the Windows and Mac operating systems now support pop-up menus but, intriguingly, these are often referred to as 'short-cuts', implying that the primary locus of action is elsewhere.

Some people retort that in (for example) a word processor, many actions apply to the document as a whole rather than to an individually selectable object. All this implies is that the designers must provide either an easy way to select the document as a whole, or a direct iconic representation of the whole document with its own pop-up menu.

A few applications picked up the original object-oriented concepts and ran with them, but they were almost all concerned with graphic design, desktop publishing and other document-related activities. Neither the original Parc researchers, nor their immediate spiritual successors in Apple, showed much interest in the world of transactional business systems that accounted for by far the bulk of computer users, worldwide, at that time. Instead, object-oriented techniques worked their way into mainstream business systems development in the form of analysis and/or design methodologies.

1.1.3 The emergence of object-oriented methodologies

The first methodologies that embodied object-oriented principles and could be applied to mainstream business systems started to appear in the late 1980s. They had common features, but also subtle differences, each with specific advantages or applicability.

Many of these methodologies applied object-oriented concepts to an existing practice. For example, Shlaer and Mellor's Object-Oriented Systems Analysis* and Rumbaugh's Object Modelling Technique* both evolved from data modelling techniques. To put this in the most positive light, these methods supported the fledgling notion of object-oriented analysis and design with proven techniques from software engineering. But conversely it can be argued that they brought with them a great deal of baggage that encumbered the object-oriented approach.

*Shlaer 1988
*Rumbaugh 1991

Despite the claims that these methodologies were well suited to mainstream business systems development, many of them were originally designed to meet the needs of large-scale engineering systems, such as defence systems (in the case of Booch's Object-Oriented Design*) or telephone exchanges (in the case of Jacobson's Object-Oriented Software Engineering*). Some of the

*Booch 1986
*Jacobson 1992

characteristics of engineering systems are considerably more demanding than those of business systems, in particular real-time performance, reliability, and safety-related issues. However, in other respects engineering systems are easier to design than business systems. The requirements for software in engineering systems will, in many cases, be specified by product engineers rather than by naïve customers; and even though the requirements may change as the overall design evolves, it is not too hard to get a reasonable first cut at the requirements specification. To those who have undertaken requirements gathering for business systems, this sounds like luxury.

In the following decade several of these methods began to converge. The Unified Modeling Language (UML), emerged as the standard way to represent object-oriented designs in graphical form, and three of the methodology pioneers (Booch, Jacobson and Rumbaugh) collaborated to specify the Unified Software Development Process*.

*Rumbaugh 1999

One approach that still stands alone is Rebecca Wirfs-Brock's notion of Responsibility-Driven Design (RDD)*. Although not fundamentally incompatible with the other methodologies, RDD places far more emphasis on the notion of object responsibilities. It teaches that objects should be conceived solely in terms of the responsibilities that they would be expected to fulfil. These can be broadly divided into things that the object is responsible for knowing, and things that the object is responsible for doing, with as much emphasis as possible placed on the latter. (Strictly speaking, even the 'know-whats' are specified in terms of what an object should know from an external perspective, not what it may or may not store internally). The use of Class-Responsibility-Collaboration or CRC cards* is a useful technique for recording these responsibilities during the early stages of analysis and/or design. The significance of both the formal approach of RDD and the lightweight technique of CRC cards is that they encourage the notion of behavioural completeness. As we shall see shortly, that is much less true of other methodologies.

*Wirfs-Brock 1989

*Beck 1989

By the beginning of the 1990s there were a number of successful large-scale business systems designed using object-oriented approaches. But the demands of object-orientation in terms of memory management and processing power relative to the capabilities of hardware and operating systems of the era posed substantial technical challenges, and pioneering organizations found themselves having to design significant amounts of new technical infrastructure from scratch. That would change in the 1990s.

1.1.4   Distributed object infrastructures

During the 1990s the emphasis switched onto the infrastructural technologies
necessary to support enterprise-level object-oriented business systems, including commercial versions of the Smalltalk language, object-oriented databases,
and various kinds of middleware to support distributed objects. The formation
of the Object Management Group (www.omg.org) led to the specification of
the Common Object Request Broker Architecture (CORBA), and a series of
other public standards, which would eventually be implemented in dozens of
products. Two proprietary technologies, Microsoft's DCOM/COM+ and Sun's
EJB/J2EE, also developed substantial installed bases during the 1990s. All three
of these technologies provide the infrastructural services needed to implement

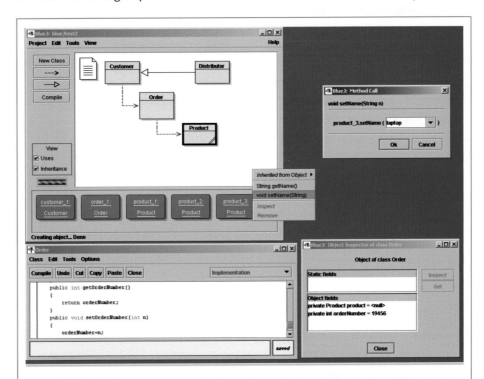

BlueJ is an open-source teaching tool for Java that is specifically designed to help
people learn Java as a true object-oriented programming language. Many Java
textbooks and development tools tend unconsciously to reinforce the traditional
procedural language paradigm. In BlueJ the user can directly inspect individual
object instances as well as the classes. The tool also eliminates the need for the
programmer to write a main method – a feature of Java that can encourage
procedural thinking. BlueJ is an excellent environment in which to learn Java, and
one that is conceptually compatible with Naked Objects thinking.

object-oriented systems on an enterprise scale, including persistence, distributed communication, security and authorization, version control, and transaction monitoring.

All three of these technologies make heavy use of object-oriented principles such as encapsulation (in the first of the two meanings described earlier), message passing, polymorphism, and in some cases even inheritance. Yet they were not primarily conceived with the intent of facilitating a greater commitment to behaviourally-complete objects. Their main intent was to enable distributed systems, implement layered architectures, and achieve platform independence.

The second half of the 1990s also saw some new developments that more directly facilitated the design of behaviourally-complete objects. One was the Java programming language, which has become very popular. Java makes object-oriented programming considerably easier to implement, because of its support for memory management and garbage collection. But the reason for Java's popularity probably has more to do with its portability across multiple platforms, its security features and its Internet-readiness than its object-oriented features. Many Java programmers actually have a very poor understanding of object-oriented techniques, and this is not helped by the fact that the Java language is often taught in the same way as procedural languages. One Java textbook*, frequently used in college courses, does not introduce the concept of classes until page 326! The BlueJ (www.bluej.org) project (see panel) is a worthy attempt to redress this situation.

*Dietel 1999

1.1.5 The state of the art

Where does this leave us, in the early years of the twenty-first century? The technical obstacles to designing and implementing object-oriented business systems have been eliminated, and object-oriented terminology has penetrated most systems development organisations to some extent. Yet core business systems design continues to separate procedure and data. They may be labelled 'procedure objects' and 'data objects' but the separation is nonetheless real. And that separation is contrary to the most important principle of object-orientation: behavioural completeness.

Some people see the idea of behaviourally-complete objects as impossibly idealistic, simply not realizable in any practical systems design. Some argue that the separation of process and data at some level is necessary and desirable for business systems: with object-oriented techniques, that separation merely occurs at a higher level of abstraction than with classical systems design. Others regard the continued separation of procedure and data as unimportant: provided that an organization is getting some benefit from the application of object-oriented principles, they say, it matters not how, or how deeply, they apply them. This point of view is an example of the relativist argument that there is no such thing as 'good' OO design, any more than 'good' English, or 'good' music – it is what works for you that counts.

*Gamma 1995
*Fowler 2000
*Meyer 1998
*Hunt 2000
*Riel 1996

Actually, there is a growing consensus about what constitutes good OO design and implementation, reflected in a range of widely-credited books on OO design patterns, heuristics and techniques. See, for example, Gamma et al*, Fowler*, Meyer*, Hunt and Thomas*, and Riel*. Although the phrase 'behavioural completeness' is not common, many of the heuristics point to this idea. Riel, for example, identifies these heuristics:

- 'Keep related data and behaviour in one place.'
- 'Distribute system intelligence horizontally as uniformly as possible, that is, the top-level classes in a design should share the work uniformly.'
- 'Do not create god classes/objects in your system. Be very suspicious of a class whose name contains Driver, Manager, System or Subsystem.'

11

Attempts to prove formally that one set of design heuristics is better than another are seldom effective, in any domain. And for business systems design there is hardly ever an opportunity to develop the same system in two different ways and compare them. Some limited experiments have produced results that support behavioural completeness. For example, one of the few documented examples of the same system being designed using the two

*Sharble 1993
*Wirfs-Brock 1994

*Deligiannis 2002

distinct approaches* when subsequently analysed using accepted metrics such as message traffic* indicated that the approach where the core business entities were more behaviourally-complete had less coupling between the objects and should therefore be easier to extend or modify. Another study compared two designs, one of which clearly featured 'god classes'* and measured the effort required (by programmers unfamiliar with either design) to introduce the same modification: again, the more behaviourally-complete style of design won.

We would not claim that such limited experiments form a conclusive proof. In any event our aim here is not to prove the advantages of behavioural completeness to those who are sceptical. Rather, we want to help the much larger community of developers who identify strongly with the goal of designing systems from behaviourally-complete objects – indeed that was what attracted them to object-orientation in the first place — but who tell us that it never quite seems to work out that way. They tell us that business system designs seem to degenerate into procedure and data with almost the same inevitability that milk decays into curds and whey, or salad dressing into oil and vinegar, and they can't explain why that should be.

1.2 Five practices that separate procedure and data

The continued separation of procedure and data could be ascribed primarily to inertia: that is how most people learned to design systems and they find it hard to think any other way. However, this individual inertia is usually reinforced by a number of specific organizational practices that tend to force the separation of procedure and data even where the software designer wants to adopt a more pure object-oriented approach. We have identified five such practices:

- Business process orientation
- Task-optimised user interfaces
- Use-case driven methodologies
- The Model-View-Controller pattern
- Component-based software development.

To say this is a controversial list is to put it mildly. Several if not all of these phenomena have the status of sacred cows within the systems development community. None of them can be dismissed as simply bad habits. All of them are conscious practices that either clearly deliver a benefit or have been designed to mitigate a known risk in the development process. We are not suggesting that any of these practices is 'bad'; merely that they have the side effect of discouraging the design of behaviourally-complete objects.

However, any alternative practice put forward to counter this separation must not lose the benefits of the incumbent approaches, nor introduce the kind of problems they were designed to overcome.

1.2.1 Business process orientation

Prior to the 1990s, the term 'process' was seldom applied to businesses except those concerned with continuous-process manufacturing such as oil and chemicals. The idea of modelling all business activities in terms of processes became popular in the early 1990s with the idea of business process reengineering*. After falling out of fashion in the late 1990s, business process thinking is experiencing its second wind, fuelled in part by the emergence of a new generation of business process modelling and management tools*.

Process-orientation really encompasses two ideas. The first is that you should focus on, and organize around, achieving an externally-defined result (such

Hammer 1993
See, for
example,
www.bpmi.org

as fulfilling an order) rather than on purely internally-defined activities. This is a useful contribution. The second idea is that processes can and should be reduced to a deterministic procedure for transforming inputs into outputs.

The problem with this notion of process orientation, as John Seeley Brown puts it, is that it tends to become 'monotheistic'*. As more than one intervie-wee has said to us, 'in our organization, if it isn't a process, management can't even see it'. Such a view is naïve and dangerous. Many things that a business does simply don't fit this sort of process model at all: there are plenty of activities where it is not possible to identify discrete inputs and outputs, let alone the sequential steps. Even within domains that can legitimately be described as processes, many of the most important activities, including most management activities and many forms of customer service, fall outside the formal process definitions. (Seeley Brown goes so far as to say that the most important people in an organization are precisely those who know how to work around the formal procedures). Social anthropologists draw a useful distinction between 'process' and 'practice', an enormous subject that is outside the scope of this book.

*Brown 2000

The Value Chain model of business, as proposed by Prof. Michael Porter in the early 1980s, is seen by many to be a universal model of business value creation. This model reinforces a process-oriented style of thinking. However the universal validity has since been strongly challenged.

One of the causes of this obsession with processes is the 'Porter' value chain*. Michael Porter proposed this as a universal model of business: margin is created through a sequential set of value adding stages. It is clear how this applies to, say, General Motors, but Porter argued that the same model applies to a bank, where 'inbound logistics' is deposit taking, 'outbound logistics' is lending, and so forth.

*Porter 1985

This idea has since been challenged by Charles Stabell and Oystein Fjeldstadt* who

*Stabell 1998

say that the value chain is actually a very poor model of many businesses, and its use can lead to dangerous mistakes at the strategic level. They suggest that there are three different mechanisms through which businesses create value: the value chain, the value shop and the value network. They also argue that the proportion of businesses that fit the chain model is declining rapidly. Value shops (such as consultancies, builders, and primary healthcare organisations) create value by applying resources to solve individual problems. Their activities seldom follow a linear sequence and are often iterative in nature. Value networks (which include many telecommunications, banking and insurance companies) create value by selling customers to each other. Their value creation shows significant network effects, which is not the same thing as the 'economies of scale' pursued by value chains.

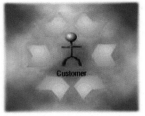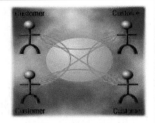

Stabell and Fjeldstadt argued that there are three fundamental models of business value creation: the value chain (left), the value shop (centre) and the value network (right). The shop model, in which resources are organised around solving an individual problem, and which represents a growing proportion of businesses, typically suffers from poor IT support.

The value chain concept emphasizes the sequential addition of value to input materials. This fits well with the software paradigm of separating the value adding procedures from the inanimate data that they operate on. If you ask IT professionals to define what an information system is, many will say it is a mechanism for transforming input information into output information through the successive application of smaller transformations. Historically that may have been an accurate description, but it is a very poor way to describe many modern IT capabilities, which are much closer conceptually to a value network or a value shop model. Metaphors that compare the role of information systems to a production line only add to the problem.

1.2.2   Task-optimized user interfaces

The same line of thinking occurs at a much smaller scale in the design of user interfaces. Most user interfaces are designed to implement a finite set of scripted tasks. This is not only implicit in the user interface design methodology, but more often than not it is also made explicit in the resulting design: the user is presented with a menu of tasks and then guided through the chosen task, selecting from sub-options as required. This style of user interface is convenient for systems developers because it maps easily onto a set of defined transactions, which in turn manipulate data structures.

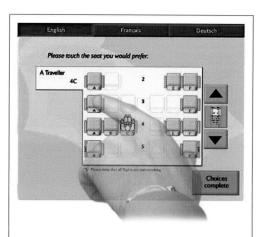

English   Français   Deutsch

Please touch the seat you would prefer.

A Traveller
4C

Choices
complete

**Self-service check-in systems, such as this
one by British Airways, can now handle
standard check-in procedures. It follows
that the systems available to the staff at the
check-in desks need to be geared primarily
towards individual problem solving, not
standard procedures.**

Another driver behind this
approach is the idea that scripting
is the key to optimization.
This can be traced directly
back to Frederick Taylor and
his principles of scientific
management* (see panel).

*Taylor 1911

Barbara Garson suggests in her
book, 'The Electronic Sweatshop:
How Computers turned the
Office of the Future into the
Factory of the Past'*, that this
paradigm isn't necessarily even
driven by efficiency: 'I had
assumed that employers automate
in order to cut costs. And indeed
cost cutting is often the result.
But I discovered in the course
of this research that neither the
designers nor the users of the highly centralized technology I was seeing knew
much about its costs and benefits, its bottom-line efficiency. The specific form
that automation is taking seems to be based less on a rational desire for profit
than on an irrational prejudice against people.'

*Garson 1988

The alternative is to design systems that treat the user as a problem solver.
Most businesses already have some systems that are problem-solving in nature.
All drawing programs, from PowerPoint through to complex CAD/CAE systems,
take this form, as do spreadsheets. However, in most businesses these systems
are not considered to be 'core'. The core systems are typically concerned with
processing standard business transactions, and they are optimized to a finite set
of tasks, which are almost always implemented as scripted procedures.

Many people feel that problem solving and transactional systems reflect two
very different needs within the business, that there is no need to merge the
two, and that doing so would likely de-optimise the processing of the standard
tasks that represent the bulk of business activities. We suggest that there is a
very real need to bring the two ideas closer together: in other words to make
even core transactional systems as 'expressive' as a drawing program*.

*Pawson 1995

Bringing these two ideas together does not mean just putting graphical user
interfaces on core transactional systems. In fact, as several airlines discovered

The legacy of Frederick Winslow Taylor

Frederick Taylor's quest for 'the one best way' of working began with the technology itself. In the machine shop where he worked, initially as an artisan and then as a foreman, he conducted thousands of experiments to find the optimum cutting speeds for various kinds of machine operation. His results showed significant improvements in possible productivity rates compared to the rule-of-thumb methods in use by the workers of the day. His next target was the organization of the work. Again using thousands of experiments he sought to find the optimal answer to every aspect of organizing manual work: from the optimal size of a shovel to the optimal

frequency of work breaks. To encourage workers to adopt his best practices, he advocated the introduction of differential piece rates, where the incremental rate of pay rose with performance. Still Taylor was not satisfied. The workers were making use of his techniques, but not consistently. The solution was to remove all the decision rights from the workers: to script their every action. Taylor realized that the workers would not give up their self-determination lightly. To get them to do exactly his bidding – to order their tasks as he said, arrange their space as he said, work when he said, and rest when he said – he would need to increase their overall rate of pay. The amount of this pay increase was just another value to be determined scientifically: it turned out to be 35%. Biographer Robert Kanigel calls this the 'Faustian pact' (Kanigel 1997). Taylor believed that he was empowering the workers, in the specific sense of empowering them to earn a better living. But in the modern sense of the word, he was clearly dis-empowering them.

Taylor's scripted instructions were provided on index cards. We can only speculate how he might have reacted to modern information technology, but we suspect that he would have been delighted by its capacity for extending his methods in both their range and their reach. Most business systems treat the user as simply a process-follower. The system controls the whole procedure, subcontracting to the user only those subtasks that it is not able to fulfil autonomously.

The Incredible Machine (www.sierra.com) is a great example of a problem-solving system, and one that clearly reveals its object-oriented structure to the user.

The user is presented with a problem to solve – in this case, pop the silver balloon …

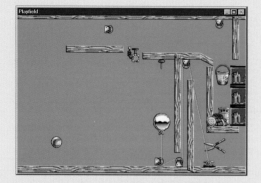

… using any of the available parts (objects), each of which can be inspected to reveal its physical properties and behaviours:

First, we use an anti-gravity pad and a block of wood to bounce the ball onto the plunger …

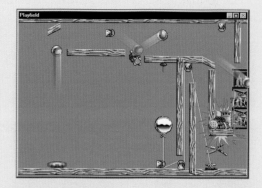

… which will detonate the TNT by remote control. Using a rope and two pulleys and a counterweight, we tie up the bucket so that it will catch the ball:

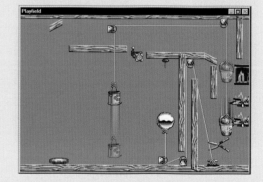

The counterweight is a leaky bucket, and when enough water has leaked out, the bucket and ball fall onto the shears, releasing the balloon, to pop itself on the pin above:

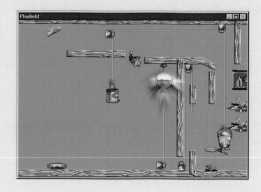

to their cost, the first generation of GUI-based reservation systems were in fact less expressive than the old style command line interfaces – which may have been difficult to learn, but afforded the user a high degree of control. Such experiences can give rise to the wrong conclusion that 'users don't really like GUIs'. What users really don't like is bad GUIs.

Another prejudice is that introducing more expressiveness into core transactional systems will reduce efficiency. This may be true in the narrow context of specific standard tasks, but in a broader sense efficiency can actually increase.

Consider the area of customer service. Everyone can relate to the frustration of dealing with a customer service representative, perhaps in a call centre, where the whole interaction is both defined and constrained by the computer system's script. Sometimes the problem that the customer wants to solve (using 'problem' in the broadest sense of the word) does not seem to fit one of the standard scripts; or tasks cannot be fulfilled without an unpredictable number of side-excursions in completing a task-step; or the customer would prefer to give the information in a different order from that which the computer expects. Most frustrating of all is when the customer needs an intermediate result to be able to answer a question:

- Customer: How long does it take to get from London to Sydney?

- Agent: What date are you leaving London?

- Customer: That depends on what my options are for getting to Sydney . . .

This approach to tightly-scripted interactions is becoming ever more common (and frustrating). In customer service, an increasing proportion of 'standard' problems are now addressed through self-service. If the customer just wants to order a book, report a fault on a telephone line, or check-in to a flight, then a web-interface, interactive voice-response system, or kiosk, respectively, can handle it. It follows that a growing proportion of calls or visits to a customer service centre are about non-standard problems, or are from people who simply do not wish to work within the narrow confines of such an approach. And yet call centre systems continue to strive to shave seconds off the average call length by 'optimizing the script'.

1.2.3   Use-case driven methodologies

The concept of a use-case was defined by Ivar Jacobson as 'a sequence of transactions in a system whose task is to yield a measurable value to an individual actor of the system'*. A use-case driven approach to systems development writes use-cases that capture the requirements of a system, and then seeks to identify the common objects from them. The most popular object-oriented methodologies are use-case driven.

*Jacobson 19

The case against use-cases is well summarized by Don Firesmith*: 'Use cases are not object-oriented. Each use case captures a major functional abstraction that can cause numerous problems with functional decomposition that object technology was supposed to avoid ... Since they are created ... before objects and classes have been identified, use cases ignore the encapsulation of attributes and operations into objects.' He goes on to say that a use-case driven approach results in 'the archetypal subsystem architecture ... a single functional control object representing the logic of an individual use-case and several dumb entity objects controlled by the controller object ... Such an architecture typically exhibits poor encapsulation, excessive coupling, and an inadequate distribution of the intelligence of the application between the classes'.

*Firesmith 19

Jacobson also saw use-cases as serving another purpose: testing the resulting system. 'The use cases constitute an excellent tool for integration test since they explicitly interconnect several classes and blocks. When all use cases have been tested (at various levels) the system is tested in its entirety'*. This concept has no negative impact on the quality of the object modelling, and we would consider this to be good practice.

*Jacobson 199

We suggest that use-cases are most powerful when they are written in terms of operations upon objects that have already been identified and specified, and are used to test that object model. Conversely, use-cases are most dangerous when they are written before the object model and used to identify the objects and their shared responsibilities – which is precisely what use-case driven approaches advocate.

The question then arises: how are the business objects to be identified? The answer is through direct and unstructured conversations between the users and developers. The idea of direct interaction or the 'on-site customer' is advocated by all of the modern 'agile' methodologies, though not specifically to enable what has been suggested here. There is ample evidence that good object modellers, given a context like this, are able to identify the objects directly without the need for other formal artefacts*.

*Rosson 1989

The criticism levelled at this approach is that it depends upon expert object modellers. By contrast, systems development methodologies are designed to avoid the need for such expertise. (In fact, there is a kind of vicious circle:

prescriptive methodologies reduce both the need for, and the possibility of, design intuition.)

We suggest that our approach does not need super-human object modelling expertise. All it really needs is the right medium to capture an emerging object model in the form of a working prototype that both users and developers can understand and contribute to. This does not mean a conventional prototype that captures the user's task requirements in terms of forms and menus, but a prototype of a object-oriented user interface (OOUI), where what the user sees on screen bears a direct relationship to the underlying business objects – in terms not only of attributes and associations, but also of behaviour. Previous work relating to this concept includes IBM's Common User Access* and OVID methodology*, and Oliver Sims' work on Newi and the 'Lite' version Business Object Facility**.

BM 1991
Roberts 1998
Sims 1994
Eeles 1998

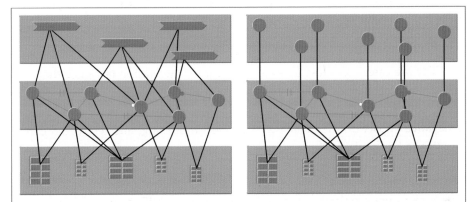

(Left) With use-case driven approaches there is a strong tendency for the use-cases to end up being implemented as explicit software constructs (top layer) that mask the objects (middle layer) from the user. The result is that natural responsibilities of the business objects get usurped by the user-interface layer. (Right) By adopting an object-oriented user interface (OOUI) it is possible to preserve a 1:1 correspondence between the constructs of the user interface and the underlying business object model. This helps to maintain the concept of behaviourally-complete business objects.

1.2.4 The Model-View-Controller pattern

As discussed in the previous point, use cases get translated all too easily into controller objects that sit on top of dumb entity-objects. This effect is reinforced by a common architectural pattern that explicitly separates three roles: the core business objects that correspond to business entities, objects that provide the user with views of the model, and objects that control the interaction between the user and the model. One version of this pattern is Model-View-Controller, or MVC*; another (as used in the Unified Process) is Entity-Boundary-Controller*. There are subtle distinctions between these two patterns, but they are broadly similar. We shall use MVC as an example.

*Krasner 1988
*Jacobson 199

The motivation for using MVC is the separation of concerns. The argument is that any given core class of business object will be viewed in many different ways: on different platforms, in different contexts, and using different visual representations. Embedding knowledge of all these different views, as well as the knowledge of how to effect them, into the business objects themselves would make for bloated objects and heavy duplication of functionality between objects. Using MVC, the Model objects have no knowledge of these different views. Dedicated View objects specify what is to appear in each view, and in what form, and have the know-how to create the visual display. Controller objects provide the glue between the two: populating the views with attributes from the business entity objects, and invoking methods on those objects in response to events from the user.

This is sound thinking, but it has some negative side effects. Although it is not the original intent of the MVC approach, the Controller objects tend to become an explicit representation of business tasks − especially if the design approach is use-case driven, but also in other cases. When that happens the role of the Controller objects ceases to be limited to the technical 'glue' between the user interface and the business objects. Increasingly they take on the role of task-scripts, incorporating not only the optimized sequence of activities, but business rules also − thereby usurping what ought to be responsibilities of the core business objects. And whilst the View objects cannot be said to contain business logic in the sense of algorithms, they can nonetheless end up incorporating a form of business-specific knowledge in the selection and layout of fields presented for a particular task, and (sometimes) minor business logic such as maintaining a running total of entered data.

The net effect is that business-specific knowledge is scattered across the model, view and controller domains. Any change to the core business object model will potentially entail changes to a large set of the View and Controller objects*. Of course this problem is not restricted to object-oriented design − it applies to most forms of multi-tiered architectures. Also, there is nothing inherent in MVC that forces this trend, but the fact that it is common practice suggests that the pursuit of behaviourally-complete objects requires an explicit means to counter it.

*Holub 1999

As with the other forces, any alternative proposal must avoid falling into the trap that MVC was designed to avoid: it must still be easy to port an application across multiple technical platforms and even multiple styles of interaction, without requiring the business model to be edited. At the same time, it must accommodate the need for multiple visual representations of the model on the same platform, where these are genuinely needed. The use of the word 'genuinely' is a reference to a minority but growing belief that the emphasis in recent years on user-customisation has become excessive: that it consumes vast development resources with limited benefits. As Raskin points out*, what is the point of a vendor investing heavily in the design of user interface patterns to maximize comprehensibility and minimize stress, only to let the user, or the user's agent, customize those benefits out again?

Raskin 2000

Instead, supply a generic viewing mechanism, embodying the roles of View and Controller objects. This means writing a viewing mechanism for each required client platform (Windows, Linux, web browser or Palm Pilot, for example). But once a generic viewing mechanism exists for the target platform, all a developer needs write are the business Model objects. The generic viewing mechanism automatically translates the business Model objects, including the available behaviours, into a user representation. The Model objects and their various associations might show up as icons, for example, with the methods or behaviours made available as options on a pop-up menu. This approach does not violate the essence of MVC, but is a radical reinterpretation of how to apply it. One way to look at this is that it renders the View and Controller objects agnostic with respect to the Model, as well as vice versa.

23

The idea of auto-generating the user interface from an underlying model is not new. The concept existed in many proprietary fourth-generation languages and application generators, and is re-emerging in various XML-based initiatives such as the W3C's Xforms (www.w3.org/MarkUp/Forms/). However, few of these approaches are object-oriented: the user interface is typically an explicit representation of data structures and functional modules or processes. They continue to encourage the separation of procedure and data.

Perhaps the closest approach to our solution, and certainly one of the best challenges to the hegemony of MVC, is the Morphic user interface*. Using Morphic, application objects can inherit the ability to render themselves visible to, and manipulable by, the user. Morphic was originally developed as part of the Self language*, and subsequently taken forward within the Squeak language* – see figure. Squeak provides the user with a very strong sense of direct interaction with the application objects themselves. The user can select any object and invoke display-related as well as business-specific behaviours

Maloney 1995

Smith 1995

Ingalls 1997

directly – even when the objects are moving around the screen. Hence Squeak has blurred the line between programming and using a system. However, although Squeak clearly has general-purpose potential (in the words of the Squeak central team, Squeak is 'Smalltalk as it was meant to be'), most of the emphasis to date has been on educational applications, animated graphics, and multi-media authoring tools. It has yet to be applied to the design of transactional business systems.

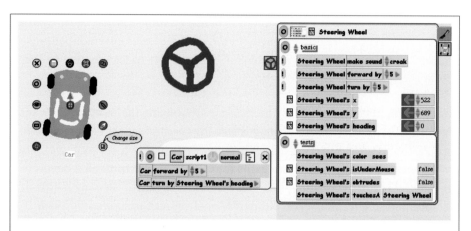

The Morphic user interface, originally developed as part of the Self language and now adopted by Squeak (pictured) is one of the most comprehensive challenges to the Model-View-Controller paradigm. All Morphic objects inherit the ability to display themselves and to render their behaviours visible and accessible. As shown in this screenshot, when the user clicks on an object (in this case the red car), it displays a 'halo' of small icons around it, which provide standard manipulation functions. See www.squeak.org and www.squeakland.org for more details of this exciting open-source project.

1.2.5 Component-based systems development

We are not opposed to the idea of component-based systems development, but we are concerned about the way in which this idea gets confused with object-oriented design. Certainly they have elements in common, just as any two ideas in software development have elements in common. But object-oriented design and component-based systems development are quite different concepts.

Component-based systems development is primarily concerned with enabling a plug-and-play approach to systems development. Plug-and-play gives you, in theory, more flexibility in sourcing your systems: you will be able to purchase components on the market, copy them from a public library, or re-use components that you have written in-house with multiple applications in mind. Such flexibility can potentially save direct expenditure, reduce development effort, improve quality, and promote standardization.

Object-oriented modelling is not, or should not be, concerned with plug-and-play. It is concerned with matching the structure of the software to the structure of the real-world business domain that the system is modelling. The motivation is to make it easier to change that model, either periodically in response to changing business requirements, or dynamically in response to a particular problem.

The components model has been very successful at the level of technical services – in the sense that you can now change your database without necessarily having to change other layers in the architecture. At the business level there is now a much greater degree of compatibility between application suites: you can choose your manufacturing planning package independently of your parts ordering system and so forth. But attempts to decrease the granularity of business components have been much less successful. Where it has happened at all, the components have not ended up looking like objects – at least in the sense of behaviourally-complete instantiable entities – but like sub-routines – chunks of code that can transform an input into an output. This form of components marries well with the idea of business process modelling, neatly completing the circle.

There have been some attempts to marry the concept of business objects with plug-and-play software assembly (notably by Oliver Sims and colleagues**). However, combining two paradigms into one is always risky: the more widely accepted paradigm (assembly of components) is likely to dominate the less well accepted one (behaviourally complete objects). Our view is that these two concepts are best kept apart. Apply the concept of component assembly to your technical infrastructure, and stick to pure object modelling for the business layer.

*Eeles 1998
*Herzum 200●

Arguably, one of the main reasons why so many organizations have come down on the components side of the 'object vs. components' debate is that they have developed an almost pathological fear of doing their own design and development. They have painful memories of analysis paralysis, of drawn-out development, and of systems finally delivered to specification but failing to address the real business need. We hope to demonstrate that it doesn't have to be that way. Developing your own business object model need not be a painful experience at all.

1.3 Defining a new approach

If we are going to encourage the design of business systems from behaviourally-complete objects, then we need to overcome a number of forces that discourage people from doing proper object modelling, and/or that tend to separate procedure and data even in so-called object-oriented designs. Overcoming these forces will require new tools and techniques, and these must demonstrate that they do not re-expose us to risks or problems that the established tools and techniques were designed to overcome. Specifically:

- Instead of envisaging the role of business systems solely as a means of executing a deterministic process, transforming input information into output information through a sequence of value-added steps, we need to find alternative metaphors. One such metaphor is the value shop, where the user constructs a solution to an individual problem. (It is a lot easier to add optimized scripts to a value shop model where necessary than it is to add problem solving to a value chain model.)

- Instead of pursuing optimal efficiency in the execution of each of a finite set of scripted tasks, design a form of user interaction that maximizes the overall effectiveness of the users in fulfilling their broader responsibilities. This means giving the users more control, for example over the order in which capabilities are invoked in order to achieve a goal. We should also design systems that allow users to become more expert as they learn, rather than constraining everyone to the lowest common denominator.

- Instead of capturing the requirements for a system as a set of use-cases and then using these to identify the shared objects and their responsibilities, aim to identify the objects and their responsibilities directly, in conversation with the users and other stakeholders. We also need some means of capturing the emerging object model in a concrete form that the users can identify with and gain value from.

- Instead of allowing the business logic to become scattered across Model, View and Controller objects, find a way to make the View and Controller roles generic, so that the developer writes only the Model objects and all user interaction is derived from this automatically.

- Instead of allowing the architecture of our systems to become dominated by the idea of being able to buy it piecemeal from different suppliers, recognize that real agility demands a homogeneous business object model that cannot be purchased, but has to be designed in-house to reflect true business needs.

Case study: Government benefits processing

In 1999 we had the opportunity to design a set of behaviourally-complete objects that modelled the business of a large organization, and to create a system that met users' requirements simply by exposing these business objects directly to the user.

The Department of Social and Family Affairs (DSFA) is the Irish social security administration. Prior to 1998 it was known as the Department of Social Welfare. The Department depends heavily upon information technology to fulfil its tasks. It has some 2000 PCs, but its core transaction processing programs (both on-line and batch) are all mainframe-based, and accessed via some 4000 green-screen dumb terminals. These systems are technologically out-of-date and increasingly expensive to maintain. For example, they require manual re-programming every time the government changes the benefit rates or rules. Currently, there is a separate system for each major type of benefit – Child Benefit, Disability, Unemployment and so on. Although there is a Central Records System (a customer database, effectively), there is much less sharing of both information and functionality than there could be. For example, many systems have their own separate mechanisms for generating payments. Word processing, email and calendar facilities are provided through the mainframe-based All-in-One suite, and there is no integration between this and the transactional systems.

Demand for greater organizational agility within the Department has been growing for some years, and this translates into demand for greater agility within the information systems. Technological developments such as the Internet and smartcards offer significant potential benefits both to the DSFA and its customers, including ease of access, richness of information, and cost savings. The government has also been pressing for more agility, both in the ability to introduce new forms of benefits, and in improving service to the customer. There are various e-government initiatives in Ireland, of which the most significant is the REACH programme, which will provide a common 'e-broker' for accessing information about the services offered by multiple government agencies, a central means of identification and authentication, and a personal data vault that gives the customers greater control over their own privacy.

In response to these various demands, in 1999 the DSFA conceived a new Service Delivery Model (SDM) that emphasizes electronic commerce, agility and customer-responsiveness. The SDM highlighted the need for a complete new architecture for the core systems. It would not only support the specific needs of the SDM, but would also be more adaptable to future, as yet unforeseen, business changes. Early on it was decided that new architecture should be multi-tiered, and object-oriented. The DSFA's IS department had experimented with object-oriented techniques some three or four years previously, focussing on the idea that object-orientation could improve development productivity through re-use, but had produced little in the way of tangible output or results. In retrospect, the IS management felt that the previous initiative had been focussed much too inwardly on the IS department itself. This time, the motivation for thinking about objects would be to improve business agility.

Early experimentation

Early in 1999 the IS management became aware of the emerging set of ideas that would eventually become embodied in Naked Objects. They were attracted to the concept for several reasons. First, it advocated a very pure version of object-orientation, based on the idea of behavioural completeness, and the motivation for this was clearly to facilitate business agility, rather than to promote re-use. Although the management did not necessarily accept the full argument at that stage, it was clear that the objectives were well aligned with what they wanted to achieve. Secondly, the IS management were attracted to the visual concreteness of the approach. They felt that this would make it easier to get non-IT managers more involved with crucial design decisions.

Early in 1999, the IS department initiated some educational workshops on object-oriented concepts for some of its senior managers, both IT and business, with the help of one of the authors (Richard Pawson). Given that the Naked Objects framework did not exist at this point, and there were no known examples of transactional business systems having been built this way, The Incredible Machine* was used as a metaphor throughout the workshop. In The Incredible Machine, the user is presented with a series of physical challenges, and must construct a simulation of a complex, improbable-looking, machine (in the style of the artists Heath Robinson or Rube Goldberg) to solve them.

*See page 18

As well as clearly demonstrating the notion of a problem-solving system, The Incredible Machine is also very clearly object-oriented from the perspective of the user: the elements that the user drags from a parts catalogue into the workspace are not just visual representations, but bring with them the complete simulated physical behaviours of that part.

One of the workshops (a one-day exercise involving six managers) attempted to identify the core business objects that could potentially model the DSFA's business. The participants were invited to suggest object categories directly: no attempt was made to capture requirements or to specify use-cases up front. By the end of the morning a list of approximately twenty candidates had been produced. During the afternoon this list was reduced by identifying candidates that were duplicates, declaring certain candidates as sub-classes of others, and eliminating candidates that, with further discussion, turned out not to be core business objects, because they could be better represented as simple attributes or as methods of other objects. The result was a list of seven core classes: Customer, Case, Scheme (meaning a Benefit Scheme), Payment, Service (a non-monetary benefit such as a bus pass), Community, and Officer.

The group was next asked to imagine how users would interact with each object, by asking such questions as: What will this object look like on the screen? Where might a user want to drag it? and What actions will a user want to be able to invoke by right-clicking on this object? The result was a list of 'know-what' and 'know-how' responsibilities, with emphasis on the latter to avoid thinking of the objects merely as complex data sets. The result was a very crude definition of a set of behaviourally-rich objects.

These draft object responsibility definitions were translated into a crude visual mock-up of a system that might be used by a 'deciding officer'. The mock-up was actually a series of hand-drawn screenshots held as Powerpoint slides, but a well-rehearsed demo managed to create quite a realistic effect, with the impression of icons being dragged around the screen and menus popping up in response to a right mouse-click.

The mock-up was demonstrated to a group of senior managers who had not been involved in the modelling workshop. A few of the responses sum up its impact:

- 'I can see how everyone in the entire organization, right up to the minister himself, could use the same system'. This did not mean that all users would perform the same operations, or indeed have the same levels of authorization. Rather, everything the organization does could be represented as actions on the handful of key objects. Such a consistent interface could help to break down some of the divisional barriers, as well as making it easier for individuals to move into different areas of responsibility.

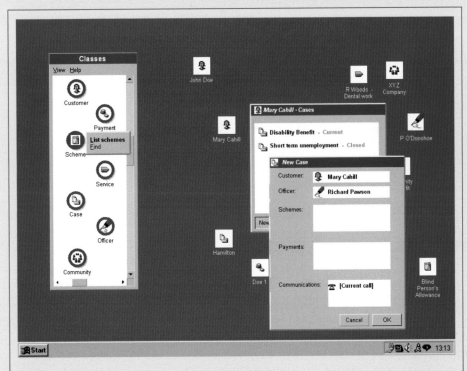

This mock-up of the DSFA system was created in Powerpoint in full-screen mode. Using a carefully scripted demo, the mock-up created the illusion of mouse-clicks, pop-up menus and new windows appearing.

- 'This interface might be sub-optimal for high volume data entry tasks'. There was some debate about this, until someone pointed out that the DSFA's commitment to electronic access (via the web, smartcards and telephone call centre), plus a more integrated approach to the systems themselves, means that most of the data entry work will disappear anyway.

- 'This system reinforces the message we have been sending to the workforce about changing the style of working'. The DSFA is committed to moving away from a conventional assembly-line approach to claims processing, where each person performs a small step in the process, towards a model where more of its officers can handle a complete claim, and appropriately-trained officers might in future handle all the benefits for one customer. The managers at the demonstration felt that even this simple mock-up could help to convey to users the message that they are problem solvers, not process followers. This was in marked contrast to the approach proposed by some vendors, which emphasised using rules-based technology or 'intelligent software agents' to automate as much decision making as possible. Instead, the object-based mock-up suggested an environment where the users' natural problem skills would be highly leveraged. In this sense, the design of the system could be seen as helping to facilitate a fundamental cultural change.

In addition to this positive reaction from the user representatives, the IS management were also impressed with speed of this exercise compared to previous attempts at department-wide modelling (whether as objects, data, or processes). They were only too familiar with the phrase 'analysis paralysis'. Although the DSFA was by no means ready to commit to this new approach for a full-scale implementation at that stage, all agreed that the concept should be explored in more depth.

The Child Benefit system

At the beginning of 2000 the business case for action became more urgent. The existing Child Benefit Administration system needed to be replaced with some urgency. The Government had indicated possible future changes to Child Benefit that the existing system could not be modified to address. Child Benefit is one of the simpler schemes that the DSFA administers and is relatively small in scale: the existing system had just 50 users. Yet it also has much in common with other schemes. It seemed an ideal opportunity to start the deployment of a new approach.

In a series of workshops involving both senior managers and user representatives, the responsibilities outlined in the original object model (from the one-day workshop) were now fleshed out from the particular perspective of Child Benefit Administration. These ideas were immediately prototyped using a very early version of a prototyping tool designed by the authors.

During the workshops, object responsibilities were refined and new responsibilities identified. New sub-classes and secondary (or 'aggregated') objects were also added. And the whole model was crudely tested against a number of business scenarios. Some screenshots from this prototype and an example use-case for processing a straightforward application for Child Benefit are shown on this page.

Additionally, the model was crudely tested against a variety of scenarios of how the DSFA's business might change in future. What is remarkable is how well the initial model from the one-day workshop stood up to these subsequent demands and tests.

The prototype of the Child Benefit system was created using a very early version of the framework that would eventually become Naked Objects, though this name was not used at the time. It had no persistence mechanism but had sufficient functionality to simulate some real operational business scenarios.

Technology demonstrators

Meanwhile, another group was looking at how to translate these concepts into a working infrastructure that would fit in with the DSFA's technical requirements. As a public sector agency, all procurement is subject to the European Union tendering rules. Accordingly, the DSFA published an RFT (Request For Tender) for 'technology demonstrators' that would implement all the main layers of a scaleable enterprise architecture (including message broking, transaction monitoring, and persistence) using a relational database, whilst at the same time reflecting the design ethos of the prototype. The Department commissioned three such demonstrators, each using different object technologies: EJB, COM+, and a proprietary object-oriented package.

Phase I implementation

Having evaluated the demonstrators, the DSFA put out a new RFT for the design and implementation of a full-scale 'Expressive Object Architecture' and the business functionality necessary to replace the existing Child Benefit Administration system. Interestingly, the RFT did not provide a full functional specification, but it did provide a description of the high-level responsibilities required of the core business objects, which is reproduced in this section. The contractor would be required to undertake a detailed requirements specification at the start of the project, using those object descriptions. This was deemed to be sufficient information for the contractors to place fixed-price bids.

The contract was awarded in February 2001 to DMR Consulting (now known as Fujitsu Consulting) – with the original intent that the new system would go live in March 2002. Following some industrial relations issues to do with the business changes being introduced, the switchover was postponed until the summer of 2002.

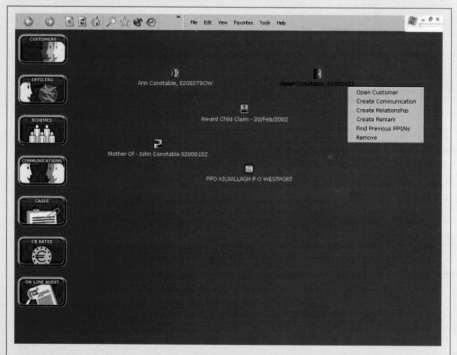

This screenshot is taken from the implemented Child Benefit system. On the left side of the screen are the icons representing the core business object classes; elsewhere on the desktop are icons representing individual instances. One of the customer icons has been right-clicked to reveal the pop-up menu of instance methods available to this user.

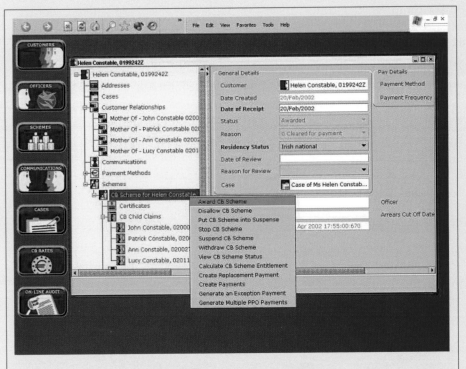

The opened view of a customer object reveals both simple data attributes and the various associated objects in a navigation pane on the left. The pop-up menu for the associated CB (Child Benefit) Scheme shows that all the relevant behaviours can be invoked in that context without necessarily opening a view of that object.

The user interface of the implemented Child Benefit system is not identical to that of the prototype shown earlier, but it clearly adheres to the same principles: business objects show directly through to the user interface, both as classes and instances, and all business actions are initiated either via pop-up menus from the objects or via drag-and-drop. Moreover, the entire user interface is auto-generated, dynamically, from the underlying business objects. Screenshots from the implemented system are shown on this page.

Moving into Phase II

At the beginning of 2002, when a substantial amount of the Phase I development had been completed but before it went live, the DSFA started to plan Phase II, to replace the current systems for administering the state pension schemes. This will use the Expressive Object Architecture built for Phase I, but is considerably larger in both scale and scope.

At the very beginning of the original project in 1999, Richard Pawson advised the DSFA that re-use should not be treated as an objective. He recommended that the objective should be agility: strategic business agility, operational business agility, and agility in the development process. If these goals were pursued, and the object modelling was done well, then re-use would be a positive side effect. And so it proved. The preliminary object modelling for Phase II, conducted early in 2002, has shown levels of re-use from Phase I that have startled even the most passionate of the object-modellers. The message: re-use is a good result, and a poor objective.

The DSFA's Business Object Model

The DSFA's Business Object Model identifies six primary object classes: Customer, Case, Officer, Communication, Scheme and Payment. The primary object classes in turn make use of several other objects, which can be considered secondary in role, but which are nonetheless still capable of being manipulated as objects by the user. In other words, the secondary objects are usually 'aggregated' into the primary objects. Objects are defined in terms of a set of responsibilities that they fulfil. The 'know-what' responsibilities indicate the attributes and associations with other objects that a user might expect to see and/or edit when that object is viewed on the screen. The 'know-how-to' responsibilities summarize the behaviour of the object. These 'know-how-to' responsibilities will typically translate into methods on the object, though not necessarily one-for-one.

We have listed the know-what and the know-how-to responsibilities for each of the six primary business object classes below. We are grateful to the DSFA for allowing this to be reproduced.

The responsibilities of the secondary objects were defined in similar manner, but are not included here for space reasons. We have also edited out certain details that are not important to understanding the object model.

Some of these responsibilities are not slated for implementation until Phase II of the project, which was going out for tender as this book went to press.

We have included this model as a good example of how to go about designing a system in terms of a small set of behaviourally-complete business objects. There is no implication that this particular model is suitable for use outside of the DSFA, although there are certainly patterns within the model that could have broader application.

Customer object

A customer is anyone who has dealings with the State and has been assigned a Personal Public Service Number (PPSN). The intent of the Customer object is to provide a single point of access to any and all customer-related information that might be of value in more than one context (e.g. for more than one scheme). Where information is clearly specific to one scheme, such as the recording of a mouth-map for Dental Benefit, then this information may be held in the scheme itself — but the guiding principle is to favour the Customer as the repository. The Customer is also the point through which any action that pertains directly to the customer (e.g. authenticate and communicate) is initiated.

The bulk of the data underlying the Customer object, and of some of the new secondary objects such as Contribution History, is held on the Department's existing Central Records database (CRS). However, with the advent of the REACH (www.reach.ie) initiative (the framework for E-government in Ireland) the Customer object should also be seen as the interface to the 'public service broker' that forms a major facet of REACH. Several of the responsibilities listed below are being explicitly planned for the public service broker.

This underlines the importance of specifying the responsibilities of the Customer object, and hence the interface to other objects, primarily in terms of 'know-how-to' responsibilities, rather than 'know-what'. Over time, several of these know-how-to responsibilities will be delegated to the public service broker, or to other systems, and the intent of the design is to make this transfer invisible to the rest of the system that is interfacing with the Customer objects. In the long run, it may be that the only responsibilities of Customer objects fulfilled within the DSFA's own systems are the knowledge of other DSFA-specific objects (see below). In the short to medium term, the Customer object will have to fulfil most of these responsibilities directly.

Know-what responsibilities

- Cases in which the customer is cited.

- Relationships to other Customers, including 'mother of', 'spouse of', 'nominee for', 'legal guardian of'.

- Communications to and from the customer (that are not held within a specific Case e.g. advice of change of address).

- Payment Methods – methods through which payments can be made to the customer e.g. bank account, Post Office details.

- Addresses for communication.

- Schemes in which the Customer is cited.

- Overpayment recovery objects pertaining to the Customer.

- Whether the Customer is an employee of the DSFA or other civil servant – in which case the object may only be accessed by a special unit of officers.

- Contribution History – summary yearly details of the Customers social insurance contributions.

- Means Assessments.

Know-how-to responsibilities

- **Find and Retrieve**. This method allows the user to find an existing customer instance using any variety of search criteria available. It is implemented by wrapping an OpenVMS based specialised search facility and making it available through the Customer Object.

- **Communicate**. The Customer object provides the ability to Communicate with the customer, using any of the specified media and addresses (currently surface mail, e-mail and telephone). This method creates a new Communication object which looks after the transmission and filing of that Communication. Communication can be in Irish if the Customer desires, so the Customer object knows the preferred language of the customer.

- **Authenticate**. This means the responsibility to ascertain that the customer you are dealing with (for example by phone, face to face, on the web, or by mail) is the person who they say they are. This facility may use direct input from the customer in the form of a password, PIN, PKI, smart card, digitized written signature, or biometrics. At some point in the future it could evolve full facilities for the issue and maintenance of Public Services Cards. Authentication is likely to be implemented in conjunction with the REACH initiative.

- **Create a statement**. The customer should be able to list all Payments (including overpayments) made in a specified period.

- **Update**. An officer should be able to request, through the Customer object, that the customer checks their held information and updates it as appropriate (subject to the rules for verifying individual fields). This will usually produce an electronic or paper communication to the customer and may, in future, initiate and process data from other applications.

- **Register life event**. There should be specific methods for dealing with the major life events such as birth, marriage, retirement, or death.

- **Respond to life event** e.g. notify the Customer of the need to claim entitlements three months before their 66th birthday.

Scheme object

A Scheme object is responsible for the administration of a particular benefit or set of Benefits. Scheme is an interface. Each benefit scheme that the DSFA administers will be represented by a Scheme object that implements this interface.

There are, broadly, two different forms of Scheme: composite Schemes and component Schemes. Component Schemes model individual benefits.

Composite Schemes are containers that hold one or more component Schemes. Thus, an instance of a Component Scheme can only exist in the context of a Composite Scheme. Individual Schemes will vary in the kind of support that they provide to the Officer handling the claim. At the simplest level, the Scheme instance merely provides a convenient place for recording the facts and decisions taken. At a more sophisticated level, the Scheme could implement some form of rules engine and/or a spreadsheet-like calculator. However, the underlying philosophy of the design is that the system provides a workbench to leverage the skills, and increase the productivity of the Officer – not to attempt to automate a process that necessarily involves judgement.

A composite Scheme will always exist inside a Case, creating a new one if necessary, in order to be processed by an Officer. However, once the Scheme is 'In Payment', then the Case will usually not play an active role. The batch system will interact directly with the Schemes. Certain Schemes will need the ability to bring themselves up for review after a certain period, or upon certain events – via the Case mechanism.

Any Scheme (composite or component) must implement the following generic responsibilities, plus any additional responsibilities specific to their own needs:

Know-what responsibilities

- The Customer who is claiming the benefit and any other Customers cited in the claim. (Component Schemes do not need the former since they can get it from the composite Scheme they can belong to, but they may need the latter e.g. the Customer object representing the Child or the Qualified Adult.)

- The Payment Method that the Customer wishes to be paid by, including nominee payments. (Component Schemes will default to the Payment Method specified in their parent Composite Scheme, but this can be overridden if, for example, the customer wishes different components to be paid to different parties or different accounts. Note that for the Free Schemes, the Payment Method specifies the Service Provider and knows how to deal with that Service Provider.)

- Component Schemes held within this Scheme (if it is composite).

- Start and End dates.

- Status.

- Any other information specific to this Scheme (or shared by its component Schemes) that cannot be obtained from the relevant Customer object.

- The Case within which the Scheme is currently held.

- All Payments made against this Scheme.

- Certificates for various decisions made by the officer, including eligibility and review date.

Know-how-to responsibilities

- **Request needed information**. In line with the Service Delivery Model, this capability could generate a personalized form (paper or electronic) on which the customer could confirm relevant existing details and supply any missing ones. For some schemes, this request could be going to other agencies (e.g. a school/college or doctor). The request would usually generate a standardized Communication object, filling in the fields as appropriate. Where the missing information should be held within the Customer object, then the responsibility to request the needed information is delegated to the Customer object.

- **Record the eligibility decision**. This is equivalent to ruling the customer's eligibility for the Scheme. It involves creating a Certificate which represents the legal decision of the Deciding Officer. The claim cannot proceed until this stage has been passed. If the claim is disallowed, then the Scheme object continues to exist, but the Case that contains it may be closed. Deciding the claim may automatically generate an advice note, using the Customer's communicate capability. (Note: it will usually be necessary for the Officer to formally decide the eligibility for the composite Scheme and for each of the component Schemes that it contains.)

- **Calculate entitlement** for any specified period. This responsibility is carried out by reference to the particular Scheme being processed. It implies that the Scheme must know the rates and rules for previous years, not just the current year. It must also know the payment frequencies which apply to the particular scheme. As new rates and rules come into force, these will be added to the Scheme definition. If the new rules and rates follow the same structure as the previous ones, then this can be thought of as just adding a row to a table. If they introduce new structures then the modifications will be more complex. Note, however, that all changes to scheme rates and rules are contained within the particular Scheme – they do not spill over into the

Customer or Payment objects. The calculate entitlement responsibility is used as a prelude to generating a payment for that period, but may also be used just to advise the Customer of how much they are due.

- **Calculate claim start date**. Where there has been a delay in submitting a claim, some backdating of entitlement is permitted. A set of rules exists to calculate the backdated start date.

- **Generate new payment** for a given period. Depending on the Payment Method selected, this capability will typically be invoked by an external batch process running at a range of frequencies e.g. weekly, fortnightly or monthly. Application of taxation rules (with reference to the Customer's taxation status) may be an embedded part of this responsibility.

- **Generate a schedule of payments**. This method will be used when the preferred method of payment is a book (i.e. it is necessary to generate payment vouchers at regular intervals – say, every 6 months or every year – or one-off payments such as a Christmas Bonus. The frequency of voucher generation and the number of vouchers in a book will vary from scheme to scheme). It may also be used during transition, for compatibility with existing systems.

- **Generate difference payment** for a given period. This method will invoke the Generate New Payment, but will then net the amount against any existing payments for that Scheme for the same period. This will be used when, for example, the customer's circumstances change after a schedule of forward payments has been generated (e.g. new child born during the year). This responsibility can also produce a negative Payment (i.e. an overpayment to be recovered). Note: This is only for making corrections to future payments, and within a single scheme. In general, overpayment recovery is handled by a dedicated Overpayment Recovery Scheme.

- **Split payments** in accordance with individualization or other legal requirements. This could be achieved by generating separate payments based upon a percentage split agreed with the Customers involved.

- **Correct an overlap**. This means generating an Overlap object that will, effectively, transfer surplus payments made under this Scheme onto another Scheme.

- **Guide the user**. This means permitting the user to look up the relevant legislation, or more likely staff guidance notes, relevant to processing the claim. This may be implemented as context-specific business help.

The following responsibilities apply only to composite Schemes:

- **Add component Schemes**. This includes enforcing rules as to which such component Schemes can be added

- **Manage interdependencies** between component Schemes. A simple example of this is that the CB Scheme needs to assign an 'eligibility order' to each of the (component) Child Claim objects – since they cannot calculate this for themselves.

- **Cascade methods** on to the component Schemes. The most common one of these is the regular Generate Payment method.

- **Aggregate Payments** generated by component Schemes. Most of this responsibility is delegated to the Payment objects themselves. However, the composite Scheme will need to enforce certain rules about which Payments can and can't be aggregated (e.g. because they are legally paid on different days of the week).

- **Bring itself up for review** based upon certain events or the passage of time.

Communication object

The Communication object models a single communication, for example between an Officer and a Customer, or between two Officers. The role of the Communication object is not just to allow such communications to be created, but also to allow them to be filed.

Communications may be incoming or outgoing. In addition, the Communication Object is used to record remarks.

The transmission mechanism for a Communication is achieved through the Address object. The same user interface is used regardless of the transmission channel chosen.

A Remark is a Communication that has no recipient. It is typically made within a Scheme, Case or Customer object.

Know-what responsibilities

- Recipient's Address (obtained from the list of Addresses contained by the recipient object i.e. a Customer, Officer or any other object that is communicable). The user may choose the particular address, but it will default to the first entry in the list.

- Sender's Address (obtained from the sending object). This will default to the first entry in the sender's address list that is the same type as the recipient's address (although all written communications will list various ways of replying).

- Subject. If the Communication was generated inside a Case, then that object will be recorded as the subject. This will not only allow the Communication to be filed in the right place, but will also potentially allow any reply to be matched up. This field could also hold other context objects.

- Date

- Status: draft, sent, received, returned, standard letter (read-only) etc.

- Content. Text will be held in some generalised mark-up language (e.g. HTML).

- Certificate (i.e. digital signature) if required.

- Attachments. In a wide variety of formats (e.g. Word, Acrobat) that are themselves capable of being transformed into various forms such as paper and electronic image. Additionally, the content can include pointers to any expressive objects in the system, though these will only be of use to recipients who are on the system (i.e. internal mail). Attachments could also include digitized voice recordings.

- Language of content. (English or Irish, initially).

Know-how-to responsibilities

- **Transmit**. Execution of this responsibility is fulfilled through the Address object.

- **Edit**. Allows text contents to be created and edited.

- **Reply**.

- **Forward**. This is done by creating a new communication that has the current one as the Subject.

- **Retrieve** (class responsibility). Previous communications will be retrieved from lists held in the Customer, Officer or Case objects.

- **Attach** a file such as a scanned image to a Communication.

- **Confirm** successful delivery (also fulfilled in collaboration with Address).

- **Sign**. Create a Certificate digital signature of the sender. This responsibility may append a digitised image of a physical signature, if desired.

- **Copy**. This copies a whole Communication.

- **Lock**. This turns a Communication into a standard read-only communication that can be copied.

- **Append**. Used to create a letter from standard paragraphs.

Officer object

The Officer object is the single point of contact for information and functionality associated with an individual (an employee of the Department or an associate) who may use the information system. There is one instance for each such individual.

Users of the system have their own Officer object readily accessible, as this is the means for logging on and off, and for storing their personal desktop view. In addition the Officer object provides access to their current workload.

An Officer object may be 'virtual', that is, it may represent roles and/or departmental sections (e.g. the Claims Registration Section).

Know-what responsibilities

- Relationships to other Officers. This includes supervisors, supervised, and peers.

- Cases. This means cases that are currently assigned to the officer.

- Communications to or from the Officer.

- Addresses for communication.

- Roles fulfilled.

Know-how-to responsibilities

- **Find and Retrieve**. These responsibilities are broadly similar to those specified for Customer.

- **Log-on and off**.

- **Capture and recall the user's desktop**.

- **Present caseload**. This responsibility can show all cases currently assigned to the Officer broken down by various categories including current status.

- **Manage in and out boxes**.

- **Manage authorization levels**. Authorization (to perform a specific method on a specific object) will be done by a system-wide authentication and authorization server. However, the Officer object will be a principal user interface onto this server (i.e. the means through which the authorization levels for specific roles and/or individuals are specified).

- **Communicate**. This works in the same way as the Communicate responsibility of the Customer object.

- **Create a Certificate** to record the basis of the Officer's decision.

Payment object

A Payment object represents a single payment from a payer (by default, the Department) to the payee (usually a Customer). A Payment is in many ways analogous to a Communication and shares some of its structure. Thus, the role of the Address in a Communication is replaced by a Payment Method, where that may represent a cheque, electronic funds transfer, electronic information transfer or a voucher (the latter usually forming part of a payment book).

The amount of the payment will have been determined by whatever created the Payment object (e.g. a Scheme, or, in rare cases, an authorised Officer), along with the date due. Payment can represent negative amounts for the purposes of recovering an overpayment

Payments are generally created at the lowest level possible to enable them to be posted accurately into the financial accounting system. Thus, a claim may give rise to the creation of several Payment objects representing different component Schemes such as Retirement Pension, Contributory Pension, Qualified Adult Allowance or Child Dependent Allowance. Payments that have been created but not yet executed and which have the same payee and date may be combined or merged with other Payments within the same payment period to form a single net transfer.

Know-what responsibilities

- Scheme that caused the Payment to be created.

- Payee's Payment Method. The descriptive label of the Payment Method includes the name of the Payee, and can provide direct access to the object representing the payee (e.g. a Customer or Agency).

- Payment identification. For example, cheque number or voucher number.

- Component Payments. This means that any composite payment knows what other payments it has been made up from.

- Amount (expressed in a currency).

- Status (issued, paid, stopped, reconciled).

- Stop Reason, if status indicates that the payment has been stopped.

- Payment Type. This indicates if the payment is a regular payment, a replacement payment, grant payment etc. This is a free-form field whose contents are typically determined by the Scheme that creates the Payment.

- Payment period that it relates to.

- Date due. (It may be that this is a function of the payment period e.g. first Tuesday in the period).

Know-how-to responsibilities

- **Merge with another payment** (subject to rules). Typically, Payment instances are created at the level of Scheme elements (e.g. child dependent, fuel allowance) and then merged to form a single payment which is transferred to the Customer.

- **Post** into the financial accounting systems.

- **Authorize**. Most payments will be generated within Schemes, which will look after their own levels of authorization. However, it may be appropriate to put some additional generic concepts of authorization into the Payment object itself (e.g. for payments over 5,000 Euros).

- **Stop** the individual payment or the entire book of payment vouchers.

- **Issue** in the manner appropriate to the Payment Method.

- **Deduct tax**, if appropriate, by reference to the taxable status of the payee and/or the reason for payment. (This can be thought of as splitting the payment between the payee and the taxation authority).

- **Advise**. Generate an advice or payment to the payee, by generating an appropriate Communication object or by generating an advice note for inclusion in the PPO Book.

Case object

The Case Object is currently used to hold Scheme instances and is the mechanism whereby a Scheme instance can be linked to an Officer. Case can act as a holder for any supporting communications (including Remarks) and could in future hold scanned images of other documents associated with Schemes being processed, but which may not be explicitly held within the Scheme. However, the work contained in a Case does not have to be related to a Scheme. Instead it can be any type of Departmental work from correspondence to investigations.

Case provides certain workflow-like characteristics, including the ability to forward the case on to another officer.

Know-what responsibilities

- The Officer currently responsible for the case.

- The Officer to whom the Case was previously assigned (if any).

- Schemes that form part of the case (which in turn know the Customers).

- Communications relating to the case.

- Other relevant documents (including, potentially, scanned images) and notes.

- Current status. For example: Pending – customer; Pending – other; In payment; Closed.

- Review Date – the date when the case is to be brought to attention for review. This date will usually be determined by the Officer.

Know-how-to responsibilities

- **Refer to another Officer**. This referral may be temporary (e.g. for authorization to proceed) or a permanent handoff. The nature of the referral will make that clear. The referral may be initiated merely by dragging the Case object onto the appropriate Officer object. As well as changing the Officer assigned, the referral will generate a standardized Communication to appear in the in-tray of the recipient.

- **Alert**. Publish and subscribe is a generic capability of the Expressive Object Architecture. Case is expected to be a significant user of this capability – using a specified event on an object within a Case that may change the status of the case itself.

- **Maintain history**. All objects maintain a full history of both accesses and changes for audit purposes. However, for the Case object, the history of changes needs to be maintained in a form that is easily accessible by an officer – for example whilst dealing with a customer on the phone.

Section 2:
Introducing 'naked objects'

The DSFA project was our first demonstration that it was possible to design a large-scale mission-critical business system from a set of behaviourally-complete business objects, that were exposed directly to the user instead of being masked behind a conventional user interface. During the project we found ourselves referring to such business objects as 'naked objects'.

Following that success, we wanted to create a general-purpose framework to enable this concept to be more broadly applied. We took the simple Java-based prototyping framework that we had used to build the Child Benefit prototype illustrated in the case study, and re-built it from scratch to make it viable as an implementation tool. This meant addressing the issues of object persistence, sharing and distribution.

That framework is now known as Naked Objects.

2.1 The Naked Objects framework

To develop an application using Naked Objects, all that the developer writes are the naked objects: the business objects that model the domain. Each class of business object (for example, Customer, Product, and Order) must be written as a Java class, and must implement an interface called NakedObject that is provided by the framework. The simplest way to do this is to declare each of your business classes to be a sub-class of the AbstractNakedObject class provided with the framework. The programmer must write the necessary code to specify each business object's attributes, associations with other business objects, and business behaviours. The code must follow a few simple conventions, but in general the business objects are coded in the same way that behaviourally-complete business objects would be written for the business model tier of any multi-tiered system.

When the set of business classes is compiled and run, the framework's generic 'viewing mechanism' provides the user with a view of the business objects in a form like that shown in the screenshots below. Individual business object instances show up as icons; the style of the icon indicates which class it belongs to, and a unique title (specified by the programmer and usually derived from one or more of the object's primitive attributes, such as the name, date and reference number) distinguishes that instance. Any of these icons can be double-clicked to open a more detailed view of the object's attributes and associations with other objects (which show up as icons in their own right).

Right-clicking on any object will produce a pop-up menu of actions (instance methods) that users can invoke on that object. Right-click on a Customer object and you might be able to 'communicate' with that customer (via one of the customer's communication addresses) or perhaps 'assess the value' of the customer to the business based on past orders.

In addition to these business methods, the pop-up menu may offer the user different ways to view the object. For example, you might be able to view a Product object as a photographic image; a collection of similar objects as a table, rather than a list; or a set of numerical values as a graph. And if the object has spatial coordinates associated with it (e.g. Latitude and Longitude) then you might want to view it on a map or graphical layout. These viewing options are created automatically, based upon the type of the object: they do not have to be written by the developer. (The framework can be extended to create new ways of visualizing an object, but this should not be necessary for a straightforward application).

To develop this early-stage prototype for an expenses processing system using the Naked Objects framework, the developers had only to write the code specifying the 'naked' business object classes. These are shown in the classes window. Individual instances take the icon of their class by default. They can be opened to reveal their attributes and associations, dragged and dropped onto other objects or specific fields, and right-clicked to reveal a pop-up menu of actions that includes both generic operations and business behaviours.

As well as via pop-up menu actions, behaviours can also be initiated by user drag and drop actions. The user can drag an object onto another object, which will trigger a pre-defined operation involving the two objects; or drag an object into a specific field within another object, usually to specify an association between the two. If the user attempts to drop the wrong type of object, the drop-zone will flash red and the drop will not work. Similarly a menu action may be greyed-out if the action is impermissible, usually because of the current state of the object. The set of menu actions, attributes and associations that the user sees may also be customized according to the role(s) that they fulfil.

In addition to the individual instances, and collections of instances, the system presents the user with a direct representation of the classes themselves – shown in the screenshot as the Classes window. This is where the user goes to invoke behaviours that don't belong to a single instance: such as to create a new instance of that class, to find a specific instance, or to list the instances of that class that match some specified criteria.

That's all there is to it. Everything the user does is a direct operation upon one of the business objects, or its class. There is nothing getting between the user and the naked objects. There are no top-level menus, no scripts. There aren't even any dialog boxes.

Naked Objects encourages the design of behaviourally-complete objects in two ways. First, positively: the concrete visual representation of the business objects helps users identify with the object model and makes it much easier to envisage behaviourally-complete objects. Second, negatively: if there is no other way to build business functionality into the system, then the designers are forced to associate all required behaviour with a business object.

2.2 The benefits of naked objects

The Naked Objects framework directly encourages the design of behaviourally-complete business objects. But what is the net benefit? Behavioural completeness may satisfy some intellectual objective, but does our approach deliver any concrete business benefits?

Our experience to date has demonstrated four such benefits:

- Naked objects can better accommodate future changes to business requirements.
- Naked objects empower the user.
- Naked objects improve communication between developers and users.
- Naked objects can speed up the development process.

We'll look at each of these in turn.

2.2.1 Naked objects can better accommodate future changes to business requirements

Systems built from naked objects are more agile, in the sense that they can more easily accommodate future changes to the business requirements – changes to product specifications, the organization chart, internal rules and external regulations, business processes, and relationships with suppliers and customers.

There are many techniques for building greater agility into business systems. A common approach is to identify the thing that is most likely to change, extricate it from the workings of the system, and represent it in explicit and editable form. Workflow and other business process modelling tools extract a representation of the flow of work between people and between systems and make it editable. Rules engines do the same for, say, product configuration rules. However, the limitation of this approach is that business changes don't often fit into neat parcels.

An alternative approach is to break up the whole system into fine-grained components, of many different kinds, and then use a general-purpose architecture to stitch them together into usable systems. This, in essence, is the web services approach. Whilst this technique may offer more flexibility than huge monolithic systems, it is a fallacy to assume that finer-grained equals more agile. A seemingly simple business change can easily require modifications to dozens of components – and if those components are not well isolated from each other, there can easily be a domino effect.

There is no such thing as a general-purpose representation that can effortlessly accommodate any kind of unforeseen change. However, good object modelling is probably the closest you can get towards this ideal. This is because when object modelling is done well, the responsibilities of the objects are not driven primarily by the specific business requirements. Instead, the designers aim to identify the inherent responsibilities that can be envisioned for such an object. The initial implementation of those responsibilities may be optimized to the immediate need, but the more abstract notion will have been preserved in the design.

Take a simple example: it is natural when specifying a Customer object to state that it needs to know the postal address of the customer. But a responsibility-driven approach would suggest that the real responsibility of a Customer object should be to know how to communicate with the customer (even if the first iteration of the system will cover only postal communication). If the object's message interface is defined as:

communicateViaTheCustomersPreferredChannel(thisContent)

(we've exaggerated the method name to make the point) rather than as:

getPostalAddress()

then if new forms of communication are introduced (e.g. email, fax, instant message) only the code defining the Customer class need be changed. All the other business objects that need to communicate with the customer can continue to call the same method on the Customer object without having to worry about specifying which of several options to use (although the option of specifying the channel could be added). As Alec Sharp observes: 'Procedural code gets information then makes decisions. Object-oriented code tells objects to do things.'*

*Sharp 1997

2.2.2   Naked objects empower the user

Empowerment is a much-abused term in business. Often it is merely a euphemism for downsizing, de-layering or plain old-fashioned delegation. But the fact that it is often abused does not negate the importance of the idea. To understand what naked objects contribute we need to look more closely at the fundamental nature of empowerment.

Andrew Clement argues that empowerment takes two distinct forms: functional and democratic*. Functional empowerment 'is oriented to improving performance toward organizational goals that are assumed to be shared unproblematically by all participants' – for example, when a customer service representative is given greater authority to resolve a customer's problem in the interests of customer retention and the firm's reputation. Democratic empowerment (we prefer to call this 'intrinsic' empowerment) has to do with giving the individual a 'greater grasp and sense of their own powers'. It is done in the interests of the individual and is not oriented towards achieving any explicit external goal, though there may be an indirect benefit to the business in improved motivation and staff retention. Intrinsic empowerment is clearly a more subtle and elusive notion. Most initiatives aimed at strengthening empowerment are, despite the rhetoric, purely functional. Clement claims that 'For empowerment to offer an authentic promise of enhancing work experiences and outcomes, it needs to combine the attention to job effectiveness aspects of the functional approach with the emancipatory aspirations of the democratic approach.'

How naked objects support functional empowerment

The principal way in which naked objects support functional empowerment is by reducing modality. Most systems are strongly modal, and this can often infuriate users. The oft-told story of the Bravo word processor illustrates one form of this problem: if you typed the word 'EDIT' whilst in the wrong mode, it would be interpreted as 'select Everything; Delete it, then Insert the letter 'T'!* A more commonplace form of the problem occurs in many transactional business systems where users are forced to complete one task script before they can initiate another. Discrete applications are themselves a form of modality: users have to switch applications to invoke a particular function or piece of information.

Apart from causing frustration, modality can be functionally dis-empowering because the modes often cut across the way in which the user thinks about the problem, or the order in which information becomes available. Task oriented user interfaces, as discussed in (section 1) are always strongly modal. Modality cannot be eliminated, but if designers are conscious of the problem, they can make it less obstructive.

One of the most effective ways to reduce modality is to adopt the 'noun-verb' form of interaction. Almost all core business systems today follow the opposite 'verb-noun' style of interaction: the user selects a verb or task from an initial menu (such as 'Modify customer record' or 'Register new claim') and then

Clement 1996

Hiltzik 1999

55

supplies the data needed, in response to the system's prompts. In a noun-verb style of interaction, the user selects a noun and then chooses one of the available verbs to apply to it. The desktop metaphor adopts this style of interaction: the file icons represent nouns and the right-click pop-up menus provide the verbs such as Open, Print and Mail. However, most applications launched from the desktop show much less commitment to the noun-verb form. Although noun-verb interaction is not necessarily more efficient than verb-noun, there are several arguments suggesting that it is closer to the way people think, especially in problem solving activities.

The noun-verb style of interaction fits well with an object-oriented user interface (OOUI). But tools to support the design of OOUIs (as distinct from object-oriented tools to support the design of conventional GUIs) are few and far between. Naked objects, by definition, provide an OOUI. The Naked Objects framework enables you to produce this OOUI automatically from the business object definitions.

Functional empowerment, or treating the user as a problem solver, does not imply the elimination of all constraints. Certain rules need to be enforced for both legislative and business reasons. But when the business objects are naked, all such rules and constraints are encapsulated into those objects rather than being associated with scripts or procedures that sit on top of them. This is a better solution all round. It gives the users much more freedom to decide how to go about tackling the problem. It forces the designers to distinguish more clearly between an absolute rule and a mere procedural convention. And having decided that something is an absolute rule, embedding it into the business object it applies to makes it much harder for users to circumvent it. The panel illustrates the perils of using scripted procedures to implement business rules rather than encapsulating them in the underlying object.

How naked objects support intrinsic empowerment

Brenda Laurel states that 'Operating a computer program is all too often a second-person experience: a person makes imperative statements or pleas to the system, and the system takes action, completely usurping the role of agency.'* Over time this has a subtle but cumulative impact on the users' sense of their own self-worth and motivation. Naked objects contribute to the users' sense of intrinsic empowerment by seeking to give the user a first-person experience.

*Laurel 1991

Taking this a stage further, Hutchins, Hollan and Norman state that 'There are two major metaphors for human-computer interaction: a conversation metaphor and a model world metaphor. In a system built on the conversation metaphor, the interface is a language medium in which the user and the computer have a conversation about an assumed, but not explicitly represented world. In this case, the interface is an implied intermediary between the user and the world about which things are said. In a system built on the model world metaphor, the interface itself is a world where the user can act, and that changes in state in response to user actions ... Appropriate use of the model world metaphor can create the sensation in the user of acting on the objects of the task domain themselves'*. They might have been describing naked objects!

*Hutchins 1986

The Naked Objects framework provides mechanisms that reinforce the model-world metaphor and that make it positively difficult to adopt the conversational approach. For example, the reason why the framework makes extensive use of drag and drop has nothing to do with efficiency, but is because physical gestures aid this sense of direct engagement or intrinsic empowerment.

Physical actions aid understanding and memory: child psychologists tell us that children develop a stronger mental representation of things that they can physically move than things that they can't – what Bruner called an 'enactive representation'*. (Bruner's ideas were one of the inspirations behind the work of the Learning Research Group at Parc*). As children develop they make increasing use of the symbolic and visual representations, but enactive representations still play a role. Take the situation where two people are travelling by car to a new destination: one is driving, the other is navigating by reading the map, observing road signs and giving directions. Ask both individuals subsequently to follow the same route from memory and it is the driver who finds the task easier: the movement of the muscles play an important role in memorizing where to take the necessary turns.

*Bruner 1966
*Kay 1990

The Naked Objects approach seeks to avoid verbal messages wherever possible. Rather than waiting for the user to make an error then popping up an intrusive error message, it prevents the user from making the error. For example, dragging an object across a series of fields will cause each field to colour red or green to indicate if the object can be dropped there.

Finding ways around verbal messages requires some creative thinking. The best way to avoid annoying 'Are you sure?' messages is to provide the user with a generic 'undo' function. But there are situations where this would be very difficult to implement – what then? In the physical world, if a button or switch has serious consequences it is usually coloured red, and if it has very serious consequences then it will probably have a flip-cover. Putting a mouse-operated flip cover over a software button or menu command would be easy: it would have the same positive effect as an 'Are you sure?' message, but without the *sense* of intrusion, or patronization. (We hope to implement this in a future version of the framework.)

We do not claim that the user interface produced by the Naked Objects framework is the epitome of user friendliness, at least in the conventional sense of that phrase. There are well-established design principles (such as Shneiderman's 10 golden rules*) and specific techniques for designing user interfaces that are more aesthetically pleasing, more efficient in terms of the number of mouse-clicks or keystrokes required to perform a task*, easier for the beginner to understand, and less prone to user error. We have adopted some of these principles; we could do more. But some are incompatible with the auto-generation of the user interface that is part of our approach. Some commentators have been strongly critical of the Naked Objects framework for this reason.

*Shneiderman 1998

*Raskin 2000

Yet users continue to tell us that they really like the systems that have been built using the framework. We conclude that what they like is the sense of empowerment, both functional and intrinsic, that naked objects provide, and that they value this more highly than conventional notions of 'friendliness' and optimization.

Auto-generated user interfaces inevitably have limitations, and some applications will require a handcrafted user interface – although it will interface to the same business objects. However, as the case studies in this book testify, the Naked Objects auto-generated user interface has proven to be both highly effective and broadly applicable.

2.2.3 Naked objects improve communication between developers and users

The first and most noticeable benefit of using our approach to design and development is that the naked objects facilitate communication between user and developer.

It has long been claimed that object-orientation bridges the communication gap (sometimes called the 'semantic gap') between users and developers. But in practice this has meant bridging the gap between different stages in the software development cycle – for example between analysis and design – not between what the user speaks about and what the programmer codes. The end user representation of systems developed using object-oriented techniques is seldom itself object-oriented. Conversely, in many systems that have object-oriented user interfaces the objects seen by the user do not necessarily mirror the objects in the business layer.

Naked objects provide a genuine common language between the developers and the end users of the system, and this makes it a lot easier for users to become involved in the design of the system, which is one of the tenets of most modern development methodologies.

In all the projects where we have deployed this approach, the users involved in the design process have quickly become comfortable with the language of objects. This is not limited to the idea of business objects (such as Customers, Products, Orders, Payments, and so forth) but also with concepts such as 'instance', 'class' and 'subclass', 'instance method' and 'class method', 'attribute' and 'association'. After only a few hours of involvement in a Naked Objects project, the users start to express their ideas and requests for new functionality in object terms: 'Would it be possible to have a new action on the Promotion object to visualize the leaflet?'; 'We need another sub-class of Store to represent our Petrol Filling Stations'; 'I want to be able to associate an individual Payment Method (object) with each different Benefit (object), not just with the Scheme (object) overall'; and so forth. The naked objects render the core business objects visible to the users, so users talk of them quite naturally.

Contrast this with the normal state of affairs, where users specify requirements in terms of alterations to processes: new menu items, new reports, alterations to forms. Someone (maybe the developers, or maybe an intermediary such as a systems analyst) must translate such requests not only into the changes needed to the underlying data and functions, but into all the screens and user interaction controllers that are affected.

2.2.4 Naked objects can speed up the development process

The fact that the user interface is auto-generated from the business object definitions makes it possible to prototype very rapidly. Using our framework, simple requests for changes to the prototype (such as a new attribute, association, or a simpler method) can often be implemented in real time, in front of the users who are making the suggestion. Not all the prototyping can or should be done that way – sometimes it will be necessary to break for a couple of hours or a couple of days, to knock up the necessary code. But we have found that it is possible to get through many iterations in the time that most approaches would permit only one.

The idea of rapid prototyping tools is hardly new, but with most such tools you are merely developing the user interface. With naked objects you are prototyping the underlying object model at the same time as the user interface, because they are effectively the same thing. During the prototyping, all the attributes, associations and methods are rendered immediately visible to the user. (The finished system may hide some of them again, but that comes later). This has the advantage that the prototype itself documents the object model.

Anything that can eliminate documentation will be welcomed by development organizations. An outsider observing most software development methodologies in operation could be forgiven for thinking that their purpose was to generate documentation. The tasks of creating, editing, formatting, circulating and checking these documents consume huge amounts of time and effort. But the real problem with documentation-heavy methodologies is keeping the documents consistent with each other. The more recent 'agile' methodologies typically generate less documentation overall, and fewer types of document that need to be kept in synchronization.

2.3 Frequently Asked Questions

In this section we address some of the questions that people often raise when they are first shown the concept of naked objects – but before they have started to use the framework for themselves. Most of the questions relate to whether the approach is suitable for their kind of systems or their business environment in general.

2.3.1 What types of business systems benefit most from being designed as naked objects?

Naked objects work well wherever:

- It is recognised that the resulting business system needs to support a form of problem solving.

- There is considerable uncertainty in the business requirements for the system.

One could argue that both of these apply to any new business systems project, but the degree varies.

Systems at the customer interface are good candidates for a problem-solving approach. That said, it must be recognized that the empowering, expressive nature of the resulting systems assume a reasonable degree of familiarity on the part of the user. We do not claim that naked object systems are 'intuitive'. In fact, we subscribe to Jeff Raskin's view that there is no such thing as intuitiveness (at least in the way that most people mean), but only familiarity*. If the users are customer service representatives who interact with the system frequently, if not continuously, then they will quickly become familiar enough with the system to gain the advantage of having direct access to the objects. If they use the system only occasionally, lack of familiarity may become a problem.

For this reason, naked objects are seldom appropriate for systems that will be directly used by the customers – they are probably better off with a more scripted approach. There are some exceptions, such as on-line banking combined with Quicken-style personal financial management, or on-line grocery shopping. Both of these involve frequent and quite intensive use, and it is possible to see how naked objects could benefit both.

However, once you have developed a system from naked objects, there is nothing to stop you from developing a more conventional scripted user interface that invokes the capabilities of the same objects (on the

Raskin 2000

61

server) – either to provide restricted interaction for a specific class of users, or to cope with the limitations of a browser interface.

The customer interface is not the only area that benefits from a problem-solving style of interaction. Resource scheduling is another, especially in the intersection between planning and operations. Airlines, for example, have sophisticated tools for planning and running the schedule. But when significant disruption occurs, caused by a storm perhaps, the systems provide very limited support for simulating and then executing live workarounds. Pricing and promotions, trading, network operations, and risk management are also examples of intense operational activities that demand a problem-solving approach. Look also for anything that fits the value shop model of business: project management, emergency response, campaign management, and so forth.

Even where there is not an explicit demand for a problem-solving style of user interaction, naked objects can be a highly effective approach for any systems project where the system requirements are uncertain. (In several projects of this nature that we've been involved with, the sponsors have eventually recognized that a problem-solving interface was actually one of the keys to success).

Our experience suggests that business systems projects broadly fit into two categories: the engineering dominated and the requirements dominated. (Some fit both categories; they are invariably a nightmare, but fortunately they are rare). Engineering dominated applications (such as a new credit card transaction clearing system, an airline reservation system, or any form of infrastructural service) need a rigorous, heavyweight methodology. But many new business applications do not make heavy demands upon the technology. Instead, the challenge comes from changing functional requirements, and even the purpose of the system. Naked objects are particularly well suited to these problems.

2.3.2 Doesn't expressiveness come at the expense of business efficiency?

If you have an absolutely standardized task then providing the user with multiple ways of tackling this task will be less efficient than optimizing the system to the one best solution. But the ratio of non-standard to standard tasks is increasing, because problems that can be completely standardized are either being fully automated, removing the human from the loop, or, through the use of self-service technologies, are being delegated to users outside the organization. The armies of clerks performing high volume 'data entry' tasks are disappearing fast.

Consider the example of checking-in at an airport. Self-check-in kiosks are increasingly common. Passengers retrieve their bookings, check their seat assignments or change them to any available seat, then print out their boarding passes and self-adhesive luggage labels as required. For everyone except those with out-of-the-ordinary requirements, the kiosks save considerable time. As use of these machines grows, a growing proportion of the passengers queuing at the regular check-in desks have non-standard problems: excess luggage, a routing change, or colleagues on different bookings they want to sit with. It follows that the systems used by the check-in staff need to be designed primarily for problem solving rather than optimized for the routine transactions that are increasingly being undertaken on the self-service kiosks.

At the DSFA, when the implemented system was first submitted for user acceptance tests, one of the first users reported that he could now process a 'standard' child benefit in just six minutes, compared to twenty on the old system, and he could process a '16+ extension' (a child staying on for further education) in one minute rather than five. This was a single user's report, not a comprehensive analysis. But what is interesting about this story is that the system was not explicitly designed to optimize the handling of standard cases!

It is commonly asserted that power users prefer keyboard shortcuts to mouse-driven operations. There is some truth to this, but it needs more careful examination. One of the great ironies in the history of personal computing is that the inventor of the mouse (Doug Englebart) was not seeking to make computers easier for beginners to use, but to make computers more expressive for power users*. The mouse was only half of his invention. On the other side of the keyboard lay a 'chording' device with five piano-style keys, which the user depressed simultaneously in memorized combinations to invoke different operations on the items being pointed at with the mouse. In fact, the mouse (or equivalent pointing device) is a highly efficient mechanism for assigning relationships between objects. But keyboard shortcuts can sometimes be a lot more efficient than mouse-activated pop up menus. This is something else that will be provided in a future release of the Naked Objects framework.

*Englebart
1968

2.3.3 Are our staff up to using this style of system?

Not everyone wants more responsibility or more freedom of expression. Some may prefer the comfortable position of not having to think. But business managers must not jump to conclusions about this. As one systems manager of a bank told us during an interview: 'For years we've told the users that they can't do anything unless it is expressed in terms of the seven core transactions that our mainframe banking system can support. Now we have this all-singing all-dancing client-server system with a fancy user interface and guess what ... the users are complaining that they don't know what to do with it. We've drummed all the creativity out of them!'

The whole concept of naked objects undoubtedly embodies an optimistic view of the user's capabilities. It will not succeed everywhere. But we find the opposite philosophy too awful to contemplate.

At the end of the day, we must all recognize that any transition to a more empowered style of working requires a great deal of education, and may dictate a transitional period where there is more guidance and handholding. As we said earlier, if you design a system from naked objects, then it is always possible to layer scripted procedures on top of those objects – in fact they are very easy to write. But if you design a system around scripted procedures, you will find it very hard indeed to make the system more expressive later.

2.3.4 How can we still implement necessary business controls?

All of the examples contained in this book show some form of business controls in operation: you cannot create a Payment except in the context of a Benefit Scheme that has been signed off by an Officer; you cannot violate the minimum connecting time between Flight Segments at any Airport (at least not within a single Booking); you cannot create two different Price Adjustments on the same Product Group, unless they are of the Cumulative type. With naked objects these controls or constraints must be implemented within the business object(s) to which they apply. By contrast, most business systems enforce controls at the level of the scripted interaction. Enforcing them at the level of the business objects not only gives the users more freedom to invoke the objects in the order that best suits the problem they are addressing, but actually permits a stronger level of control.

This approach will not be welcomed by advocates of 'rules-based' systems design, where the principle is to extract all business rules into a separate representation so that the rules can more readily be changed. We do not like that approach for two reasons. The first is that you can end up with an awful lot of rules (even down to the level of checking the validity of a date), with the result that finding all the rules affected by a proposed business change can actually be harder. The second is that the rules-based approach seems to encourage those whose goal is to remove all decision rights from the users.

Implementing a rule or constraint inside the object or the relationship to which it applies makes it easy to find when it needs to be changed. And if you practice the disciplines of writing code that is easy to read and alter, then the rules will be easy to edit.

2.3.5 How do you get around the need for dialog boxes?

Designing systems without access to dialog boxes is quite a challenge. It is even more extreme than not allowing the separation of entity and controller objects. But once you accept these constraints, it leads to better object modelling.

Consider the example of a banking system – a perennial favourite in object textbooks. Account is clearly an object, and it is natural to think of Checking Account and Savings Account as specialized sub-classes. A conventional use-case analysis will suggest that all Accounts will need methods for depositing, withdrawing, generating statements and applying charges, amongst others. But how should the system handle a transfer of funds between accounts?

Many people argue that this functionality belongs in some kind of a process, not to either of the Account objects.

If we don't allow the addition of scripts or controllers on top of the entity objects, then another option is to implement TransferTo(Account, Currency-Value) as a method on both the Account classes. This could then generate a dialog box wherein the user could specify the Account to be transferred to and the amount. But the Naked Objects framework doesn't support dialog boxes. It can translate a zero-parameter method into an action on the pop-up menu for that object, and realize a one-parameter method by dragging one object onto another. But it cannot translate a multi-parameter method into a user action.

The solution is to implement Transfer as a class of object in its own right. Its attributes are the two accounts, the amount to transfer, and the date/time. The methods on the two account objects then become, effectively, 'Create New Transfer', which creates a new instance of Transfer, ready populated with the 'from' account. Alternatively, the user could shortcut this by dragging one account onto the other, which returns a new Transfer object with both the 'from' and 'to' fields populated. After specifying the amount to transfer, the user then invokes the 'Execute' or 'Make it so' method on the Transfer object.

Critics will say that all we have done is created a Transfer process, or even a Transfer dialog box, and called it an object; but they are missing an important point. Because each transfer is now modelled as an instantiated object, it can be directly referred to in future, for purposes of audit, or even reversal. In fact, for our banking application, Withdrawals and Deposits should similarly be treated as noun-objects not as verbs. (It would be legitimate to refer to all of these examples as 'form' objects, where the form provides a permanent record of that instance of a process). If you treat each of those concepts as merely a verb or process then you cannot refer directly to, say, a particular withdrawal, but must reconstruct it, in effect, from the audit trail.

Many good object modellers would have seen that solution immediately. For the rest – Naked Objects will not automatically present them with the best solution, but it will make it considerably harder to implement some of the poorer ones.

2.3.6 How can Naked Objects meet the requirement for multiple views?

Using Naked Objects, all user views are generated automatically from the business object definitions; but it is a common requirement for a system to provide multiple views of the same business object. How does Naked Objects address this?

We need to distinguish two different kinds of alternative views. The first we shall call multiple representations: we might want to view a collection of objects as a list, or as a table, or perhaps as a graph. The Viewing Mechanism that forms part of the Naked Objects framework already provides several alternative generic views of objects. The default view is a small icon. The 'opened' view lists the attributes and shows all the associated objects as active icons. Alternatively, an object can be portrayed as plain text, or, if it implements the 'hasImage' interface, it can be displayed as an image. Collections of objects can be shown as a single icon or a list. If the objects in the list are all of the same type then the collection can be viewed as a table, or a tiled layout of images. If the objects in the collection implement the 'mappable' interface, then they can be located on a two-dimensional geographic or schematic map. All of these generic views are automatically provided, without any explicit programming, and users can select any of them. This capability is conceptually the same as the Windows (or equivalent) capability to view the contents of a folder as icons, a summarized list, thumbnails or details. We expect that a broader range of generic views will be added in time – for example, the ability to view any array of numbers as a chart, as in a spreadsheet application. Capable programmers can extend the framework themselves to add new kinds of generic views.

The second concept we shall call selective views: providing the user with a partial view of an object, showing only certain of its attributes, associations, and methods. This may be because a certain user is not authorized to see other information, or simply in order to reduce screen clutter.

The Naked Objects framework does permit you to customize views through the use of About objects – you can specify which attributes, associations and methods are available to a given user or role. The same mechanisms could also be used to control the view, or behaviour, of an object according to its state (where that state is either explicitly represented, or derived from other attributes and associations).

But in general, the idea of designing systems from naked objects is to avoid too much contextualizing. The aim is to give the user as rich a potential view of any object as possible unless the screen gets too cluttered. This is in marked contrast to the usual approach to systems design, which is to give the user the minimum information necessary to complete a particular task – thereby limiting the users' opportunity to learn to see the big picture.

A positive side effect of naked objects is that they help to preserve the integrity of the object model. For example, a conventionally-designed system may display on an invoice the name and address of the customer, which will have been extracted from the Customer object. Whilst this may not be breaking the rule of encapsulation in the technical sense, it is certainly damages the user's understanding of the object model. Using naked objects, the Invoice will not display the customer's name and address as separate fields: it will display an icon representing the Customer within the Invoice. To check, or alter the customer's address, the user must open the Customer object and make the alteration there.

2.3.7 How do you avoid shared business objects becoming 'bloated'?

If the only way that the user can invoke an action is by selecting a method upon a core business object, and if objects are going to be shared across different uses or departments, then aren't those core business objects quickly going to become bloated with methods, attributes and associations?

An object with too many methods, attributes and associations smells suspiciously like a monolithic program – suggesting that agility will be reduced. The answer, in most cases is to use the technique of aggregation: split a single object into natural components, even if those components are never accessed outside the context of their parent object, and aggregate those components. Thus, the Customer object might have components to model the Identity information, Medical history, and so forth. This also helps with performance. An object with too many attributes takes a long time to load into memory from secondary storage. Using aggregation, the object can choose to load only pointers to its component objects, and load their attributes only if a component object is to be viewed by the user, or invoked by a method on the main object.

2.3.8   Can Naked Objects work in a 'thin client' architecture?

More and more organizations claim to have adopted a 'thin client' policy, but the meaning of that term varies considerably. To some people it means that every application must run within a browser; but then to some large plug-ins are acceptable, while to others they are unacceptable; and some even take the view that the client must run pure HTML, with no Java code. Alternatively, thin client may not imply operation within a browser, but within other architectural or hardware constraints.

The Naked Objects framework can work within any of these constraints – although this may involve writing an alternative generic viewing mechanism for your preferred client architecture. For example, a pure HTML implementation might portray each object as a web page, with the action methods shown as buttons. Drag and drop would not be possible, but point and click would be. Multiple panes, including a tree view of recently visited objects, would permit all the same operations to be conducted. But it would not feel nearly as expressive to the user.

However, we believe that the 'thin client' idea (or, at least, most interpretations of it) needs to be challenged. When first proposed, the idea of running everything within a browser held considerable appeal, because it eliminated the need to maintain software directly on client machines. But there are now several technical means of achieving this goal. Another motivation was to provide a standardized user interface environment, but, as we have seen, there is very little standardization in the user interaction model offered by different browser-based applications. Moreover, the basic HTML interface is not a good interface for undertaking any kind of problem-solving activity. It was intended only for browsing published information. Transactional capabilities have gradually been added, but they are something of a kludge in user interface design terms. The third motivation for standardization on a browser interface is for consumer access. However, naked objects are best suited for frequent-use applications, which primarily means in-house users.

2.3.9 Would Naked Objects permit users to develop their own applications?

Many people have pointed out that whilst naked objects improve the expressiveness of the system for the end-user, the Naked Objects framework does not do the same for the developer. Why make the developer write code in a text editor, when much of the initial development could also be done with techniques such as drag and drop?

For several reasons. The first is that we were anxious not to let the idea of developer expressiveness and end-user expressiveness become confused. Tools such as VisualBasic already offer a great deal of expressiveness to the developer, but the user interfaces that result are frequently not very expressive for the end-user. By deliberately contrasting the developer environment and the end-user environment, our aim was to keep the developers focussed on creating expressive systems for their users, not for themselves.

Secondly, it's not clear that graphical representations and drag and drop (or equivalent) gestures are particularly relevant to developers. Certainly, they are relevant to designing screen layouts, but the whole idea of Naked Objects is that you don't design screen layouts – they are auto-generated by the system. Graphical representations can also help developers navigate around large amounts of code; but so too do state-of-the-art integrated development environments such as VisualAge, Eclipse, or TogetherJ which can all be used in conjunction with Naked Objects to develop applications. All that's left is writing functional code in a programming language such as Java. At this stage, graphical representations add little value – what the developers benefit from most at this stage are advanced code-support tools such as automated test suites and refactoring browsers.

We think that attempts to make programming an entirely graphical operation are misguided. They are generally aimed at end-user programming; but is that what we need? Naked objects were conceived to support problem solving by end-users, not programming by end-users. Problem solving means finding a solution for a single specific context. Programming involves finding an abstract solution to a whole class of problems. These are different skills. The spreadsheet is an extraordinarily powerful tool for solving individual problems and is simple to use, but writing a spreadsheet template that is robust enough for others to use too requires a different degree of discipline. Is that what we want end-users to be doing?

Case study: Travel bookings

Executive Car Services (ECS) is a large limousine company with a call centre servicing operations in multiple cities. (ECS is a fictional organisation, but this case is based upon real experiences.) Although the company enjoys a reputation for excellent customer service, the standard call centre approach of attempting to cover all customer interactions using standardized, optimized scripts can sometimes lead to considerable frustration – for both customer and booking agent – as the following example reveals:

- **How can I help you?** I'd like a car from mid-town Manhattan to JFK airport early this afternoon, please.

- **May I have your first name?** Richard.

- **Last name?** Pawson.

- **I see you've booked with us before. Are you still with CSC?** Yes.

- **In that case I'll need a project number for the invoice.** I don't have a project number to hand, can I pay by credit card?

- **Certainly. Type of credit card?** American Express.

- **Number on the card?** 3791 xxxxxx xxxxx.

- **Expiry date?** 01.04

- **Name as printed on the card?** Richard W Pawson.

- **Date of travel?** Today.

- **Time?** 2.30pm.

- **Location?** It's the Pfizer building on East 42nd St – I don't know the number.

- **I can look that up for you . . . just a moment . . . yes, it's 234 East 42nd St.**

- **And you are going to?** JFK airport.

- **Which airline?** British Airways.

- **Which flight number?** I don't know the flight number, it is the one going to London at 18.00.

70

- **I can look that up also ... just a moment ... yes, it's the BA218.**

- **And finally, I need a contact telephone number for you.** I'm staying at the Grand Hyatt on 42nd and Park Avenue. I don't know the number.

- **I can look that up ... yes, its 212 XXX XXXX. And what is your room number?** 1634.

- **Thank you, that's all I need. Just a moment please ... Sorry, sir, it seems that we have no cars available!**

The point is that the system ought to have been able to capture the information provided in the very first sentence and ascertain whether a car was available first — and only then ask for all the further information. It is not enough to put a new step into the script to check availability as early as possible in the interaction. Rather, the operator should be able to handle each call in any way that suits the customer or the particular problem in hand.

The screen shown below is from a simple prototype that we produced to demonstrate how designing a reservations system from naked objects might address this issue.

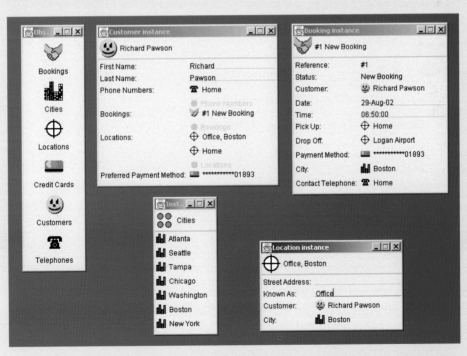

The mock-up uses just six core business object classes and these are now briefly explained.

The six classes used in the ECS prototype

 Booking Knows the details of a customer's booking. Knows how to check availability and confirm.

 Customer Knows identification details, and object instances frequently used by customer (e.g. Locations, Telephones). Knows how to communicate with the customer.

 City Knows frequently-used Locations in that city. Knows how to look up today's weather and traffic conditions.

 Location Knows the street address and a nickname (e.g. 'Head office'). Knows how to obtain driving directions.

 Credit Card Knows the card details. Knows how to hide the number, and how to obtain authorization for a given amount. (Other Payment Methods such as Company Account to be added later).

 Telephone Knows the number and nickname (e.g. 'My office'). Knows how to place the call. (Email, Fax objects would be added later, all sharing a common interface).

From this simple prototype we can illustrate three of the four benefits of naked objects:

- Naked objects empower the user.

- Naked objects can better accommodate future changes to business requirements.

- Naked objects improve communication between developers and users.

First, we'll look at empowering the user. The prototype allows the agent to construct a booking in several different ways, according to the particular context or the customer's preference. Here are just three possible scenarios:

- Right-click on the **Bookings** class and select **New Instance**.... Then fill in the fields one by one (but in any order that suits the customer or user). The **Check Availability** method can be invoked at any point from the pop-up menu. If all the necessary details are provided, this method will return a firm yes or no. If not, it will give an indication of availability during the day. The Booking object could also have methods to estimate journey time and adjust the pick-up time accordingly, or arrange to pick-up from a flight. (And because Flight would also be an object, it could easily be designed to monitor the predicted arrival from the appropriate airline's website).

- Go to the **Customers** class and retrieve the object representing this repeat customer. Expand the list of the customer's recent bookings and 'clone' the one desired, filling in only the new date and time. Alternatively, drag the **Customer** onto the **Bookings** class as a shortcut – this will pre-populate the booking with the customer details.

- Right-click on the **City** where the journey is to be made, which offers you the option of checking today's availability, and also the weather forecast and traffic news (which the customer may want to know in order to decide the time of travel). The **City** can then be used to show the most frequent locations booked by all customers within that city, including generalizations such as 'Downtown' that can subsequently be made more specific.

Secondly, the prototype shows how it becomes easier to accommodate future business change. Since the company often takes bookings for cars at both ends of a flight, might it not in future also make the flight booking? For an extra fee, why not add a concierge service to book theatre tickets or dinner reservations? All of these could be accommodated by generating new classes of business object that could be associated with a Booking as needed. Or, as another example, currently the two methods of payment are credit card and company account. Only one of these has been implemented on the prototype as shown, but both are sub-types of PaymentMethod. Further sub-types could easily be added to enable a gift certificate service, for example.

The third major benefit, of providing a common language between developer and user, is illustrated over the next few pages.

User and developer views of the system

What follows is a series of views illustrating different aspects of the system from the perspectives of the user and the developer. This is not a programming tutorial. Rather, it is an attempt to show the close correspondence that exists between the two views of a business system developed with the Naked Objects framework. From these screenshots it is possible to get a sense of just how easily a user-request can be translated into the necessary code changes.

Classes

An 'application' consists of nothing more than a set of business object classes. All user operations take the form of actions invoked upon an instance of one of those classes or upon the class as a whole. Any class that could form the start-point of a user activity is shown in the user's 'Classes' window, shown here on the left of the screen.

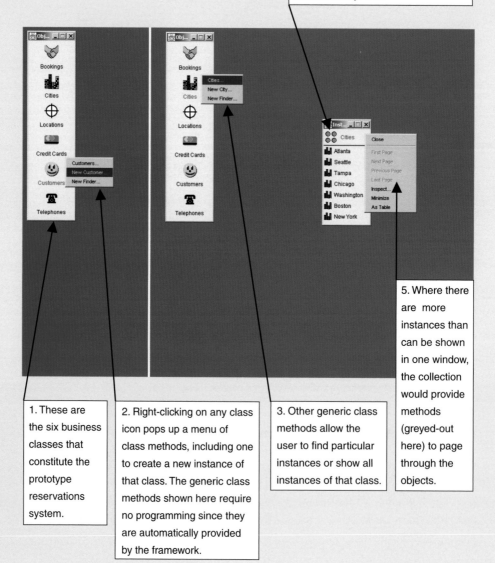

4. This symbol represents a collection of objects: in this case, all seven of the cities in the system.

5. Where there are more instances than can be shown in one window, the collection would provide methods (greyed-out here) to page through the objects.

1. These are the six business classes that constitute the prototype reservations system.

2. Right-clicking on any class icon pops up a menu of class methods, including one to create a new instance of that class. The generic class methods shown here require no programming since they are automatically provided by the framework.

3. Other generic class methods allow the user to find particular instances or show all instances of that class.

8. Each business object class must implement the NakedObject interface in order for the viewing mechanism and/or persistence mechanism to be able to use it. The easiest way to achieve this is to make each business class inherit from the AbstractNakedObject class provided with the framework.

6. The code for this application is all held in a project folder called ecs.delivery.

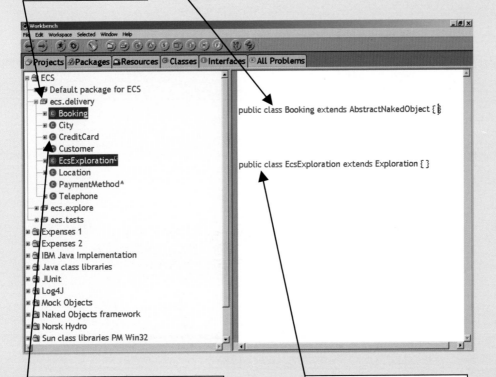

75

7. There is one Java class corresponding to each of the business object classes presented to the user. The label on the user's class icon is (by default) automatically derived from Java class name. Here CreditCard has been converted into Credit Cards. (Irregular plurals must be manually specified.)

9. The only code in this project that is not a business class is EcsExploration which is needed to run the application. Almost everything that this class needs is provided by the framework's Exploration class. When the application is deployed this EcsExploration will be replaced by a simple configuration file.

Instances

For most business scenarios, the user of the system will be dealing with individual instances of the business classes, and sometimes with collections of instances of the same type. By default, an instance uses the same icon as its class, but has an individual title. It is also possible to vary the icon according to the identity or the status of the object.

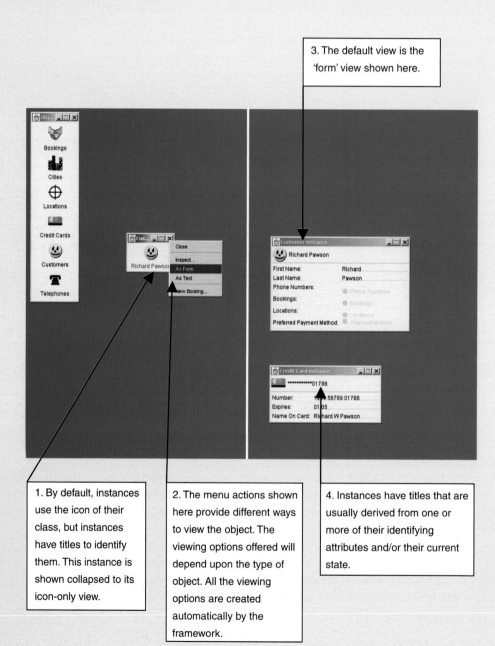

3. The default view is the 'form' view shown here.

1. By default, instances use the icon of their class, but instances have titles to identify them. This instance is shown collapsed to its icon-only view.

2. The menu actions shown here provide different ways to view the object. The viewing options offered will depend upon the type of object. All the viewing options are created automatically by the framework.

4. Instances have titles that are usually derived from one or more of their identifying attributes and/or their current state.

5. Each class is defined by the set of methods it can fulfil. All these methods deliver specific business value, and result directly from a user requirement. The underlying technical methods needed to manage the objects can all be inherited from the framework and need never be seen by application developers

8. CreditCard has a more complex title method that masks all but the last five digits of the number.

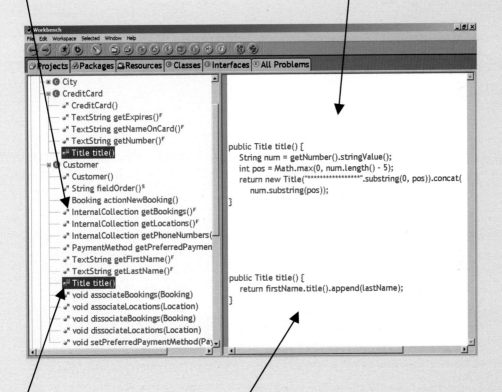

6. Each business class needs a title method to generate the title that appears next to the icon. This is normally derived from one or more of its attributes such as name, status, or reference number.

7. The title method must return a Title. Here the firstName is turned into a Title object (using an inherited method), then the lastName is appended to it. The append method looks after leading and trailing spaces automatically.

Fields

Open a view of any object and you will see a set of fields. Some of these fields contain simple values (such as dates, numbers or text strings), which the user may be able to enter or edit. Other fields will contain business objects, shown as icons. Even where an icon appears inside another object view, that icon still represents a fully functional object: you can invoke its behaviours in situ or open up a new view of it.

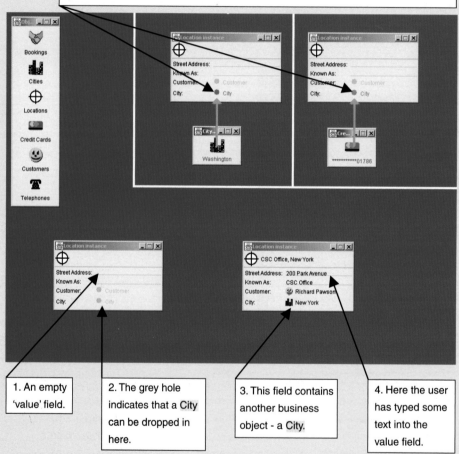

5. If you attempt to drag the right type of object into a field, (here a City) the drop zone will flash green. A red flash indicates that the framework will not let you drop that object there, either because it is the wrong type or due to some other programmer-specifed rule.

1. An empty 'value' field.

2. The grey hole indicates that a City can be dropped in here.

3. This field contains another business object - a City.

4. Here the user has typed some text into the value field.

6. Each field in the user view is determined by the existence of a get method in the Java class definition. The field name is, by default, a formatted version of the method name.

9. The framework provides a set of generic NakedValue classes including TextString, WholeNumber, Date and Money. Such fields require only a get method because the value object itself provides the methods for changing contents.

10. NakedValue objects are typically initialized within the constructor method for the business object they are contained in.

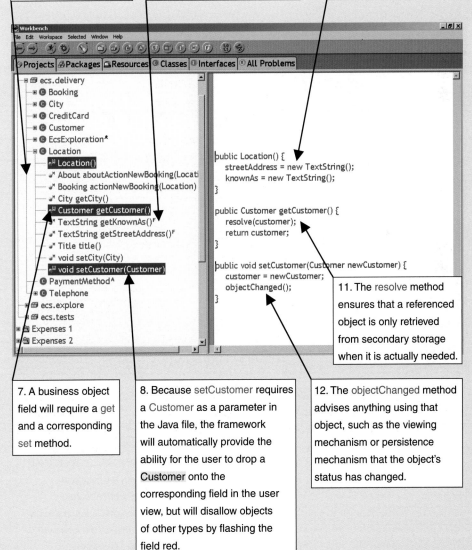

```
public Location() {
    streetAddress = new TextString();
    knownAs = new TextString();
}

public Customer getCustomer() {
    resolve(customer);
    return customer;
}

public void setCustomer(Customer newCustomer) {
    customer = newCustomer;
    objectChanged();
}
```

11. The resolve method ensures that a referenced object is only retrieved from secondary storage when it is actually needed.

7. A business object field will require a get and a corresponding set method.

8. Because setCustomer requires a Customer as a parameter in the Java file, the framework will automatically provide the ability for the user to drop a Customer onto the corresponding field in the user view, but will disallow objects of other types by flashing the field red.

12. The objectChanged method advises anything using that object, such as the viewing mechanism or persistence mechanism that the object's status has changed.

Associations

We have just seen how a field can contain a reference to another business object. Naked Objects can also handle more complex relationships such as multiple associations, where one object knows multiple instances of another type, and bi-directional associations, where two objects both know about each other.

1. The Customer can have multiple Locations associated with it.

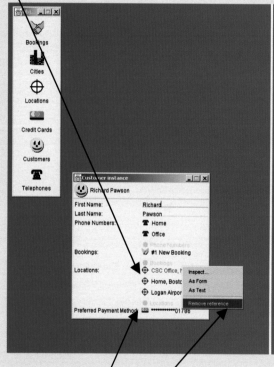
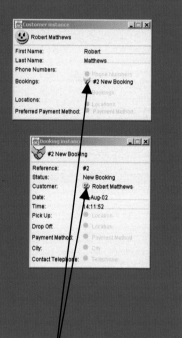

2. A new Location can be associated by dropping it onto the grey hole at the bottom of the collection.

3. Right clicking on any member of this collection offers the option to Remove Reference.

4. This is an example of a bi-directional association. When a Customer is associated with a Booking, a reference to that Booking is automatically added to the customer's list of bookings.

9. Adding a fieldOrder method to an object allows us to control the order in which fields are presented to the user.

5. A multiple association is managed by an InternalCollection (provided by the framework) which can hold only objects of a specified type.

6. A multiple association needs only a get method to return the InternalCollection, which then provides its own methods for accessing the objects it contains.

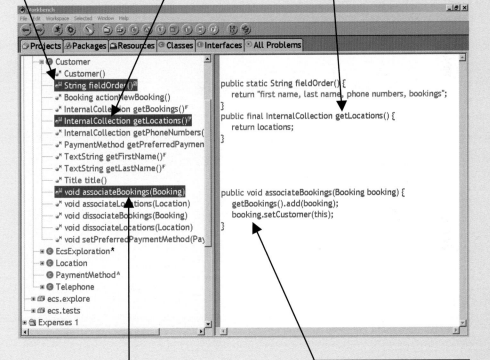

7. Bi-directional associations (whether singular or multiple) require the provision of associate and dissociate methods.

8. associateBooking on the Customer first adds the new Booking to the internal collection of bookings, then sets the customer field on that Booking to point to this (Customer). In a bi-directional association, one object manages the association and the other one delegates responsibility to it.

Behaviour

The two principal mechanisms by which a user can invoke a business behaviour are by selecting an action from a pop-up menu on a business object and by dragging one object onto another. (The latter is not the same as dragging an object into an empty field inside an object.) It is also possible to invoke business behaviours at the class level – through the pop-up menu on that class – or by dragging an instance icon onto the class icon.

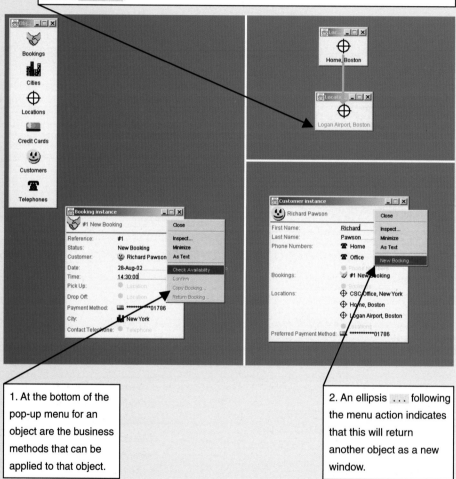

3. Dragging Home, Boston directly onto Logan Airport, Boston will trigger the creation of a new Booking that uses those two locations as Pick Up and Drop Off respectively. This shortcut is most useful when both locations show up in a list of frequently-used locations inside a Customer.

1. At the bottom of the pop-up menu for an object are the business methods that can be applied to that object.

2. An ellipsis ... following the menu action indicates that this will return another object as a new window.

4. The method name actionReturnBooking is stripped of its action prefix and reformatted to generate the menu option Return Booking. . . automatically. For language localization it is possible to over-ride this automatic correspondence. The ellipsis in the menu option reflects the fact that an object wiil be returned by this method - in this case a Booking.

5. createInstance creates a new instance of the Booking class, called returnBooking. Just using the simple Java new keyword instead of createInstance would not perform all the necessary initialisation.

6. This code swaps the pick-up and drop-off locations for the return booking.

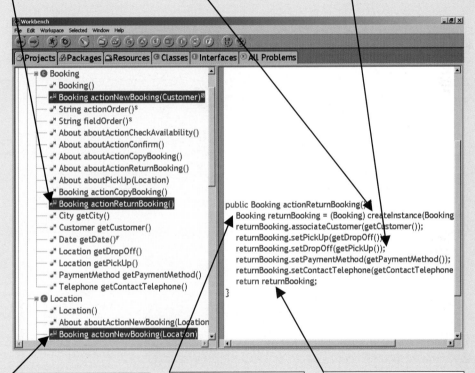

7. If an action method requires an input parameter (in this case another Location) then this behaviour will not show up on the pop-up menu. Instead, it will be automatically invoked when the user drops an object of the required type onto this object.

8. This method creates a return booking from an existing booking.

9. If another object has invoked this method then the newly created Booking will be passed back to it. If the method was invoked by the user from the menu, then the returned object will automatically show up as a new window.

Control

Naked objects empower the user but that does not imply an absence of controls. Different users will need access to different objects, different fields within those objects and different behaviours on those objects. It will also be necessary to enforce certain business rules, such as preventing an action from being invoked unless the object is in the right state. In Naked Objects these forms of control are implemented using about methods and About objects.

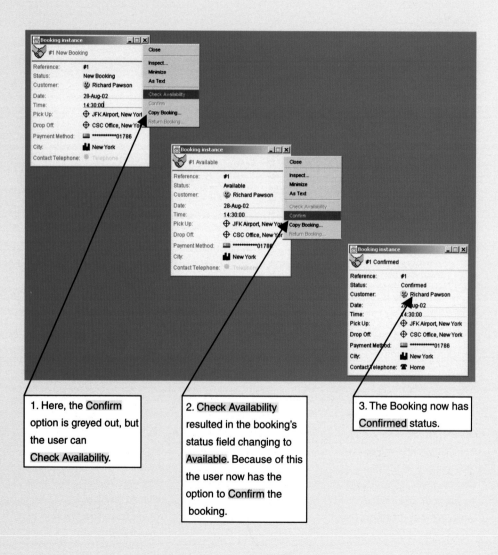

1. Here, the Confirm option is greyed out, but the user can Check Availability.

2. Check Availability resulted in the booking's status field changing to Available. Because of this the user now has the option to Confirm the booking.

3. The Booking now has Confirmed status.

4. The actionConfirm method has a corresponding aboutActionConfirm method that determines whether the former can be accessed. If access is denied then the viewing mechanism will grey out this menu option.

6. Availability may be determined by business rules or by user authorisation. The whole determination could be sub-contracted to an authorisation server.

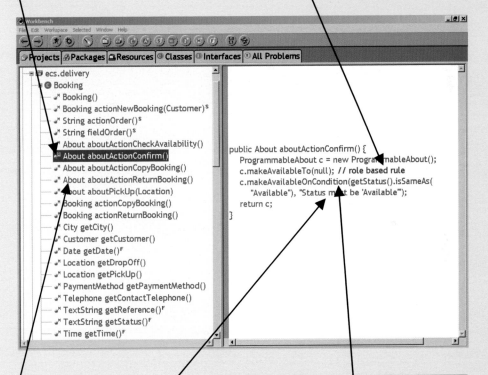

```
public About aboutActionConfirm() {
    ProgrammableAbout c = new ProgrammableAbout();
    c.makeAvailableTo(null); // role based rule
    c.makeAvailableOnCondition(getStatus().isSameAs(
        "Available"), "Status must be 'Available'");
    return c;
}
```

(Workbench window showing ecs.delivery → Booking class tree:
- Booking()
- Booking actionNewBooking(Customer)ˢ
- String actionOrder()ˢ
- String fieldOrder()ˢ
- About aboutActionCheckAvailability()
- About aboutActionConfirm()
- About aboutActionCopyBooking()
- About aboutActionReturnBooking()
- About aboutPickUp(Location)
- Booking actionCopyBooking()
- Booking actionReturnBooking()
- City getCity()
- Customer getCustomer()
- Date getDate()ᶠ
- Location getDropOff()
- Location getPickUp()
- PaymentMethod getPaymentMethod()
- Telephone getContactTelephone()
- TextString getReference()ᶠ
- TextString getStatus()ᶠ
- Time getTime()ᶠ)

5. about methods return an About object, which contains data about the availability of a method, class or instance it applies to. Generic forms of About are provided with the framework.

8. Here, a reason is provided for the unavailability of the method. In the current version of the framework, this message shows up in the system log window. In a future release better use will be made of this capability, perhaps in the form of optional balloon help.

7. Here, aboutAction Confirm checks to see if the Booking object's status field is set to Available. If so, Action Confirm will be made accessible to the user.

Section 3:
Programming with Naked Objects

In this section we will look at how to write a business system using the Naked Objects framework.

Most of the code examples in this section are taken from the Executive Car Services (ECS) application, the complete code for which is distributed with the Naked Objects framework.

We will start by looking at the anatomy of a naked object – the interface that it must present to its external users. Naked object classes are written in Java and build on Java's inherent structure by adopting certain coding conventions. Because we name and structure methods in a standard way, the framework can recognize the fields and behaviours of an object and make those objects available to the user, identify them and manipulate them.

We then look at how to make your naked object classes available to users in the form of a simple standalone application that is suitable for exploration and testing.

The third part looks at making the same objects available as part of a finished business system. This section addresses the issues of sharing objects between multiple users, making the objects persistent (typically via a database), and handling transactions.

In the fourth part we look at writing unit and acceptance tests. We show how Naked Objects makes it feasible to write your acceptance tests before you commence writing any of the operational code.

The last part looks at the detail of coding business functionality into a business object. This includes manipulating value objects and collections inside your methods, building more complex titles for an object, and using About objects to implement business controls.

In order to follow this section you will need to have some familiarity with Java already. Our aim in developing the framework was to build on the way Java classes are defined, make use of recognized good practices and minimize the number of new restrictions. Most of the burden of using the objects – displaying, distributing and persisting them – is therefore shifted onto the framework, leaving you free to code just the business objects.

Throughout this section we often talk about naked objects from the user's perspective. For example, we talk about one-parameter action... methods as enabling one object to be dropped onto another. This way of describing naked objects comes naturally because the objects we are defining are the objects the user manipulates. But it is important to understand that the naming convention required by the Naked Objects framework is not in fact directed at the user interface. Those same one-parameter action... methods might also be called by other objects or by a batch program with no user interface. The coding conventions are our way of exposing the object, laying it bare, making it naked. Then the naked object can be seen by the system, and hence shown to the user.

Furthermore, the style of graphical interface that we show throughout this book is the one generated by the first viewing mechanism that we have written. We expect to write other viewing mechanisms that will take the same business objects and render them in quite different styles – perhaps via an HTML-only browser interface, or even a via speech synthesiser and voice recognition system.

If you have not already used Naked Objects, we suggest that before working through this section you follow our step by step instructions for downloading and installing the framework and then developing a very simple application from scratch*.

*See page 223

Notes for experienced Java programmers

If you are an experienced Java programmer then you will be able to work through much of this section fairly quickly. But be aware that the coding for Naked Objects does differ in a number of small but important ways from writing Java classes in general:

- All fields usable by the user need to be of type org.nakedobjects.object.Naked. The framework does not know how to display or persist the standard Java types. The framework does provide a number of generic Naked types such as TextString, Money, WholeNumber and Date (all part of the org.nakedobjects.object.value package), which both encompass and extend the types provided by Java.

- It is important to access variables through their accessor (get... and set...) methods rather than directly. The persistence mechanism relies on such methods to store away and reload the object's data.

- To create an initialized and persistent object, use the factory method createInstance. New instances of business objects should not be created using just the standard Java new operator – this would not initialize them properly. Related to this, a persisted object's constructor will be invoked every time it is restored.

- Every persistent object must have a unique ID that does not change between instantiations. The equals and hashCode methods are based on this ID and should not be changed.

3.1 The anatomy of a naked object

A Naked Object system is simply a collection of classes that are made available to the user. To be rendered visible to the user, an object must be of the type org.nakedobjects.object.Naked. This interface is defined within the Naked Objects framework along with two sub-interfaces. The first is org.nakedobjects.object.NakedValue, for value objects, which store simple data values (such as text, numbers, currency and dates) and are only used inside other objects. The framework provides a number of ready-made classes that implement this interface, several of which we shall be introducing in this section. Programmers can add new NakedValue classes if needed. The second sub-interface is org.nakedobjects.object.NakedObject. This is used for objects that need to be referenced in multiple contexts, which typically means your business objects.

The simplest way to ensure that your business objects conform to the NakedObject definition is to make them sub-classes of org.nakedobjects.object.AbstractNakedObject — a class provided by the framework. If you cannot do this, because your business object must inherit from some other hierarchy, then you will have to implement the methods required by NakedObject yourself.

AbstractNakedObject implements all of the methods in the NakedObject interface except for title, which we will discuss shortly. Thus it provides you with a foundation for building your business objects. We will use this class throughout our discussions.

If a business object class is defined as a subclass of AbstractNakedObject, then you must also do the following in order for the framework to be able to access and manipulate these objects, and thereby make them available to users:

- Declare the class as public.

- Ensure the class has a zero-parameter constructor (this is often referred to as the default constructor).

- Declare as public all of its methods that are to be made available to the framework.

- Implement the abstract title method from the superclass so that it returns a non-null reference. The title method will help users to distinguish each object from the rest of the instances of a specific type — but it could also be used for other purposes, such as searching or report generation.

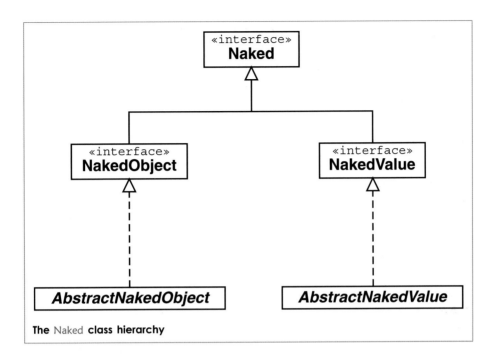

The Naked **class hierarchy**

3.1.1 Naked object classes

Here is a typical class declaration for a business object class written using the Naked Objects framework. It is shown here without any method bodies, and with the required members in bold. The zero-parameter constructor is shown to reinforce the point that one is always required (although if you don't declare any other constructors then Java will provide this one for you.)

```
import org.nakedobjects.object.AbstractNakedObject;
import org.nakedobjects.object.Title;
import org.nakedobjects.object.control.About;

public class Parcel extends AbstractNakedObject {
    public static final long serialVersionUID = 1L;

    public static About aboutParcel() {}

    public Parcel() {}

    public About about() {}

    public void created() {}

    public Title title() {}
}
```

The class variable is the version number for this serializable class, which is used when the object is serialized (as happens when it is transferred across the network). Although there is little that will cause serialization to fail, the default serial numbers can be different on different JVMs, so it is good practice to set this variable up for each new class. (However, to keep things brief we do not show this in the examples that follow.) As the Naked Objects framework uses quite a coarse-grained serialization algorithm, this serial number can be set (to any arbitrary value) and left, even when the class is changed.

The two about... methods are used to control the accessibility of the class and its instances.

The created method is only called following the creation of a new logical instance of the class and not every time that that logical object is recreated in memory by the persistence mechanism. By contrast, the constructor will be called every time Java instantiates that particular persistent object, which will happen each time the object is retrieved from the persistent store. Thus, the created method is where you would put any code for initializing a business object.

Making a class uninstantiable

By default, users will be given the ability to create new instances of any business class. To prevent this you can add the static about method to your class. For example, in the ECS application the set of City objects is fixed by means of the following code:

```
public static About aboutCity() {
    return ClassAbout.UNINSTANTIABLE;
}
```

(org.nakedobjects.object.control.ClassAbout is a special type of org.nakedobjects.object.control.About object provided by the framework.)

In consequence, the pop-up menu on the Cities icon will show New Instance... as disabled. Dragging the class onto the desktop or into a field to create an object will not work either.

The About can also be used to prohibit access, by making the class invisible to certain types of user, or to all users.

Making an object read-only

It is also possible to control access to individual instances. An object can be made unchangeable, so that all the fields are set to read-only; and it can be made inaccessible, so that it will not appear on the screen. This is done through the about object method (as opposed to the about *class* method such as aboutCity in the example above). The following method, again taken from the City class, makes any instance of city un-editable:

```
public About about() {
    return ObjectAbout.READ_ONLY;
}
```

Class names

Classes are usually represented to the user in two places when Naked Objects is run. The first, and most obvious, is the list of classes. The second is in each empty field, where the class indicates the type of object that can be placed in that field. The screenshot below shows both. Note that the **Customer** field takes a Customer object and the **Pick Up** and **Drop Off** fields both take Location objects.

The titles shown for the classes are automatically generated from the name of the class by removing the package name, adding spaces in front of subsequent upper case letters, to separate the words, and adding an 's' on the end. If the class name takes an irregular plural then you can use the class method pluralName to specify the plural version manually. For example, the following code shows the method set up to return the correct plural for the class Calf:

```
public static String pluralName() {
    return "Calves";
}
```

You can also specify a class title to be shown to the users that is different from the name of the Java class, by using a singularName method. This could be wise in languages that use accents and ligatures. As Java source code is compiled using Unicode instead of ASCII, it is possible to use both of these within identifiers, but it is not recommended because identifiers are easily mis-spelt or corrupted when source code files are transferred. Instead, give your identifiers simple ASCII names, as shown in the example below, which embeds the german 'ä' into the plural string as a unicode character:

```
public class City extends AbstractNakedObject {
    public static String singularName() {
        return "Stadt";
    }

    public static String pluralName() {
        return "St\u00e4dte";
    }
}
```

3.1.2 Fields

When the framework's viewing mechanism portrays a business object in one of its opened views (most commonly the 'form' view), it looks to see if the object has any publicly available accessor methods that return an object of the org.nakedobjects.object.Naked type, and if so displays that object in a field. These accessor methods have many uses: they are used by the persistence mechanism, and may be called by other objects. But it is often convenient to think of them, in the first instance, as rendering an internal attribute visible to the user.

Fields can be divided into three categories: values, associations, and multiple associations. These can all be seen in the screenshot below, where the values appear as characters on a line and are editable, and the associations show up as icons. For a multiple association, the field can show more than one icon.

The label, or field name, is generated from the name of the accessor method (it is the method name without its 'get' prefix, and with spaces added where a capital letter is found). An accessor method often shares the same name as the variable it accesses, but not always. Remember that it is the method name and not the variable name that is used by the framework to label the field displayed to the user.

Values

Simple unshared data values are restricted to classes of the type
org.nakedobjects.object.NakedValue. The framework provides TextString,
Date, Time, WholeNumber (in the org.nakedobjects.object.value package) and
several others*. Use these classes to model all values that might need to be   *See page 126
accessed outside the business object – for example to be displayed to the user
or made persistent in a database. Programmers may define new NakedValue
types, for example to handle scientific units of measurement. You may use
other Java classes and primitives such as java.lang.String or int inside a method
for strictly local purposes, but you cannot display them directly via the viewing
mechanism.

Each value object must be declared and initialized, and must be made available
through an accessor method:

```
public class Customer extends AbstractNakedObject {
    private final TextString lastName;
    private final TextString firstName;

    public Customer() {
        firstName = new TextString();
        lastName = new TextString();
    }

    public TextString getLastName() {
        return lastName;
    }

    public TextString getFirstName() {
        return firstName;
    }
}
```

The lastName and firstName variables are both TextString objects and are used
to store simple textual information. All value objects are mutable and should be
declared as private and final so that a specific value object referenced by a field
is never replaced. The value that it contains (e.g. the last name) may change,
but only by getting hold of the value object and invoking one of the change
methods that it provides. This convention helps to ensure that value objects
are not inadvertently shared between business objects by attempting to copy a
value from one field to another.

Since they are marked as final, these variables must be initialized before the containing object can be used. This must be done either after the declaration or, as we have shown, in a suitable constructor. All value object classes have a zero parameter constructor, so they can be instantiated without you having to provide an initial value.

As all fields containing a value object are marked as final, only a get... method is required. The beauty of the value objects is that the framework takes complete care of them. If the user wants to change a value then the framework asks the value object to change itself. If the user interface needs to know what possible values there are (for the org.nakedobjects.object.value.Option value object, say) then the framework asks that value object directly. As programmers our job is done when we decide to use a specific type of value object and declare it as described.

Value fields can be made read-only, so the field cannot be edited. This is indicated to the user by the removal of the light grey line underneath the field's text. The field can be set at any time by a call to the setAbout method on the value object and passing in an About object – after which it cannot be changed. Suitable org.nakedobjects.object.control.About objects to make a field read-only or read-write can be obtained from the org.nakedobjects.object.control.FieldAbout class and are called READ_ONLY and READ_WRITE respectively. Commonly, value objects are set to read-only when they are created, as shown in the following code taken from the Booking class:

```
public Booking() {
    reference = new TextString();
    reference.setAbout(FieldAbout.READ_ONLY);
    status = new TextString();
    status.setAbout(FieldAbout.READ_ONLY);
}
```

One-to-one associations

A one-to-one association is where one business object has a field that contains a reference to another business object. (A business object is an object of the type org.nakedobjects.object.NakedObject – any other type of object is ignored by the framework). This association is essentially achieved just by implementing the standard accessor methods get**Variable** and set**Variable**. The following code, taken from the Booking class, shows a reference variable and its two accessor

methods. You will see also that both the getDropOff and the setDropOff methods have had specific calls added within them:

```
public class Booking extends AbstractNakedObject {
    private Location dropOff;

    public Location getDropOff() {
        resolve(dropOff);
        return dropOff;
    }

    public void setDropOff(Location newDropOff) {
        dropOff = newDropOff;
        objectChanged();
    }
}
```

In the getDropOff method, we can see a resolve call, which is a static method
provided in the superclass hierarchy. The purpose of the resolve call is to ensure
that the referenced object (in this case the Location held in the DropOff field)
actually exists, fully formed, in memory. The fact that the Booking object has
all its data loaded does not imply that all the other objects it references are also
complete: if the framework operated that way, loading a single object could
take a long time! Instead the framework endeavours to load objects from storage only when they are needed.

This is best explained with an example. In the image below the left hand side
(with the blue background) shows the user's view. The right hand side (grey
background) is a portrayal of what is happening in working memory:

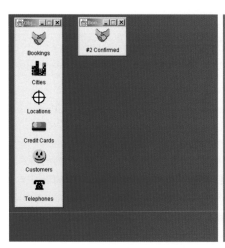

In this first screen, the user has retrieved the **#2 Confirmed** booking from storage and displayed it as an icon. On the right-hand side we can see that a booking object has been instantiated in memory, and that the value fields, which are an integral part of the object, have been retrieved from storage. In this case, those value fields provide sufficient information for the booking object's title to be generated (specifically from the **Reference** and **Status** fields). For each of the objects associated with that booking, a new instance of the appropriate type has been created within the association field, but none of those objects have yet been resolved. We have portrayed this graphically by using icons without titles.

The user now opens up the booking object to show the form view. All value fields and all associated objects are now displayed:

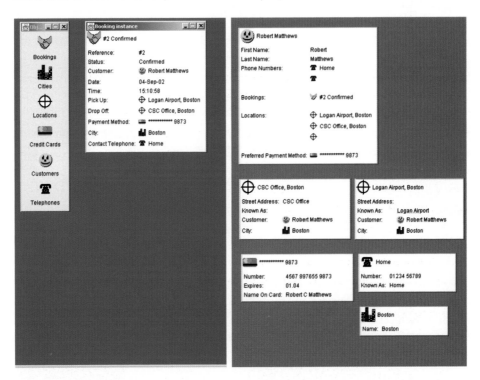

In order to display the titles of each of the associated objects (such as the customer for that booking) the framework has automatically resolved those objects. (The booking object still exists in memory, but this is not shown for reasons of space). Each of these objects has now had each of its value fields retrieved from storage, but where the objects contain references (associations) to other objects, these have been instantiated, but not themselves resolved. If the associated object has already been retrieved then that reference is used. In our example this has happened with the **Home** telephone, the first two locations and the credit card because they have all been used by the booking. The second telephone and the third location have not been used yet and therefore exist only as skeletal objects.

The user now opens up a form view of the customer object, in this case as a new window:

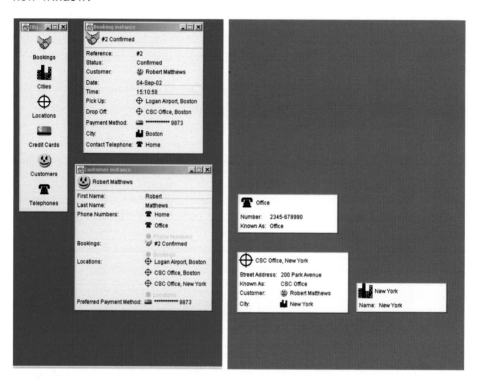

On the right hand side we can see that this object has now been resolved in memory. Most of the objects that it refers to are already available as they have been used previously, except for the **Office** telephone and **CSC Office** location which now must be read in. Note that the location object has a title that uses both the **Known As** value field and the **City** association field. The generation of the title therefore forces the automatic retrieval of the **New York** object.

In consequence, accessors for fields that reference other business objects (such as the getDropOff in the last piece of code we looked at) should start with an explicit attempt to resolve the referenced object. The resolve method checks the reference, and if it is valid but has not yet been resolved, the framework issues a resolve request to the object store. The object store responds to this by loading the missing data into the object. Alternatively, if the argument is null, or if the referenced object has already been resolved, then the request is simply ignored. Hence, when this method returns we can be assured that the referenced object has been resolved and can be used safely. After the reference has been resolved it is returned to the caller of the accessor method in the normal way.

In the setDropOff method above, after the assignment has been made, objectChanged is called. This notifies the framework that the object has changed. In response the framework updates the persisted version of the object, and notifies the other viewers of this object so that their displays can be updated. If you forget to include the objectChanged call within a set... method then you could find that changes to the object are not being persisted, your display is not updating properly, and, if the object is being shared, that other users are working with non-current information.

It is common to control association fields so they can be made inaccessible or read-only, or so that they will only accept certain objects. When an association is marked as inaccessible the field in which it would be normally shown will not show up in the view. If the field is read-only it will not allow objects (of its type) to be dropped into it, flashing red if the user attempts to do so.

An association field is controlled through an about... method whose name is based on the field's name without the 'get' or 'set' prefix. This method must accept one parameter, which must be the same type as specified in the get... and set... methods, and return an About object. The following example would make the **Drop Off** field (as identified from the getDropOff method) read-only:

```
public About aboutDropOff(Location location) {
    return FieldAbout.READ_ONLY;
}
```

In addition to the control that is exerted over the accessor method, the About object can supply a name that is used to replace the field's label. This mechanism can be used to localize the names of the fields when the system is used internationally.

One-to-many associations

A one-to-many association is where a field contains references to a number of other business objects. This is achieved by specifying the field as containing an org.nakedobjects.object.collection.InternalCollection – a specialized collection that is provided by the Naked Objects framework. This InternalCollection is itself a type of org.nakedobjects.object.NakedObject, and can therefore be 'seen' by other elements of the framework such as the viewing and persistence mechanisms. The InternalCollection becomes a composite part of the business object and is responsible for managing the references to the other business objects. It provides methods to add and remove references to business objects and ensures that they all conform to a specified business type. In a future release it will provide additional methods for sorting and other operations.

The following example, taken from the Customer class, shows two collections being declared along with the appropriate accessor methods. The collections are being set up to maintain a number of Location and Telephone objects:

```
public class Customer extends AbstractNakedObject {
    private final InternalCollection locations;
    private final InternalCollection phoneNumbers;

    public Customer() {
        locations = new InternalCollection(Location.class, this);
        phoneNumbers = new InternalCollection(Telephone.class, this);
    }

    public final InternalCollection getLocations() {
        return locations;
    }

    public final InternalCollection getPhoneNumbers() {
        return phoneNumbers;
    }
}
```

The org.nakedobjects.object.collection.InternalCollection variables are marked as final to ensure that they remain part of the customer object and are never replaced. The contents of the collections are changed by invoking methods upon the collection object itself. A normal get... accessor is declared, but being marked final there is no set... method.

As the collection is a composite part of the customer object it is created when the customer is created. The InternalCollection's own constructor requires us to specify the type of objects it will hold, as a java.lang.Class object; and which object it belongs to. (Unlike the other fields, the type cannot be specified within the variable declaration, nor does it figure in the method signature.)

As with the value objects, the framework takes care of managing the collections. Whenever the user adds an object to a field that uses an InternalCollection, or a method adds an element to the collection, the framework checks the type, adds the object to the collection, and notifies the object store so the persisted data can be updated. Whenever the user uses an element from the field, or another method accesses the collection's elements, then those elements are resolved before they are made available.

One-to-many associations can also be made inaccessible or read-only, in the same way as one-to-one associations. Additional control over the adding and removing of specific objects from the collection will be added to the frame-work in the near future. When an association is marked as inaccessible the field in which it would be normally shown will not be added to the view. When marked as read-only a field will not allow objects (even of the correct type) to be dropped into it; the grey 'hole' on the screen that normally shows where an object can be dropped will not be there.

Controlling a one-to-many association field is done through an about... method whose name is based on the field's name without the 'get' prefix. This method must return an About object and have no parameters. The following example would make the Locations field (as identified from the getLocations method) read-only:

```
public About aboutLocations() {
    return FieldAbout.READ_ONLY;
}
```

Bidirectional associations

So far we have considered how one object knows about another object – a one-way association. Often this is enough, but sometimes the object that is being referenced also needs to know about the object that is referencing it. Take, for example, an ordering system. An order object will typically hold a reference to the customer who placed the order. However, it may also be useful to be able to get directly from a customer object to his current order, perhaps even to all his orders. To allow this, the customer needs to keep a reference to the order object. This can be achieved by adding a field to the customer class, containing either a single order object, or a collection of orders.

Keeping references within both objects in a relationship means that the user can find all of the related objects when given either of the objects as a starting point. That is, the association between the objects is bidirectional.

In principle this is simple to implement: you define the fields and suitable accessor methods in both objects, each holding reference to objects of the other type. However, in order to specify such a relationship the user would first have to drop one object into the appropriate field in a second object, and then drop the second object back into the corresponding field in the first object.

This would be tedious and prone to error. The obvious solution would be to modify the set... methods so that they call each other, thus causing both references to be set... up in one operation. However, you then need to ensure that you don't go into an infinite loop by calling the other object's set method repeatedly. You would also need to write the functionality needed to delete or clear a relationship when required. This complex process gets even worse if one side is an InternalCollection.

The Naked Objects framework simplifies all this through the optional use of a pair of associate**Variable** and dissociate**Variable** methods to set and reset the association respectively. If present these two methods will be called in preference to the set method, or instead of accessing the internal collection and adding a reference to it or removing one from it. Both of these new methods must correspond to the get**Variable** method in name and accept one parameter. The parameter should be of the type of business object returned by the accessors, or if the field contains an org.nakedobjects.object.collection.InternalCollection, the type that the collection was initialized with.

The relationship between the Customer and the Booking objects in the ECS application shows how this works. The following code from the Customer class shows the InternalCollection being declared, initialized and made accessible. It also shows how the association methods associateBookings and dissociateBookings are both specified to expect a Booking object as this is the type specified when the internal collection was initialized.

```
public class Customer extends AbstractNakedObject {
    private final InternalCollection bookings;

    public Customer() {
        bookings = new InternalCollection(Booking.class, this);
    }

    public final InternalCollection getBookings() {
        return bookings;
    }

    public void associateBookings(Booking booking) {
        getBookings().add(booking);
        booking.setCustomer(this);
    }

    public void dissociateBookings(Booking booking) {
        getBookings().remove(booking);
        booking.setCustomer(null);
    }

}
```

With the two association methods in place, dropping a **Booking** object onto the grey hole on the **Bookings** field within a **Customer** object will cause the associateBookings method to be invoked rather than getBookings.

When the associateBookings method is called it takes on the responsibility of adding the Booking object to the customer's collection of bookings, thereby setting up the forward link. In addition this method asks that booking to set its own customer field to refer to this booking, which forms the backlink.

The dissociate method is used to reverse this by removing the booking from the collection and setting the booking's customer field to null, i.e. removing the forward and backlinks.

We probably also want to be able to initiate this bi-directional association from the other object – that is, when a **Customer** object is dropped onto the **Customer** field within the **Booking**, then the customer field is set up with that customer object, and the **Booking** object adds itself to the set of bookings for that customer.

The following code shows the associate and dissociate methods that we must add to the Booking class to achieve this. To keep them simple they are implemented so that they only call the corresponding method in the Customer class. This avoids duplicating the code that manages the association. As in the Customer class, the original accessor and mutator methods remain as they are. These are called by the association methods, and are also used for persisting the object:

```
public class Booking extends AbstractNakedObject {
    private Customer customer;

    public void associateCustomer(Customer customer) {
        customer.associateBookings(this);
    }

    public void dissociateCustomer(Customer customer) {
        customer.dissociateBookings(this);
    }

    public Customer getCustomer() {
        resolve(customer);
        return customer;
    }

    public void setCustomer(Customer newCustomer) {
        customer = newCustomer;
        objectChanged();
    }
}
```

Now dropping a **Customer** object onto the grey hole in the **Customer** field within a **Booking** object will cause the associateCustomer method to be called instead of setCustomer. This invokes the associateBookings method (in the Customer object) that we looked at earlier. As before this method adds the booking object to its bookings collection, setting up the backlink, and then calls the setCustomer method back in the Booking object, thereby setting up the forward link.

Bidirectional associations are coded in the same way whether they are one-to-one, one-to-many, or many-to-many. All that differs is whether we are adding or removing elements from a collection or a single object.

The prefixes 'add' and 'remove' can be used instead of the prefixes 'associate' and 'dissociate'. Methods using these prefixes read more easily when used with an internal collection. For example the Customer class could equally be written as follows:

```
public class Customer extends AbstractNakedObject {
    private final InternalCollection bookings;

    public Customer() {
        bookings = new InternalCollection(Booking.class, this);
    }

    public void addBookings(Booking booking) {
        getBookings().add(booking);
        booking.setCustomer(this);
    }

    public void removeBookings(Booking booking) {
        getBookings().remove(booking);
        booking.setCustomer(null);
    }

    public final InternalCollection getBookings() {
        return bookings;
    }
}
```

The associate and dissociate methods can be used for other purposes as well, such as setting two fields at once. For example in the Booking object when a Location is dropped onto the **Pick Up** or **Drop Off** field, then as well as setting the targeted field, the booking's **City** field will also be set with the same City as that contained in the Location object just dropped. This is achieved through the following code:

```
public void associateDropOff(Location newDropOff) {
    setDropOff(newDropOff);
    setCity(newDropOff.getCity());
}

public void associatePickUp(Location newPickUp) {
    setPickUp(newPickUp);
    setCity(newPickUp.getCity());
}
```

Derived fields

If a field needs to be derived dynamically from other fields within the object then it is better to use the prefix 'derive' instead of 'get'. This will make the field read-only and non-persistent, avoiding any potential problems that could arise from the persistence mechanism attempting to store or retrieve that field from storage.

In the following example a 'due' date is calculated as being 14 days after the date held by the ordered field. The important thing here is that a new Date object is created from the existing one. This copy is then used to do the calculations and it is this copy that is returned to the framework. The principle here is that by creating a new value object you will avoid corrupting the object's other fields.

```
public Date deriveDue() {
    Date due = new Date(ordered);
    due.add(14,0,0);
    return due;
}
```

Ordering fields

The ordering of the fields when an object is displayed is based on the array of accessor methods that is produced by Java's reflection mechanism. This means the ordering depends on how the JVM you are running collects the data about your class, and you have no direct contol over this. You may, however, specify an order within your class definition, which the viewing mechanism then interprets. This is done by adding a static method called fieldOrder that returns a String listing the names of the fields separated by commas. These need to be the reflected names and not the method names. For example the string 'Pick Up' would be used to refer to the getPickUp method. (Case is ignored.)

The following example from the Booking class specifies an order for its fields:

```
public static String fieldOrder() {
    return "reference, status, customer, date, time, pick up, drop off, payment method";
}
```

Any listed name that does not match a field is simply ignored, and fields that are not listed will be placed after all the specified fields.

3.1.3   Behaviours

Any method within a naked object that is prefixed with 'action', and that returns either a NakedObject type or void, is made available to the user. Methods defined this way that take no arguments are displayed on the object's pop-up menu, as shown in the example below. The name used on the menu defaults to the method name stripped of its prefix and with spaces added where uppercase characters are found.

Methods that take a single parameter (which must be of the type NakedObject) are made available through drag and drop gestures.

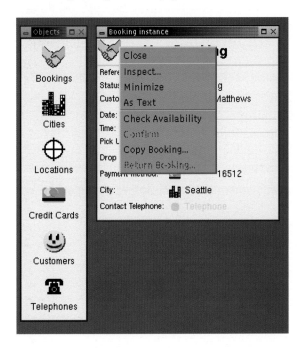

When one of these action methods returns a non-null value, the framework will attempt to show that returned object to the user – typically in a new window. This is indicated on the pop-up menu by an ellipsis (...) being added to the menu name, e.g. the Return Booking... option shown above will display a new object, whereas Check Availability won't.

Instance methods

A typical action method (taken from the City class) is shown below. It creates a new Location object and sets its city field so it refers to the city object that the method was called on. This newly created and persisted object is then returned to the user. This method shows itself as **New Location**... on the city's pop-up menu and is invoked when that menu item is selected.

```
public Location actionNewLocation() {
    Location loc = (Location) createInstance(Location.class);
    loc.setCity(this);
    return loc;
}
```

The next method (taken from the Location class) creates a new booking object. This method requires another location object to be provided as an argument, so that it can set up both the new booking's pick up and drop off fields. This method is invoked by dropping one location object onto another.

```
public Booking actionNewBooking(Location location) {
    Booking booking = (Booking) createInstance(Booking.class);
    Customer customer = location.getCustomer();
    booking.setPickUp(location);
    booking.setDropOff(this);
    if (customer != null) {
        booking.setCustomer(customer);
        booking.setPaymentMethod(customer.getPreferredPaymentMethod());
    }
    booking.setCity(location.getCity());
    return booking;
}
```

On the screenshot below you can see the dragged object, whose title and labels have changed to purple; the object it was dropped on, whose title and labels flash green to indicate a valid drop; and the resulting new booking with its Customer, Pick Up, Drop Off and City fields set up using the information from the two objects involved in the invoked method.

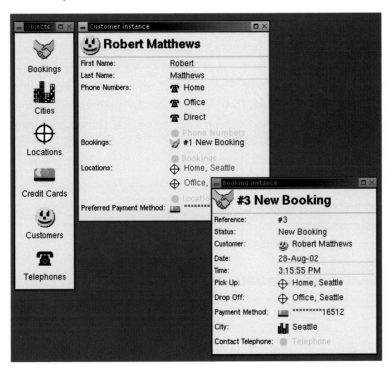

Most often, action methods are used to change the state of an object. This example from the Booking class changes the status value object and then associates the pickUp and dropOff locations, and the paymentMethod used in the newly-confirmed booking directly with the existing customer object that the booking was made for – so that they can easily be re-used in a future booking for that customer. Note that this method does not return anything; it only changes the state of the two objects:

```
public void actionConfirm() {
    getStatus().setValue("Confirmed");

    getCustomer().associateLocations(getPickUp());
    getCustomer().associateLocations(getDropOff());
    if (getCustomer().getPreferredPaymentMethod() == null) {
        getCustomer().setPreferredPaymentMethod(getPaymentMethod());
    }
}
```

Disabling methods

Action methods may be rendered unavailable because a user lacks appropriate authority, or the object is not in an appropriate state, or because of some other business rule. The availability of an action... method can be controlled by adding a corresponding about... method. This method must return an About object, have the same method name with 'about' prefixed, and have exactly the same parameter list. The following code shows two action... methods and their about... methods. The first makes the NewLocation method available if the city field contains something. The second disables the NewBooking method if the location that will be used to invoke the action method is the same location as the one the method will be invoked on, i.e. if the user attempts to drop the location object onto itself.

```
public Location actionNewLocation() {}

public About aboutActionNewLocation() {
   if(city.isEmpty()) {
      return ActionAbout.DISABLE;
   } else {
      return ActionAbout.ENABLE;
   }
}
```

```
public Booking actionNewBooking(Location location) {}

public About aboutActionNewBooking(Location location) {
   return ActionAbout.disable(location.equals(this));
}
```

When an about... method disables a zero-parameter action method, that method is greyed out on the object's menu.

When it disables a one-parameter method, the framework will flash the target object red as the user tries to drag an object (even of the right type) over it.

Method ordering

The ordering of listed methods, particularly for menu items displayed on an object's pop-up menu, is based on the array of action methods that is produced by Java's reflection mechanism. The ordering, therefore, is dependent on how the JVM you are running collects the data about your class, and you have no direct control over this. You may, however, specify an order within your class definition, which the viewing mechanism can then interpret. This is done by adding a static method called actionOrder that returns a String listing the names derived from the methods separated by commas. These need to be the reflected names and not the method identifiers. For example the string 'Call Back' would be used to refer to the actionCallBack method. (Case is ignored.)

The following example from the Booking class specifies a suitable order for its action methods:

```
public static String actionOrder() {
    return "Check Availability, Confirm, Copy Booking, Return Booking";
}
```

Any listed name that does not match a method is simply ignored, and methods that are not listed will be placed after all the specified methods.

Class methods

It is also possible to write methods that are invoked on a class rather than on a specific instance. These can be used to find instances that match given criteria – for example, to find bookings that use a specific location; or to create one object based on another, such as a city being used to create a new location in that city.

The same principles apply when defining such a method, but the method is declared as static. The following shows a typical class method (within the Booking class) that creates a new booking for a customer. This would be invoked by dropping a customer object onto the Bookings class and would result in a new booking being returned in a new window:

```
public static Booking actionNewBooking(Customer customer) {
    Booking newBooking = (Booking) createInstance(Booking.class);
    newBooking.setCustomer(customer);
    newBooking.setPaymentMethod(customer.getPreferredPaymentMethod());
    return newBooking;
}
```

Class method ordering

You can order class methods in the same manner as instance methods, but using the static method called classActionOrder.

3.2 Making the objects available to the user

During prototyping you want to translate business object ideas as quickly as possible into a form that the users can explore. For this purpose Naked Objects provides a simple class called org.nakedobjects.Exploration which is used to generate a kind of minimalist application. It starts the framework, allows you to register the business classes that you want the user to see, and then starts up the graphical interface.

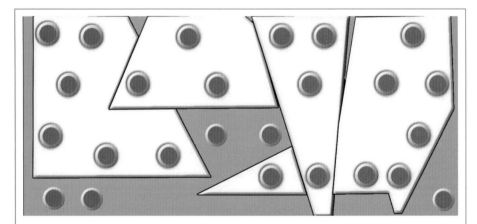

A Naked Objects application is not a purpose-written program with a dedicated user interface but rather a 'portal' into the enterprise business object model – meaning a specific set of business classes, and possibly a specific set of fields and behaviours within those classes – made available to users in a broadly-defined business context. In our ECS example, we might have a booking agent's portal, and a dispatcher's portal that allows a vehicle despatcher to match confirmed bookings to available vehicles. The despatchers would be provided with access to a Vehicle but not to the PaymentMethod classes, or any of the methods for generating new bookings.

3.2.1 Incorporating naked objects into a simple test application

The following example from the ECS system extends the Exploration class to start up an exploration application. Here you can see the registration of the business object classes (in the classSet method) and how the application is started in the main method:

package ecs.delivery;

import org.nakedobjects.Exploration;

```
import org.nakedobjects.object.NakedClassList;

public class EcsExploration extends Exploration {
    public void classSet(NakedClassList classes) {
        classes.addClass(Booking.class);
        classes.addClass(City.class);
        classes.addClass(Location.class);
        classes.addClass(CreditCard.class);
        classes.addClass(Customer.class);
        classes.addClass(Telephone.class);
    }

    public static void main(String[] args) {
        new EcsExploration();
    }
}
```

Starting an application in this way does not make use of a persistence mechanism. This is intentional so that it is easier to test an application whilst the object definitions are rapidly changing. It is possible to specify a persistor in this test environment, but it can be more useful to have the application set up a known set of objects from scratch each time it starts.

You can do this by overriding the initObjects method, as shown here for the ECS example. This creates a list of seven cities and two customers – a more realistic demonstration would need more. (The objects must be created via the Exploration class otherwise they will not be added to the framework's (transient) object store and therefore will not be made available to the user.)

```
public void initObjects() {
    String[] cities = {
        "New York", "Boston", "Washington", "Chicago",
        "Tampa", "Seattle", "Atlanta"
    };

    for (int i = 0; i < cities.length; i++) {
        City newCity = (City) createInstance(City.class);
        newCity.getName().setValue(cities[i]);
    }

    Customer newCustomer;

    newCustomer = (Customer) createInstance(Customer.class);
```

```
newCustomer.getFirstName().setValue("Richard");
newCustomer.getLastName().setValue("Pawson");

newCustomer = (Customer) createInstance(Customer.class);
newCustomer.getFirstName().setValue("Robert");
newCustomer.getLastName().setValue("Matthews");
}
```

Icons

The images for the icons are sought within a directory called images which must be located within the working directory – the directory that Java is running from. The image files are matched to the names of the classes with the addition of '16' or '32' and an extension of '.gif'. For example City16.gif and City32.gif are the two images for the City class. The numbers refer to the size of image – 16x16 and 32x32 pixels respectively. Images of both sizes are required by the framework.

You can also place these images within the resources that will be made available to the JVM – place them in the .jar file alongside the class files when you distribute your application. However, they must still be held within a sub-directory called images.

3.2.2 Creating a standalone executable demo

Having written a Naked Objects application, either as an exploratory prototype or as a delivered system, it is sometimes convenient to be able to share it with others in the form of a self-contained freestanding executable demonstration (one that does not require the prior installation of the framework, the management of source code and other resources, or any infrastructural services).

To create such an executable demo:

- First, ensure that you have created an application using the org.nakedobjects.Exploration class as your superclass.

- Create any instances that you require programmatically, as was shown above.

- Make a copy of the nakedobjects.jar file as provided in the lib directory in the distribution you downloaded (http://www.nakedobjects.org/downloads.html). Name this copy so it indicates that it is your application e.g. booking-demo.jar.

- Create a text file called manifest and place the following line within it, but specifying your application's fully qualified class name.

  Main-Class: **ecs.delivery.EcsExploration**

- Extract the Log4J classes so they can be included in your new jar file.

  jar -xf log4.jar

- Update the new jar file so that it includes your application's classes and images, the Log4J classes, and adds the manifest details into its manifest file. Following the booking example, if the images are in the images directory and all the classes are within the ecs directory, then you will run the jar utility with the following options:

  jar -umf manifest booking-demo.jar images ecs org

- Now the only file that needs to be distributed is the jar file booking-demo.jar. To run the application using Java version 1.2 or later, invoke Java using the -jar flag, for example:

  java -jar booking-demo.jar

  To make it even easier, put this into a batch file or a script. Indeed, if Microsoft Windows is suitably configured, the file's icon can be double-clicked to start it.

  If one of the more recent versions of Java is not available then the application can also be run using version 1.1. However, the Java class library has to be loaded manually and the class to run must be specified, as shown below:

  java -cp <path-to-java>\lib\classes.zip;booking-demo.jar ecs.delivery.EcsExploration

117

3.3 Building a multi-user system

Most business systems will require that the naked objects be capable of being shared amongst multiple users, and that those objects be made persistent. Both of these are features of the framework and are briefly explained here. The functionality described is all componentized and capable of being replaced by alternative implementations. For more information about how to configure alternative components, or indeed to write new ones, you should look at the documentation provided within the Naked Objects distribution and refer to our web site (www.nakedobjects.org).

3.3.1 Making naked objects persistent

Naked objects are made persistent though an object store, which normally interfaces with a persistence mechanism such as a database. Any class that implements the org.nakedobjects.object.NakedObjectStore interface can serve as an object store. At the time of writing, five alternative object stores are available (either as part of the framework or downloaded from our website) together with documentation on how to use them:

- **XML Object Store** This stores each naked object instance as a separate file in XML format. This is currently only suitable for use during prototyping, when dealing with small numbers of instances. It has the advantage that the file formats can easily be read by the programmer as well as other tools. It is also reasonably robust to changes in the object definitions during prototyping – you can usually add or delete fields without having to change the existing data files.

- **Serialized Object Store** This stores each instance as a separate file, using Java's serialization. It is only suited to prototyping or to applications with small volumes of data. However, it is more efficient than the XML store, especially for complex objects.

- **SQL Object Store** This will work with any JDBC-compliant relational database and is suitable for many business applications. If you are developing a new and straightforward application, then the SQL Object Store can manage the whole process of setting up the database and creating the necessary tables transparently: the programmer can simply define the business objects assuming that they will be stored and retrieved from a relational database as needed. If the application must use existing relational tables, or store its objects in a known fashion for access by other applications, then a programmer can manually specify a series of mapping objects. Manually-specified mappings may also be necessary on very large or complex applications, for performance reasons.

- **EJB Object Store** This object store was written by Dave Slaughter of Safeway*, and allows a Naked Objects application to take advantage of the capabilities of Enterprise Java Beans. EJBs provide very good support for scaleability, transactions and security. Using this object store, Naked Objects can interoperate with other systems built on an EJB infrastructure.

- **Transient Object Store** This provides the functionality of an object store (which is required by the framework so it can run) but without persistence, i.e. the states of the objects are only maintained while the application is running and are not saved between framework invocations. This is an integral part of the framework and is used by default when running an org.nakedobjects.Exploration application. This allows object definitions to be changed easily when initially crafting the naked objects. It is also convenient for testing as there are no unexpected objects in existence when the test application is started.

We expect that over time many more object stores will be made available for Naked Objects, as well as improved versions of the existing ones.

When the framework is run as a server it uses the persistent object store that is specified in the configuration file. Unless you need custom mappings, it is possible to swap the object store just by editing one line of that file – no changes need to be made to the coding of the naked objects themselves. The default configuration file supplied as part of the distribution specifies the XML Object Store.

As a developer there are thus three ways that you can use an object store:

- You can specify an existing object store and use it transparently.

- You can specify an existing object store and provide your own mappings or other forms of custom control over persistence.

- You can write a new object store, usually as a wrapper for an existing database or other persistence mechanism. (The requirements for an object store are detailed in the framework API and discussed on our website.)

The framework supports the philosophy that any change that a user makes to any object, whether by directly changing its attributes or associations, or by invoking an action method, is immediately made persistent. For this reason the naked objects in our examples do not have explicit 'save' or 'make persistent'

e page 155

actions. This is a deliberate design choice. The design of the Naked Objects framework means that it is possible to take this approach for many applications and still achieve desirable performance levels. The immediacy is also consistent with the expressive style of systems that Naked Objects produces.

It is possible to delay the process of making an object persistent by creating transient objects and subsequently making them persistent. For example, an order object could be created and prepared ensuring that all items are available before adding the object to the object store. Unfortunately though, once the object has been made persistent any further changes made to that object will be persisted as soon they are made.

In a future release the framework will also support the explicit saving of objects, where this may be necessary for performance or other reasons.

3.3.2   Sharing Naked Objects between multiple users

It is possible to run Naked Objects as a set of discrete client applications, each one linking directly to the persistence mechanism via an object store within the client. This is known as a 'fat client' architecture. This is not recommended unless you need to preserve compatibility with an existing fat client architecture, or your application involves a great deal of numerical processing on small numbers of object instances.

More commonly your clients will each communicate with a shared object server, which in turn will talk to the object store to access the persistence mechanism. The Naked Objects org.nakedobjects.Client and org.nakedobjects.ObjectServer are both sub-classes of org.nakedobjects.Application (as is the org.nakedobjects.Exploration used during prototyping).

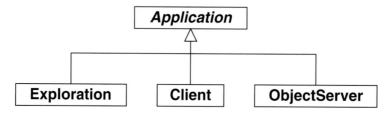

The terms 'client' and 'server' do not imply anything about physical location. A common set-up is to have the clients running on user platforms and the server running on a central machine. But it is also possible to run both the client and the server on a standalone PC for prototyping purposes. Equally you may run some clients and the server on a shared platform, with the clients communicating with user platforms via, say, a webserver. Thus the client and server should be thought of only as two tiers in an n-tier architecture.

When an object server is deployed, each naked object that is used on any client will be replicated from the server. The framework keeps the two replicas in synchronization. If two users are manipulating (or just viewing) the same object then the two client replicas of that object will be linked to the same object on the server. If one user changes an object then that change will immediately be propagated to all other client replicas. (This is one reason why it is important to include the objectChanged* statements in your methods.)

e page 97

All this happens transparently. The developer does not have to write any specific code to manage the replication, and indeed thinks of the naked objects as existing only in one place. Setting this up can be as simple as running the client on each user platform and advising it of the location of the server, then specifying the set of naked object class definitions that are to be made available. All this is done in the configuration file. In a future release it will be possible to set up the server so that the client can obtain the class configuration information and the needed class and image files directly from the server – thereby eliminating the need to update clients manually when new naked object classes are introduced.

121

The Naked Objects client and server are complete applications. The replicated objects are fully functional: the code for each of the object's methods exists on both client and server replicas. It would be possible to run all the business functionality on either client or server objects. However, if the client has been told (through the configuration file) that there is a server then it will automatically sub-contract the execution of most methods to the server version. This ensures that any resulting changes to the objects are made persistent and that all the clients using that object are immediately notified. In theory your persistence mechanism could perform this alerting function directly, but this would probably require a lot of manual programming. The Naked Objects framework ensures that this automatic alerting and updating happens whichever persistence mechanism you are using. The second reason for delegating execution of methods to the server replica is that it is likely to be physically closer to the object store and therefore yield higher performance if the method involves any retrievals or updates to persistent objects.

3.3.3 Maintaining transactional integrity

If your persistence mechanism has the ability to manage transactions (as do most relational databases, for example), then Naked Objects can make full use of this. By default, every explicit user action such as selecting an action from a pop-up menu, changing a field, or dragging and dropping an object, is assumed to be an atomic transaction even if that action triggers changes to multiple fields or other objects. When each action occurs, the framework automatically sends a 'start transaction' message to the object store, and concludes it with an 'end transaction'.

3.3.4   Providing security and authorisation

At the time of writing, Naked Objects does not have an explicit model for security and authorization. The About objects and methods allow the developer to control access to any specific class, method or attribute. This provides the foundation on which a comprehensive security/authorization model can be built. We expect that such a model will become available for Naked Objects in the near future. Meantime, if you wish to use an authentication/authorization server, then you will need to extend the org.nakedobjects.object.control.About class such that it delegates the responsibility to that server.

3.3.5   Running a multi-user system

Running Naked Objects in a multi-user environment is as simple as starting the server program and then running some clients. As the clients will commonly be run on separate machines they need to told where to find the server. They also need to be told which naked object classes to make available to the user.

Running the server

The framework's org.nakedobjects.ObjectServer class is used to run the framework as a server and is started using the following command:

```
java -cp nakedobjects.jar:log4j.jar:<object class path>
        org.nakedobjects.ObjectServer
```

(This command should all be on a single line.)

Log4J is a logging framework from Apache, which is used for logging the running of the framework. The Log4J jar-file, the framework itself, and the directory containing the naked object classes, must all be specified in the command's classpath unless they are already specified in the system's CLASSPATH variable. In addition a copy of server.properties must be in the working directory, i.e.

the directory where the above command is run. This file can be found in the conf directory in the Naked Objects distribution.

Complete
configuration
details are
included in the
Naked Objects
distribution.

Assuming the original server.properties configuration file was copied across, as the server starts it will install the default object store, a basic network service, and a graphical console for monitoring and controlling the server. All of these aspects of the server can be changed*. The following console screen will be shown allowing you to monitor the clients and to shutdown the server:

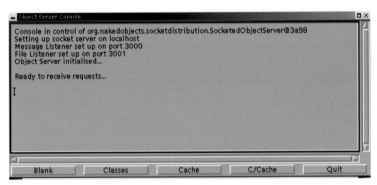

Running the client

Before running the client you must specify where the server is to be found, and tell the client which classes to make available to the user. This is done by editing the client's configuration file, client.properties. This file should copied to the working directory from the conf directory in the Naked Objects distribution. The line:

nakedobjects.socketed-proxy.address=localhost

should be changed, replacing localhost with the server's IP address or host name. For example, on our local server the line becomes:

nakedobjects.socketed-proxy.address=192.168.1.8

The naked object classes to be made available to the user are specified by appending the fully-qualified class names, separated by semicolons, to the line:

nakedobjects.classes=

For example, to configure the client to use the classes developed for the ECS application the following would be seen in the configuration file. (The backslashes at the end of each line indicate that the property is continued onto the next line.)

nakedobjects.classes=\

      org.nakedobjects.example.booking.Customer;\
      org.nakedobjects.example.booking.Booking;\
      org.nakedobjects.example.booking.Location;\
      org.nakedobjects.example.booking.Telephone;\
      org.nakedobjects.example.booking.CreditCard;\
      org.nakedobjects.example.booking.City

Before running the client the images directory, and its contents, should be copied into the working directory. The required class files should also be copied across and placed in the working directory (ideally in a specific subdirectory).

The framework's org.nakedobjects.Client class is used to run the framework as a client application. The class path is set up in the same way as the server so that the framework, Log4J and the naked object classes can be found:

java -cp nakedobjects.jar:log4j.jar:<object class path>
      org.nakedobjects.Client

(This command should all be on a single line.)

The application will appear as below.

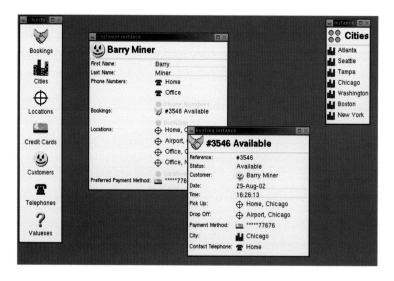

3.4 Enriching object behaviours

Having looked at the basic anatomy of naked objects and how to make them available to users, we shall now look at building more functionality into the methods of those objects, much of which will be concerned with manipulating the object's attributes and associations. As before, you must adopt some simple conventions in your Java code for these methods in order to allow the framework to do its task. However, we shall also see that the framework provides a number of useful features that make the task of writing your business methods easier.

3.4.1 Accessing fields safely

In object-oriented programming it is considered good practice always to access an internal variable through its get... and set... methods. In Naked Objects this is especially important when dealing with variables that hold other business objects. The accessor and mutator methods take care of the persistence and notification issues, so accessing a variable through its get... ensures that the object is properly loaded, and changing a variable through its set... ensures that the change is made persistent and that any view of that object, whether on the user's screen or on other users' screens, is kept consistent.

The following method from the Booking class shows this practice. Each assignment is done as a set..., while each access is done using a get.... Also note that the customer field is set up using an associate... method to set the association in the Customer class as well.

```java
public Booking actionCopyBooking() {
    Booking copiedBooking = (Booking) createInstance(Booking.class);
    copiedBooking.associateCustomer(getCustomer());
    copiedBooking.setPickUp(getPickUp());
    copiedBooking.setDropOff(getDropOff());
    copiedBooking.setPaymentMethod(getPaymentMethod());
    copiedBooking.setContactTelephone(getContactTelephone());
    return copiedBooking;
}
```

Value objects and internal collections don't strictly need to be accessed via their accessor methods as they already take care of the notification and persistence issues. It is, however, good practice always to use the accessor as this provides consistency in your code.

3.4.2 Manipulating value objects

Value objects are for holding simple, generic data values (such as a date, a string of characters, or a temperature) that belong to a single business object. All value objects must implement the org.nakedobjects.object.NakedValue interface.

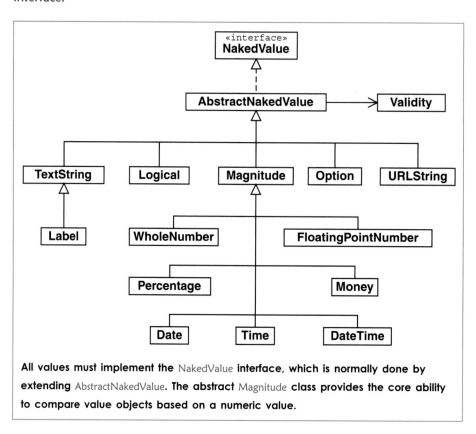

All values must implement the NakedValue **interface, which is normally done by extending** AbstractNakedValue. **The abstract** Magnitude **class provides the core ability to compare value objects based on a numeric value.**

The following value objects are defined within the framework as subclasses of the org.nakedobjects.object.value.AbstractNakedValue class and new types can be added if needed. All are self explanatory bar the Option class, which permits the object to take one of a set number of values. The current viewing mechanism portrays this to users as a set of radio buttons or a drop-down selection box, depending on how many options there are. The following classes are all members of the org.nakedobjects.object.value package:

- Date – 3-Jun-02 or 21/3/01

- FloatingPointNumber – 1,234.5 or 0.125

- Logical – set to True or False

- Money – £5,120.50 or $10.99

- Option – Saloon|SUV|Minivan|Coupe

- Percentage – 0.1% or 99.99%

- TextString – Alan McDonald

- Time – 10:50 AM or 14:15

- TimeStamp – 3-Jun-02 10:50 AM or 21/3/01 14:15

- URLString – http://www.nakedobjects.org/downloads.html

- WholeNumber – 18 or 1,200

The screenshot below shows and example of how the current viewing mechanism portrays each of these value objects to the user:

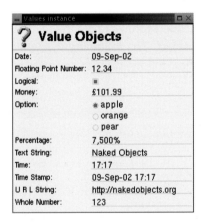

Each of these classes has three common constructors and a core set of methods. The zero-parameter constructor creates the object with its default value. The defaults are zero values for the numerical types, the current date and time for the temporal types, and an empty string for the string type. The one-parameter constructors take either an existing object of the same type and copies its value across, or a conventional Java type that can readily be mapped onto the value object type. The core methods are:

- public Title title() returns a title string – as a Title object – formatted according to the default Java Locale.

- public boolean isEmpty() determines if the object is empty: it does not contain a value.

- public void clear() clears the value so it is empty.

- public void reset() resets the object to its default value.

- public boolean isValid() determines whether a value is currently valid according to the object's Validity strategy. For example the PositiveValue strategy, applied to a WholeNumber object, ensures that the number remains positive.

- public void setValidity(Validity strategy) assigns a specific Validity strategy.

- public void setAbout(About newAbout) assigns an About strategy. This is used to control the accessibility of the value object.

- public void parse(String text) throws ValueParseException attempts to convert the specified Java String into the value object's type.

In addition to these common methods, each type has a number of **type**Value and setValue methods that accept and return various related data types. For example, the Money class includes the methods doubleValue and intValue to convert the money value into double and int Java types. It also has setValue(double) and setValue(Money) to set the value using a Java double value or another Money object. The following shows all the conversion methods for the Money class followed by an example of them in use:

```
public short shortValue();
public int intValue();
public long longValue();
public float floatValue();
public double doubleValue();

public void setValue(double amount);
public void setValue(Money value);

Money m = new Money();
m.setValue(8.4);
float f = m.floatValue();
```

The numerical types also include a set of methods to perform basic arithmetic operations. So, for example, a FloatingPointNumber can have another FloatingPointNumber or a Java double added to it using the overloaded add method. These are provided to simplify the coding of mathematical operations, avoiding the need to repeatedly convert between Java primitive types and NakedValue types. The following shows the basic four arithmetic operations (overloaded to accept both double values and FloatingPoint objects) that are available for FloatingPoint objects followed by examples of their use:

```
public void add(double value);
public void add(FloatingPointNumber number);
```

```
public void subtract(double value);
public void subtract(FloatingPointNumber number);
public void multiply(double value);
public void multiply(FloatingPointNumber number);
public void divide(double value);
public void divide(FloatingPointNumber number);

FloatingPointNumber f = new FloatingPointNumber();
f.setValue(1.5);
FloatingPointNumber g = new FloatingPointNumber();
g.setValue(1.5);
f.add(g);
f.multiply(2.0);
double d = f.doubleValue();
```

As well as the arithmetic functions, the numerical types also have methods to compare themselves against other instances. So, for example, a Percentage object can be compared to another Percentage object to see if it is greater by using the isGreaterThan method. These methods are jointly implemented in the value object classes and the Magnitude class from which they are extended. The following are all the Magnitude methods, of which isEqualTo and isLessThan must be implemented by the subclass:

```
public boolean isEqualTo(Magnitude magnitude);
public boolean isLessThan(Magnitude magnitude);
public boolean isLessThanOrEqualTo(Magnitude magnitude);
public boolean isGreaterThan(Magnitude magnitude);
public boolean isGreaterThanOrEqualTo(Magnitude magnitude);
public boolean isBetween(Magnitude minMagnitude,
        Magnitude maxMagnitude);
public Magnitude max(Magnitude magnitude);
public Magnitude min(Magnitude magnitude);
```

The TextString class, which is probably the most widely used value object, provides string methods such as contains, endsWith, isSameAs that can be invoked in either case sensitive or case insensitive manner. All the comparisons in the example below will return true:

```
public boolean isSameAs(String text);
public boolean isSameAs(String text, Case caseSensitive);
public boolean contains(String text);
public boolean contains(String text, Case caseSensitive);
```

```
public boolean startsWith(String text);
public boolean startsWith(String text, Case caseSensitive);
public boolean endsWith(String text);
public boolean endsWith(String text, Case caseSensitive);

TextString t = new TextString();
t.setValue("Form 1");
t.isSameAs("Form 1");
t.startsWith("form", Case.INSENSITIVE);
t.contains("1");
```

All the value classes and their methods are listed in their entirety in the API specification, which can be found in the Naked Objects distribution.

3.4.3 Manipulating collections

Collections within the Naked Objects framework are for storing a number of naked objects in a unique unsorted set. Some of the collections are also typed so that they will only accept a specific subtype of org.nakedobjects.object.NakedObject – i.e. a specific type of business object. There are three types of collections used within the framework (declared in the org.nakedobjects.object.collection package). All are based on the same abstract collection but differ in what type of object they store and the reason they are used. In order of frequency of use they are:

• InternalCollection, a collection of associations, which is a composite part of a business object. The objects it contains are of a type specified when the collection was created. This was described in the section on one-to-many associations*.

*See page 102

• ArbitraryCollection, a general untyped collection of objects that the user creates for his own ad hoc use. This type of collection is created when any existing collection is copied.

• InstanceCollection, a collection of instances of a specific type, generated directly by the persistence mechanism. For example, in the user view the pop-up menu on a class offers the option of listing all instances of that class, or finding instances that match given criteria. If matches are found they will be returned as an InstanceCollection.

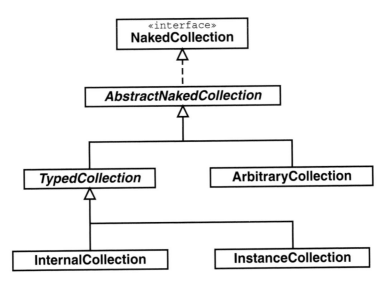

The abstract superclass AbstractNakedCollection provides methods to add and remove elements from a collection. You access the collection's elements through an Enumeration, which gives access to all the objects in the collection so that you can iterate through it. There are also some utility methods to check the size and content of a collection.

- public void add(NakedObject element) adds a new element to the collection, first calling the collection's abstract canAdd method to check whether the object can be added. The InternalCollection implements the canAdd so that only objects of the specified type, and which are not already in the collection, can be added. The same method in the ArbitraryCollection class checks only for the existence of the object. InstanceCollection, on the other hand, vetoes any addition by the programmer.

- public void remove(NakedObject element) removes a specific existing element. In the same way as for the add method, remove calls the canRemove method to check if the object is currently held and to determine whether the element can be removed. This is implemented generally so that all elements can be removed, except in the InstanceCollection where this is never allowed.

- public Enumeration elements() generates an Enumeration that can be used to iterate through the collection, as below:

```
Enumeration e = employees.elements();
while(e.hasMoreElements()){
        Employee emp;
        emp = (Employee)e.nextElement();
        :

        :

}
```

- public boolean contains(NakedObject element) checks to see if a specific element is held by the collection, returning true if it is.

- public boolean isEmpty() determines if the collection is empty and returns true if it is.

- public int size() determines how many elements the collection contains.

3.4.4 Creating persistent objects

Because of the way that objects are persisted within the framework Java's new operator should not be used to create new naked objects. Instead, create a new persistent object using the utility method createInstance provided by the org.nakedobjects.object.AbstractNakedObject superclass. Like most factory methods this returns an instance using a superclass reference – in this case org.nakedobjects.object.NakedObject – and so must be cast into its real type before it can be used. This method takes a java.lang.Class object, which specifies what class of naked object to create. The example below creates a Location object:

```
Location home;
home = (Location) createInstance(Location.class);
```

Sometimes it is necessary to create non-persistent (or 'transient') naked objects, either for use outside the shared object space or as part of a longer creation process, where the user will place the object into the shared space later. A transient object can be created using the createTransientInstance utility method. This will return a properly initialized transient object. As with the createInstance method, this will need its reference to be cast to its real type. Note also that it is illegal (because it is illogical) for any persistent object to reference a transient object. Therefore, do not attempt to set up a field within a persistent object using this method.

Calling makePersistent on a transient object will make that object, and all the objects it contains, persistent. The following example shows a non-persistent object being created, and then being made persistent:

```
Location away;
away = (Location) createTransientInstance(Location.class);
    :
    :
away.makePersistent();
```

This following method is an actual object creation example taken from the City class:

```
public Location actionNewLocation() {
    Location loc = (Location) createInstance(Location.class);
    loc.setCity(this);
    return loc;
}
```

As these two creation methods are available you should avoid using the new operator. If, however, you have not subclassed org.nakedobjects.object.AbstractNakedObject then you will have to create an object this way. It then becomes your responsibility to call the created method, and if the object is to be persisted, to call the makePersistent method as well.

3.4.5   Initializing persistent objects

When certain types of logical object are first created you will need to give their value fields specific initial values or associate other specific objects with them. In Java this would be done in the constructor as it is only ever called once during the object's lifetime. In the Naked Objects framework, however, every time a logical object is retrieved from the object store it is re-instantiated using the class's constructor. This means that the constructor will be called more than once during the 'lifetime' of the naked object. You could find yourself inadvertently resetting all the fields each time an object was retrieved from storage, overwriting any other changes.

Initialising the logical object, therefore, should not be done in the constructor, but in the created method instead. This method is only called by the framework when an object is created using the factory methods we saw in the last section. This is what actually happens when the user selects the New Instance... menu option.

The following code extract sets up the value held by the quantity field when the logical object is instantiated. The value object should already exist at this point as it should have been initialized during the variable's declaration or within the containing object's constructor:

```
public void created() {
    quantity.set(5);
}
```

This does not mean that the constructor should never be used. The value objects and internal collections still need to be created before they can be accessed, including every time an object is recreated from persistent storage, and can, therefore, be done safely within the constructor.

3.4.6 Building a title from multiple fields

All org.nakedobjects.object.Naked objects have a title that can be used when presenting the object to the user. These titles are generated by the title method, which returns a org.nakedobjects.object.Title object containing a textual title.

For value objects this is a formatted version of the value, for example "10:50 am" or "£3.50". For business objects this is some form of identifier.

Number:	3232277676
Expires:	10/02
Name On Card:	Mr Perkins

If a business objects has a field that uniquely identifies each instance, such as an invoice number, then the title method can simply get the Title object from that identifying field. The following method from the City class passes on the title held by the name value object for that city.

Name: Washington

```
public Title title() {
    return name.title();
}
```

In other cases a business object's title will be derived from multiple attributes. The Title object provides a set of useful constructors and methods that assist in creating titles from String objects, other naked objects (usually those held within an object's own fields), and other Title objects. For example, for the

Customer class, we may want to create the title from the customer's first and last names. A Title object can append various objects to itself and in true overloaded style will convert numbers, strings and other naked objects to strings before appending them, and look after all the spacing for you. Consider the following method:

```
public Title title() {
    Title title = firstName.title();
    Title fullTitle = title.append(lastName);
    return fullTitle;
}
```

Assuming that the value held by firstName is 'Robert' and lastName is 'Matthews' then the call to append will result in the title being 'Robert Matthews'. If, however, firstName is empty then the title will correctly be 'Matthews' (with no leading space). Similarly if lastName is empty then the result will be 'Robert' with no trailing space.

Simple String objects can also be appended for additional formatting. Changing the above example to:

```
public Title title() {
            Title title = lastName.title();
            Title fullTitle = title.append(",", firstName);
            return fullTitle;
}
```

changes the ordering of the names and produces the correct three variations: 'Matthews, Robert', 'Matthews' and 'Robert'. The joining string is additional to the delimiting space.

(If you do not require spaces between the elements of a title, use the concat method instead of append.)

One other useful thing to remember is that each of these methods returns the object it was called upon. This allows the append and concat methods to be chained, shortening your title method even further. This is the terse version of the previous code:

```
public Title title() {
    return lastName.title().append(",", lastName);
}
```

Remember, too, that reference variables for other business objects aren't guaranteed to refer to anything (they could be null) and could also be unresolved (they don't contain the required information). For this reason it is important not to use a reference variable directly, and to check that a reference is not null before using it. This is another reason why you should use the field's get... method even for internal operations. You can then use the returned reference (null or otherwise) as a parameter to one of the Title constructors or methods. This way the title class will check the reference and if it is null will deal with it in a suitable fashion without throwing a NullPointerException.

The Title methods that take the String default value as their last parameter will display this value when the reference passed is null. The following example shows this. This method will work whether or not the Order field has a value, and whether or not the Order object's data has been loaded yet.

```
public Title title() {
    return new Title(getOrder(), "New Order");
}
```

3.4.7 Specifying About objects to control access

We have seen several examples of controlling access to classes, objects, fields and methods using an about... method that corresponds to a class, object, accessor or action method. These methods all return an org.nakedobjects.object.control.About object. The About object provides four pieces of information about the class, object, field or method it is supporting, for potential use by the viewing mechanism or any other service. These are:

- Whether it should be accessible to the current user.

- Whether it can be used while the object is in its current state.

- The name it should be known by (if it needs to differ from the name that is automatically generated by the framework from the class or method name).

- A description of the class, object or method it is controlling.

All About objects are derived from the About interface. This interface declares four methods that represent the information mentioned above:

- canAccess

- canUse

- getName

- getDescription

The last two return String objects, whilst the first two each return a org.nakedobjects.object.control.Permission object. A Permission object is used instead of a simple boolean because in addition to specifying whether the access/use has been allowed or disallowed, it can also provide a reason, in the form of a textual message. This is further simplified by the fact that the Permission class is sub-classed as org.nakedobjects.object.control.Allow and org.nakedobjects.object.control.Veto, which simply hold a reason String and indicate the state by their type.

Using the About interface you can define your own About class and exercise complete control over your objects. However, the ready-made About classes provided by the framework will be sufficient for most purposes.

Ready-made About objects

The simplest way to apply control is to use ready-made About objects. All of the basic About classes (such as org.nakedobjects.object.control.ClassAbout, org.nakedobjects.object.control.FieldAbout and org.nakedobjects.object.control.ActionAbout) have publicly-available constants (such as UNINSTANTIABLE, READ_ONLY and ENABLE, which determine the usability of classes, fields and methods respectively).

To provide some flexibility these classes also have static methods that will provide an About object based on a flag that you supply. For example ActionAbout has the method enable that takes a boolean and will return the ENABLE object if the flag is true and the DISABLE object if false. There is also a complementary method called disable. This allows us to disable an action... method on a specified condition, as shown below:

```
public About aboutActionSell() {
    return ActionAbout.disable(getCustomer() == null);
}
```

Building About objects

When you need an About to do more than just disable something (for example, you want to change a field or method name), then the ready-made About objects we have discussed so far are not suitable as they have no provision for conveying any additional information. Things are even more complicated when there are a number of influences that each partly determine whether something should be allowed or not. For example, consider the Location class. It has a method actionNewBooking(Location) that allows two locations to be used to create a new Booking using the two locations as pick-up and drop-off points. This method should only be allowed if the two location objects are different, and that they are also in the same city. If we implement the about... method using the static About objects (as shown below) then the users will know when they can't drop an object, but will not know why:

```java
public About aboutActionNewBooking(Location location) {
    boolean differentLocations = !equals(location);
    boolean sameCity = (getCity() != null) && getCity().equals(location.getCity());

    return ActionAbout.enable(differentLocations && sameCity);
}
```

We need to be able to include the reason why something is disallowed. This is catered for in the Permission objects that we mentioned earlier. These are used within the org.nakedobjects.object.control.ProgrammableAbout class, which allows us to build up an About object by explicitly setting its state or conditionally modifying it as conditions are checked. For example, here is an alternative version of the previous method using this class:

```java
public About aboutActionNewBooking(Location location) {
    boolean differentLocations = !equals(location);
    boolean sameCity = (getCity() != null) && getCity().equals(location.getCity());

    ProgrammableAbout about = new ProgrammableAbout();
    about.makeAvailableOnCondition(differentLocations,
        "Two different locations are required");
    about.makeAvailableOnCondition(sameCity,
        "Locations must be in the same city");
    return about;
}
```

Using the same two flags we've added these conditions to the ProgrammableAbout object using the makeAvailableOnCondition method. This does nothing if the flag is true, but if it is false then this method ensures that a subsequent call to canUse will return a Veto object that includes the specified text as the reason, or part of the reason, that this option is not available. This information will be displayed to the user when the drop is invalid and describes whether the locations are the same or are in different cities.

The following version further extends the method so that the About now contains a description of the method. This is in line with our philosophy that the documentation should be part of the code and not written and maintained separately. It could be used (although it is not at the moment) within the framework to describe the option to the user at the point where he might want to use it. Alternatively, it could be used by a program that automatically generates the complete documentation for an application. This version also shows the changeNameIfAvailable method that sets up the name of the About so that it reflects the action to be performed. Using this version of the method, the name will only be changed if the action is allowed:

```
public About aboutActionNewBooking(Location location) {
    boolean differentLocations = !equals(location);
    boolean sameCity = (getCity() != null) && getCity().equals(location.getCity());

    ProgrammableAbout about = new ProgrammableAbout();
    about.setDescription("Giving one location to another location creates " +
        "a new booking going from the given location " +
        "to the receiving location.");
    about.makeAvailableOnCondition(differentLocations,
        "Two different locations are required");
    about.makeAvailableOnCondition(sameCity,
        "Locations must be in the same city");
    about.changeNameIfAvailable("New booking from " + location.title() +
        " to " + title());
    return about;
}
```

Areas of control

The following summarizes what aspects of a naked object can be controlled and how it should be done.

- **A class**

  Add a static about**Class** method to class.

  Use ClassAbout to make a class uninstantiable.

- **An object**

  Add an about method to class.

  Use ObjectAbout or the ProgrammableAbout to make an instance read-only.

- **A field**

  For value objects assign an About using the value object's setAbout method.

  For associations, add about**Variable** method to the class matching the get**Variable** method you wish to control.

  Use FieldAbout to make an field read-only or the ProgrammableAbout to make an field read-only or change the name of the field.

- **An action method**

  Add an aboutAction**Method** method to the class matching the action**Method** method.

  Use ActionAbout to disable the method or the ProgrammableAbout to disable the method or change the name of the option.

3.5 Writing tests

Modern systems development practice now demands that testing be an integral part of the development process, conducted as early as possible, and automated to the greatest extent possible. In the Java world, the Junit (http://www.junit.org) framework has been one of the most significant enablers of this concept.

The following code shows one fairly obvious approach to writing unit tests for Naked Objects using Junit. This tests the bidirectional association between a booking and the customer, and the confirm option:

```
public void testBookingForCustomer() {
        Booking booking = new Booking();
        Customer customer = new Customer();

        booking.associateCustomer(customer);

        assertEquals(customer, booking.getCustomer());
        assertTrue(customer.getBookings().contains(booking));

        assertTrue(booking.aboutActionCheckAvailability().canUse().isAllowed());
        booking.actionCheckAvailability();
        assertEquals("Available", booking.getStatus().title().toString());
}
```

The code below re-writes this using 'mock' view objects, which are provided as part of the Naked Objects framework. Mock views represent the objects within test code in the same way that graphical views represent the objects within the basic GUI, i.e. they allow the objects to be manipulated as if a user were working interactively.

As above, we start by creating two new objects, a booking and a customer. This time, though, we create the new booking by getting a mock view of the booking class itself (using the name 'Bookings' that would normally be displayed under the class icon), and then performing the equivalent of right-clicking on the menu for that class and invoking the New Instance... option. We do the same for the customer:

```
public void testBookingForCustomer() {
        View booking = getClassView("Bookings").newInstance();
        View customer = getClassView("Customers").newInstance();

        booking.drop("Customer", customer.drag());
```

```
        booking.assertFieldContains("Customer", customer);
        customer.assertFieldContains("Bookings", booking);

        booking.rightClick("Check Availability");
        booking.assertFieldContains("Status", "Available");
}
```

The advantage of this approach over the previous Junit example is not only that the test code is simpler, but that the mock views test the functionality from the perspective of the user. Thus we no longer have to worry about whether to call the set... or the associate... method; we can just ask the mock view to simulate dropping an object onto the required field and let the framework decide which method needs to be called. The framework will now also check the about... method, if there is one, and if changing the field is disabled an exception will be thrown. Similarly, if a mock view is asked to invoke one of the business object's action methods, it will only do so after first checking the corresponding about... method to see if that action method is available in that context.

The example also shows some additional assert... methods that we have added to make the checking of the objects simpler. These methods allow us to specify fields using the names as they should appear to the user. This means we can write tests before we have written the methods that we will be testing, and to compile those tests without error. When the test is run, if no method is found to match the specified name, then an exception is thrown. Some programmers like to use this style of executable unit test to guide their development process — dealing with each exception in turn.

3.5.1 Simulations using mock views

The Naked Objects testing framework makes use of three types of mock view, corresponding to the classes, the objects, and the object's fields, each simulating what can be done using the graphical interface. Thus objects can be dragged, dropped and right-clicked, and value objects edited. All of these view classes are part of the org.nakedobjects.testing package.

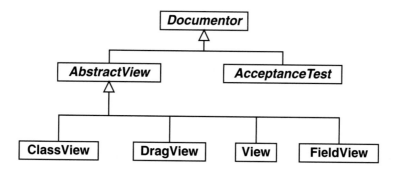

Class views

Class views are created by the test framework as each class is registered. Once a ClassView is retrieved it can be used to create new instances and access existing ones.

- public View newInstance() returns a new instance of the type represented by the ClassView. This method is a substitute for all the ways of creating an object, such as selecting the **New Instance...** option or dragging the class icon onto the desktop.

- public View instances() returns a collection of the instances as would be generated by the **Instances...** option.

- public View findInstance(String pattern) returns the first instance found of the represented type whose title matches, in whole or in part, the text in pattern. This mimics the various ways a user might find and then select an instance based on its title alone. This would include selecting an icon that already exists on the desktop, or searching manually through the collection of instances returned by the class menu **Instances...** option.

- public View drop(DragView draggedObject) takes a dragged object and invokes the class action... method for that object's type. This corresponds to dropping an object onto the class icon.

The following code simulates three class actions: the creation of a Location object; the retrieval of a Customer object with 'Pawson' in the title; and the dropping of a customer object onto the **Bookings** class icon.

```
View location = getClassView("Locations").newInstance();

View customer = getClassView("Customers").findInstance("Pawson");

View booking = getClassView("Bookings").drop(customer.drag());
```

Object views

Once an object is available through a view then all the gestures that are available to the user through the graphical user interface (such as dragging and dropping, or right-clicking and selecting a menu action) can be mimicked.

- public View rightClick(String optionName) simulates the right-clicking of an object and the selection of the named menu option. The supplied name should be the name of the action as would be seen by the user, not the method name (for example, "Return Booking" for the method actionReturnBooking). This call checks the associated about... method, if there is one, before calling the action... method. If the about... method disallows the option (i.e. it is disabled and would be shown as a grey menu option) then an IllegalActionError is thrown. If the method returns an object then this is placed in a new View before being returned.

- public DragView drag() imitates the drag part of a drag and drop gesture. This generates a DragView object that can be accepted by the drop... methods. The DragView objects may seem superfluous but were introduced to facilitate the documentation of these gestures (as described in the next section).

- public View drop(DragView dropObject) imitates the drop part of a drag and drop gesture. This accepts a view generated as a DragView object and invokes the relevant action method for that type of object. The associated about... method, if it exists, is called before the action... method is called, throwing an IllegalActionError if the action is disabled (in which case the drop zone flashes red). As before, this method will also place any returned object into a new View.

The following two lines of code simulate selecting the Return Booking... option on a booking object, and the dropping of one location instance onto another:

View returnBooking = booking.rightClick("Return Booking");

View newBooking = location.drop(fromLocation.drag());

Collections

If the object in the view is an internal collection rather than a business object then use the method public View select(String title) to select the first instance whose title matches, in whole or in part, the pattern in title. This mimics the user selecting an object from a list, scrolling through it if necessary.

Fields within an object view

An object view also has a series of methods that allow its fields to be set or accessed. For value fields, when a string is provided, it will be parsed by the value object. For association fields, these methods mimic the dropping of other objects and the dragging of icons. When any of these methods are invoked with an invalid field name, an IllegalActionError will be thrown.

- public void fieldEntry(String fieldName, String entry) sets up the specified field using the entry string. The entry has to be understood by the value object and must be entered in exactly the same way that a user would enter it – that is, it must be entered in the correct format.

- public void drop(String fieldName, DragView dropObject) attempts to set the named field so it references the object contained in the dropped view. This will invoke the appropriate set... or associate... method, or will access the collection if it is a one-to-many association, and add the item. An IllegalActionError will be thrown if the object is of the wrong type or the field already contains a reference.

- public void removeReference(String fieldName) removes the existing reference from the specified field.

- public void removeReference(String fieldName, View object) removes the existing reference, which matches the specified view's object, from the specified field that uses an internal collection.

- public DragView drag(String fieldName) creates a DragView which references the object held by the named field.

- public DragView drag(String fieldName, String title) creates a DragView which references the first object within the internal collection held by the named field that matches, in whole or in part, the text specified in title. An IllegalActionError will be thrown if the collection does not contain an item with the specified title.

The following example sets up the First Name and Last Name fields in a customer object, drops a location object into the Locations list, and drags out the Airport location object from the same list and drops it into the booking's Pick Up field:

```
customer.fieldEntry("First Name", "Richard");
customer.fieldEntry("Last Name", "Pawson");
```

customer.drop("Locations", location.drag());

booking.drop("Pick Up", customer.drag("Locations", "Airport"));

3.5.2   Unit tests

To create a view-based unit test you must subclass the
org.nakedobjects.testing.NakedTestCase class rather than the usual
junit.framework.TestCase. To set up the simulated application, the classes that
are to be used must be registered by calling the registerClass method.

The following code is taken from the unit test code from the ECS example. It
shows how the test is set up and initialized. The call to the init method inside
the main method sets up the Naked Objects framework to work locally:

```
package ecs.tests;

import junit.framework.TestSuite;
import junit.textui.TestRunner;
import org.nakedobjects.testing.NakedTestCase;
import org.nakedobjects.testing.View;
import ecs.delivery.*;

public class ECSUnitTests extends NakedTestCase {

    public static void main(java.lang.String[] args) {
        init();
        TestRunner.run(new TestSuite(ECSUnitTests.class));
    }

    public ECSUnitTests(String name) {
        super(name);
    }

    protected void setUp() {
        registerClass(Booking.class);
        registerClass(City.class);
        registerClass(Customer.class);
        registerClass(Location.class);
        registerClass(CreditCard.class);
    }
}
```

As when using Junit, each test should be written as a public method with the method name prefixed by 'test' and should make use of the mock views to simplify coding. The following example, taken from the ECS unit tests, is a test method that creates a new City instance and sets and tests its name field. It concludes by checking that the instance's title is the same as the value held by the name field:

```
public void testCity() {
        View city = getClassView("Cities").newInstance();
        city.testField("Name", "Boston");
        city.assertTitleEquals(city.getFieldTitle("Name"));
}
```

This second example tests the initial state of a booking object. It expects to have two read only fields, a specific status value, and four associations that do not yet refer to anything. Because of this state it also specifies that the Confirm option is to be disabled:

```
public void testBooking() {
        View booking = getClassView("Bookings").newInstance();
        booking.assertFieldReadOnly("Reference");
        booking.assertFieldReadOnly("Status");

        booking.assertFieldContains("Status", "New Booking");

        booking.assertCantRightClick("Confirm");

        booking.assertFieldContains("Customer", (View)null);
        booking.assertFieldContains("City", (View)null);
        booking.assertFieldContains("Pick Up", (View)null);
        booking.assertFieldContains("Drop Off", (View)null);
}
```

As in the two examples above, most tests will need to access the class objects before any useful testing can be done. The org.nakedobjects.testing.ApplicationTestCase class provides a method to get hold of the class view for a particular class:

- public ClassView getClassView(String name) retrieves a class view using the class name as it is known to the user (e.g. "Credit Cards" for the CreditCard class).

Object views are used to simulate user actions as discussed in the previous section. Additional assert… methods are provided within these views to help check fields and titles:

- public void assertTitleEquals(String message, String expectedTitle) compares the title of the view, which is the text provided by the view's object's title method, with the expected title. It throws an junit.framework.AssertionFailedError, which includes the supplied message, if the resultant strings are different.

- public void assertTitleEquals(String expectedTitle) is the same as the previous method, but without the failure message.

- public void assertFieldContains(String message, String fieldName, String expectedValue) checks the named field to confirm that it contains the expected value. If the field's value is different then an AssertionFailedError is thrown, and includes the supplied message.

- public void assertFieldContains(String fieldName, String expectedValue) is the same as the previous method, but without the failure message.

- public void assertFieldReadOnly(String fieldName) checks the named field to confirm that it is not editable. If the field is editable then an AssertionFailedError is thrown.

- public void assertFieldContains(String message, String fieldName, View expected) checks the named field to confirm that it contains the same object as the expected view. If the value of expected is null then the field is also expected to contain null.

- public void assertFieldContains(String fieldName, View expected) is the same as the previous method, but without the failure message.

- public void assertCantRightClick(String message, String option) checks that the named option cannot be selected. If the option does not exist or it is enabled an AssertionFailedError is thrown, and includes the supplied message.

- public void assertCantRightClick(String option) is the same as the previous method, but without the failure message.

- public void assertCantDrop(String message, DragView dropObject) checks that the specified object (contained by the view) cannot be dropped onto the current view. If the drop object can be dropped on this view, an AssertionFailedError is thrown, including the supplied message.

- public void assertCantDrop(DragView dropObject) is the same as the previous method, but without the failure message.

In addition to these explicit assertions there are three methods that test a field by assigning a value or an object to it and then, using the above assert methods, confirm that the information was stored properly. As for the previous methods, if the field does not exist then an exception will be thrown:

- public void testField(String fieldName, String value) tests the named attribute field by attempting to set it using the value specified in value. Once set, the value held by the object is accessed and compared to the same value.

- public void testField(String fieldName, String value, String expected) tests the named value field by attempting to set it using the value specified in value. Once set, the value held by the object is accessed and compared to the value in expected. This can be used to compensate for value objects that manipulate the set value before storing it. For example, the date object allows you specify a number of days to add to the date. So if the original date was '5-Mar-01', then after setting with it with the value '+14' the date would be '19-Mar-01'.

- public void testField(String fieldName, View setObject) tests the named association field by attempting to set it using the object contained in the specified view and then comparing the reference held by the field to the original reference.

3.5.3 Acceptance tests

Whereas unit tests are principally concerned with whether a method has been written correctly, user acceptance tests are concerned with whether the functionality can be combined to deliver a result of value to a user. We adopt the See page 193 approach of basing acceptance tests on a series of 'stories'*, which are enacted through the mock views. As well as checking that the required functionality is actually available, the acceptance test automatically generates documentation that explains how the story would play out through the real user interface. This is done through the self-commenting methods that are provided by the views. Since the acceptance tests should be based on user-specified requirements, this auto-generated documentation can serve as a significant proportion of the user training manual.

The structure of an acceptance test

Before looking at how a story is coded, we will look at how a test is set up and initiated. The following code is taken from the acceptance test code for the ECS application:

```
import org.nakedobjects.testing.AcceptanceTest;
import org.nakedobjects.testing.View;

public class ECSStories extends AcceptanceTest {

    public ECSStories(String name) {
        super(name);
    }

    public static void main(java.lang.String[] args) {
        ECSStories st = new ECSStories("ESC User Stories");
        st.start();
    }

    public void setUp() {
        registerClass(Booking.class);
        registerClass(City.class);
        registerClass(Customer.class);
        registerClass(Location.class);
        registerClass(CreditCard.class);
        registerClass(Telephone.class);

        adminCreateCities();
    }

    public void runStories() {
        story1BasicBooking();
        story2Reuse();
        story3ReturnBooking();
        story4CopyBooking();
        story5LocLoc();
    }
}
```

Acceptance tests are written by extending the
org.nakedobjects.testing.AcceptanceTest class. This class has a constructor
that takes a name for the suite of tests. Your derived class therefore needs to
implement a constructor that calls this particular superconstructor. To start the
test, call the start method in the superclass.

The start method controls the tests and creation of the documentation.
After setting up the framework it calls the setUp method where you
should register the same set of classes that will be made available to

the user in a live application. After this method has completed, the org.nakedobjects.testing.Documentor class is initialized with the name of the test suite that was passed to the superconstructor. This creates the HTML documentation file, which is given a file name based on the test suite name (for the above example the file will be ESC_User_Stories.html). Any code executed from this point on will automatically be documented. If there are any objects that need to be set up ready to be used during the tests, but which do not need to be described in the documentation, then this should be done as part of the setUp method after any required classes have been registered. (The call to adminCreateCities in the code above is an example.) Once the documentor is running, the runStories method is invoked and each of the test methods is called in turn, generating documentation as they execute. If any story fails at any point then the exception is passed back to the user and the test will stop, because in our approach to acceptance testing the stories are deemed to depend upon each other. This is in contrast to what happens in Junit where the tests run independently.

The structure of a story

There is a common pattern to most stories that reflects both the way the framework is used and how the documentation is generated. To help the development team to keep track of what they are testing, and to help the user break down each task, the stories can be split into logical steps, which can include a description of the subtask.

A story should start with a call to the story method, to mark this story as separate from the previous one and to give it a title. Each stage of the story is then started by a call to the step method, which can take a text string describing what is being done next. Then come the expected user actions, such as creating an instance, dragging and dropping objects, selecting menu options and editing fields. After the user actions it is common to check the state of the objects to ascertain that everything is progressing as expected – i.e. that requirements are being met. It is also possible to confirm that certain actions are not allowed at a certain point.

Both the actions and the checks are carried out by invoking specific methods on the views. When they run, these methods all add descriptions to the documentation, detailing the steps, explaining how to manipulate the objects, showing how their states change, and making notes of what can't be done. This process, therefore, not only checks the logic of the business object but also directs the user toward what can and can't be done with them. The following code shows the beginning of the second ECS story and demonstrates this common pattern:

```
public void story2Reuse() {
    story("A booking where the previous used locations are used");

    step("Retrieve the customer object.");
    View customer = getClassView("Customers").findInstance("Pawson");

    step("Create a booking for this customer.");
    View booking = customer.rightClick("New Booking");
    booking.checkField("Customer", customer);

    step("Retrieve the customer's home and office as the ...");
    booking.drop("Pick Up",
        customer.drag("Locations", "234 E 42nd Street, New York"));
    booking.drop("Drop Off",
        customer.drag("Locations", "JFK Airport, BA Terminal"));
    booking.checkField("City", "New York");

    step("Use the customer's mobile phone as the contact ...");
    :
    :

}
```

When the test is run and completes without any exceptions, then it will have also been documented in HTML. The following shows the output from this facility, using cascading style sheets with the HTML page to render it so the objects, field and menus can be distinguished:

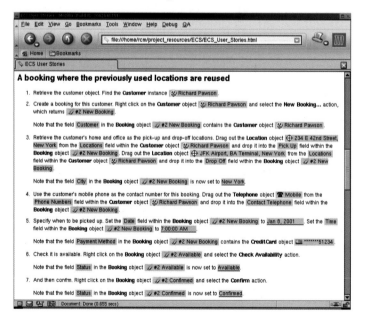

The following methods from the AcceptanceTest class structure the documentation:

- public void story(String title) creates a new story and adds a title for it to the document. In the current version this is added using the <H2> (heading level 2) tag.

- public void subtitle(String subtitle) adds a subtitle to the document using the <H3> (heading level 3) tag.

- public void step(String description) adds another step to the instructions. This is added as an <LI> (list item) tag. If the description text does not end with a full stop, then one will be added to prevent the description running into the generated text. On the first call to this method, after a call to story or subtitle, an opening <OL> (ordered list) tag is added; the closing tag is added when the next story or subtitle is invoked.

- public void step() adds another step but without a description. This works in the same way as the previous method.

- public void append(String text) adds any other text to the current step. This is added without any tags so the text is simply concatenated to the instructions as they stand at that point.

As the test runs the above methods provide the document with its structure, and the simulated interactions, by generating their own comments, describe the actions to be taken. For example the statement customer.rightClick("New Booking") produces the text "Right click on the Customer object 'Richard Pawson' and select the 'New Booking ...' action, which returns '#2 New Booking'." (The previous screenshot shows the formatted output including the icons).

The mock object views also allow the state of an object to be checked. For example the statement booking.checkField("Customer", customer) would add "Note that the field Customer in the Booking object '#2 New Booking' contains the Customer object 'Richard Pawson'" to the document. These checking methods are provided in addition to the assert... methods that can still be used even though this is not a unit test, nor is it based on the TestCase class. If any of these checks fail, then an IllegalActionError is thrown and the test will stop. As each one passes it adds an explanation to the documentation. The purpose is to explain to the user what effect the previous step would have had on the object and therefore the state it will now be in.

Unlike these check... methods, the assert... methods do not produce any documentation.

The following check methods are to be found in the org.nakedobjects.testing.View class:

- public void checkTitle(String expected) checks that the view's title (as generated by the object's title method) is equal to the value specified in expected, adding a note to the documentation to show what the title should now be.

- public void checkField(String fieldName, String expectedTitle) checks that the named field within the view has a title that matches the value specified in expectedTitle. It adds a note to the documentation showing what text should be displayed in that field, either as a value or as an object's title.

- public void checkField(String fieldName, AbstractView expected) checks that the named field, within the view, references the same object that the view specified in expected references. It adds a note to the documentation showing what text should be displayed in that field, either as a value or as an object's title.

- public void checkCantRightClick(String option) checks that the named option cannot be selected. It adds a note to the documentation explaining that this option is not available. The append method in AcceptanceTest can be used to give a reason.

- public void checkCantDrop(DragView dropObject) checks that the specified object (contained by the view) cannot be dropped onto the current view. It adds a note to the documentation explaining that this drop is not possible. The append method in AcceptanceTest can be used to give a reason.

Case study: Retail marketing and pricing

Safeway Stores is the fourth largest supermarket chain in the UK, with over 480 stores ranging from hypermarkets to local convenience outlets. Over the last couple of years Safeway has enjoyed significant growth in both total revenues and profitability, triggered in part by the appointment two years ago of a new chief executive and a more dynamic approach to merchandising and pricing.

Business background

Although Safeway is committed to using software packages for various business processes, it is also prepared to develop its own systems where it sees an opportunity to innovate or differentiate. For example, Safeway was the first of the UK store chains to introduce self-checkout for customers, using handheld barcode scanners. And its handheld Shelf-Edge Computing system, which allows staff to check prices, monitor stock and place orders whilst moving about the store, won an industry award when introduced in 2000.

Although many of Safeway's existing systems must be maintained in Cobol, Java is the preferred language for any new in-house development and integration of interactive systems. There are Java developers in most of the application areas, and also a centrally managed Java Services Team, who determine best practice and guidelines, perform research and development, provide technical assistance, and act as consultants throughout a Java project lifecycle.

The management of this team became interested in Naked Objects at the start of 2001. They did not initially see Naked Objects as a development approach, but rather as a way to train some of their Java developers to think in more object-oriented terms. (Many development managers have found that switching to an object-oriented programming language such as Java does not automatically change the way people think about systems design). They felt that more commitment to object-oriented principles would help them see greater benefit from the investment in Java technology and skills. More than 30 developers received basic training in Naked Objects over the next 3 months – with the majority reporting that it had significantly improved their understanding of object-orientation. Moreover, the experience had created considerable enthusiasm for undertaking a realistic development exercise using the framework.

Opportunity

Still under the auspices of training, a candidate project was identified in the area of promotions management, known as 'deal nominations'. Safeway changed its pricing policy a couple of years ago. Now, instead of attempting to maintain a policy of 'every day low pricing', it competes through special promotions that offer up to 50% discounts on particular food and drink lines, designed to bring more customers into the store. Each week it prints and distributes some 11 million 4-page colour flyers to households in the catchment areas. To prevent the competition from matching these offers, the set of promotions is constantly being changed. Stores are grouped into clusters, and each cluster offers a different package of around 40 special promotions each week.

Implementing these promotions involves managing the supply chain to cope with big increases in sales of the promoted items, communicating the price changes to the EPOS systems in the stores, and printing and distributing the promotional flyers, in-store banners and labels. Systems exist to manage each of these activities individually, but the overall planning and coordination of these activities is intensely manual, as is the planning process. Promotions managers are constantly exploring combinations of special offers with the intent of attracting the maximum number of shoppers who will then go on to buy regular items from the store, without merely encouraging 'cherry pickers' who take the best offers and nothing else. Each special offer must be coordinated with the supplier for logistics planning and, in some cases, to share the cost.

Ideally, these managers needed a purpose-designed system to nominate new deals, forecast sales and availability, simulate their roll-out through the store clusters, and then coordinate their execution through the supply chain and price coordination systems. Previous attempts by the systems department to analyze the requirements for such a system had not gone well. The activity did not fit well into the strongly process-oriented perspectives that are required for, say, supply chain management systems. 'Deal nominations' was much more of a problem-solving activity: any particular deal might start with a proposal from a supplier, or it might be initiated to fill a 'hole' in a partly-assembled offering. What was needed was a system that would allow users to construct multiple offerings, simulate their effect, and cut and paste them until they felt right. Then make them so!

Approach

A team consisting of developers and business area representatives was assembled and given just four weeks to design a proof-of-concept using Naked Objects. To put this into perspective, previous attempts had taken much longer than that to do a paper-based requirements-gathering exercise, only to be abandoned because the users were unconvinced that the resulting document really captured what they needed.

The new exercise made no use of that previous work: it started from scratch. After just a couple of hours spent discussing the dynamics of the business in order to give the developers some familiarity with the domain, the team got straight down to identifying the set of business objects that would best model the deal nominations area. Around twenty candidate objects were suggested but by the end of the first day this had been whittled down to below ten.

By the second morning the developers were already translating the successful object candidate descriptions into Java, using the Naked Objects framework, drawing icons suggested by the business representatives, and assembling some realistic data for Products, Stores and so forth.

The next four weeks followed an iterative pattern. The whole team met once a week and reviewed the whole object model and the state of the prototype, deciding what the priorities would be for the next iteration. During the week there would be many smaller iterations. A particularly effective way of working was to have an individual business representative sit down with a developer and evolve the prototype in real-time: adding new attributes or associations, new sub-classes, and simple new business methods. For more complex business functionality (especially those that involved searching collections of objects or navigating long chains of command) the developers would work alone, or in pairs.

Throughout this period there was almost constant demand for demonstrations, both from members of the team, and from other parties that had heard about the radical approach of the project and wanted to know more. The project manager took on the role of chief demonstrator, recording and managing a set of demonstration scripts corresponding to specific use-case scenarios. Apart from engaging the team, the demonstrations thus served the important purpose of continuously validating the object model.

Additionally, on various occasions during this exploratory period, the team was asked to identify 'what-if scenarios'. These were not requirements, nor even likely future extensions. They were purely hypothetical scenarios, relating to future changes in the business organization, strategy and relationships, as well as technology-driven scenarios. Although these were not explored in detail, the team was asked to briefly explore what changes that new scenario might require in the model. Ideally, the answer would be that the changes would be limited to just one of the object classes, or perhaps to the creation of a new class that implemented an existing interface so that it could substitute for an existing object in any context.

Key business objects

Shown below are the principal business object classes identified during the exploration of the deal nominations system and crudely implemented in the prototype.

 User The user object knows the roles that a user can fulfil, how to communicate with that person, and various HR-related information.

 Cluster Store locations are managed as regional clusters. Offerings are typically rotated between clusters so as to spread the peak in demand for a particular product.

 Location A Location models a particular store or sub-store such as an in-store coffee shop or a petrol filling station. As with Product, Location would know how to interface to other systems that provide location-specific information or functionality.

 Product There is one instance of product for each product that Safeway stocks (there are more than 40,000). As well as storing supplier data, Product holds one or more images of the product for use in advertising/marketing. The Product object could also know how to interface to the supply chain systems.

 Deal A Deal (such as a temporary discount or two-for-the-price-of-one promotion) can be nominated for any product. Deals are initially hypothetical whilst the impact on supply chain and revenues is simulated, after which they may be formally proposed. A Deal knows how to manage its own approval process.

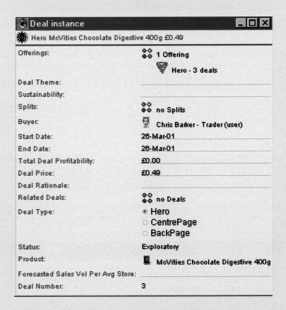

Offering An Offering is typically composed of multiple Deals. As well as knowing how to implement the price changes at the locations it is to be applied to, the Offering should know how to produce the printed promotional 'flyers' that will be distributed to local homes, and the in-store promotional display materials. Offering has various sub-classes. The 'Hero' offering, for example, is typically a collection of heavily-discounted items that would be shown on the front page of a promotional flyer.

Supplier Holds supplier details and knows how to communicate with the supplier, and to interface to supplier management systems.

Role. Knows which object classes, and which methods on those objects that someone fulfilling this role can access.

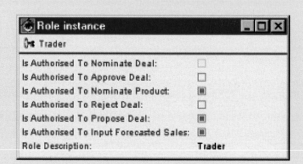

Evaluation – the business perspective

All those involved in or with the exploratory project expressed delight at what had been achieved in the short time. The user representative said that the mock-up had the right 'feel' – meaning that it gave them a great deal of operational flexibility to nominate deals and assemble Offerings in different ways, matching the reality of how they work. All commented positively on the way in which Naked Objects facilitated the dialogue between developers and business representatives. The latter had no difficulty adopting much of the object terminology.

At the end of the exercise the capabilities of the prototype were compared to the prioritized requirements produced by the previous (unsuccessful) attempt – and which had not been consulted this time. All the high priority requirements had already been addressed, and much more besides. In fact, when asked which of the prototype's features they would consider to be the highest priority for implementation if the project were to proceed to Specification and Delivery, the highest priority features had not originally been identified as requirements at all in the first exercise. For example, an Offering object contains a number of Deals – viewed as a collection of icons. During the first couple of weeks, someone had asked whether the generic icon representing a Deal could be replaced with an individual photographic image representing the actual Product to be discounted. This capability was added to the Naked Objects framework with the net result that any Offering could now be viewed as a crude form of the colour flyer that would eventually be printed. The marketing people reported that this early visualization was very helpful in evaluating the attractiveness of the offering as a whole.

Evaluation – the IT perspective

Developers reported that they found the Naked Objects framework easier to adopt than those they had previously used for developing web applications. Naked Objects allows them to concentrate on the business problem, and on the disciplines of good programming, rather than simply on how to use the technology.

Prior to an introduction to Naked Objects in 2001, the newly promoted Java Services Manager was "having difficulty justifying a migration to Java from CICS/Cobol", to himself, his peers and the IT executive. He could foresee Safeway repeating CICS/Cobol with a "nicer front end", but with no significant design and cost advantage for future development, maintainability and support. Naked Objects has changed that perspective.

The Deal Nominations system is now awaiting a decision to proceed; but there seems no question that when it does proceed, the Naked Objects approach is the best way to implement it.

The second project

Meanwhile, another group at Safeway had seen the Deal Nominations prototype and thought that the approach could help them with another difficult business problem. Naked Objects was initially seen as a way to facilitate the modelling of requirements rather than as the eventual architecture for the system. As the exploration progressed, however, it became clear that the users liked the concept very much. IT management also recognized that this system made an ideal candidate for a full-blown trial of the Naked Objects framework: the system offered high business value but had a small user base.

At that time, the Naked Objects framework lacked the enterprise services needed to implement real systems. However, Safeway made available its best Java developer to explore possibilities. It soon became clear that the object/relational mapping required between Naked Objects and Safeway's existing mainframe databases could be achieved using Enterprise Java Beans (EJB) and XML. The result was the creation of the EJB Object Store*.

*See page 118

The Exploration phase took four weeks. After a further three weeks of Specification, the Delivery phase commenced. Only the object definitions were carried forward. All the Java code needed for the release was now re-written from scratch, adopting a more rigorous approach to testing. The first release was ready for user testing after 90 days, which is remarkable given that this included developer training, Christmas breaks, and delays caused by changes and teething problems with the framework and the middleware. Initial performance was poor. However, this was because the EJB server was operating on a separate machine to the database. When the former was ported over to the mainframe, the whole system ran as fast as "anything we are used to on the mainframe running under CICS". Safeway has subsequently incorporated the testing* features of Naked Objects and is assisting with development of new features for the framework.

*See page 141

Section 4:
A development process

Our experience of applying the Naked Objects framework to a range of business problems suggests that such projects are best conceived and managed in three distinct phases: exploration, specification and delivery. For the specification and delivery phases it is possible to use a range of existing methodologies.

Although many methodologies prescribe or permit some form of exploration, our version is distinctive. What comes out of this phase is not just a better understanding of business requirements and possibilities, but an outline object model that has been tested against business scenarios, through a working prototype. You will see this in action in the following pages.

Specification and delivery are more conventional. During specification, the business requirements are formally specified and prioritized, releases planned, costs estimated, and infrastructural implications identified. In the delivery phase, the system is developed, integrated, tested and released. You could use any modern methodology for this phase, but if you choose XP, Naked Objects will make some of its disciplines easier to realize. Although no code is carried forward from the exploratory prototype, the complete outline object model gives developers more confidence to adopt the strict 'one story at a time' discipline of XP during delivery, knowing that subsequent refactoring will principally apply to methods, not to the object boundaries. And the Naked Objects testing framework makes it easy to apply 'test-first coding' both to unit testing and acceptance testing.

Within each of these phases the activities are strongly iterative. You could also iterate between the phases of exploration, specification and delivery. However this runs the risk of diluting the power of the approach and we recommend that you treat them as three distinct and sequential phases, at least until you have grown comfortable with the Naked Objects approach.

4.1 The exploration phase

The exploration phase has two main purposes: to explore business requirements and to explore object representations of the business domain. The naked objects approach is unique in making these two activities synergistic: exploring business requirements clearly helps you to identify candidate objects, but building an object model in concrete usable form also helps you explore business requirements.

Notice that we say 'explore' and not 'capture' business requirements. In our experience, the requirements specified by the user representatives after exploring the naked objects are very different from those that they would have specified, if asked to do so, at the start of the project – and also different from those they would have specified using more common forms of prototyping. The direct interaction with the object model seems to suggest new requirements and even new business possibilities. This is why a period of exploration must precede any form of specification of requirements.

4.1.1 Preparing for exploration

People often ask: 'How can you start a project without first having some idea of the scope of requirements, in order to make a first-level estimate of the overall project costs?' This line of thinking leads to many failed systems development projects. It is very difficult to get business sponsors and user representatives to specify up-front what it is that they require of a new system. This is not just – as some methodologies seem to assume – because the user has difficulty articulating the requirements; it is because the introduction of new technology into the business activity changes what is possible, but in ways that it is almost impossible to imagine in your head or on paper. Asking users to specify all their requirements for a system on paper, and to prioritize those requirements without having seen any of them implemented, or even simulated, just invites future problems.

Making the case for action

Using the Naked Objects approach, every project starts with a period of exploration, which is strictly time-boxed and which, once you have some experience of using the approach, can be fixed-price without needing to know anything about the application.

'Making the case for action' for a Naked Objects project should therefore mean making the case for undertaking an exploration phase. We recommend that you write this in a single paragraph or presentation slide that spells out the one most compelling reason for doing the exploration: a changing regulatory environment, a new line of business, a sudden and dramatic need for cost reduction, or simply a compelling vision of a new way of working. If you can't write a single paragraph (or slide) that is persuasive enough to justify a fixed-price four-week exploration exercise, then the project is probably not worthwhile.

Although this takes courage, it is more honest to refuse to make any estimate of overall implementation costs before the exploration phase has been undertaken, than to make a crude estimate and have to revise it by a factor of three, or ten, as the true requirements and complexity emerge. We are not the first to say this. However, one of the big advantages of the Naked Objects approach is that the customer gets a lot of value from the exploration: not just a specification, or feasibility study, or a set of static UML diagrams, but a working prototype that's fun to play with, and an object model that might also yield new insights into the business itself.

By the time you start the specification stage you will not only have a clearer idea of what's required and what's possible, but also of the costs involved in implementation. If necessary you can then write a more detailed justification for proceeding to the delivery phase.

Forming the exploration team

The exploration team includes systems developers and user representatives working closely together. Because the developers will be writing code and making modifications directly in front of the users, they need to be fluent with their tools: the Java programming language, the Naked Objects framework, and the chosen development environment. (Training developers by exploring a hypothetical business problem can be very effective, but we do not recommend going into a real business exploration phase until they have achieved some fluency with the tools).

The user representatives need to have a broad and deep understanding of their own business domain, and the trust of those they represent. Ideally they will be selected for their willingness to explore new ways of working, and will be confident and experienced users of information technology. And ideally, the group will include at least one person who is going to be an everyday user of the proposed system. Sometimes, the user representative will be an IT person such as an account manager, business analyst or consultant (sometimes known as 'subject-matter experts'). However, understand that the user representative is there to provide broad and deep business knowledge, and to represent the users, not to perform some kind of translation role between users and IT.

The exploration team also needs an experienced object modeller to lead all the modelling sessions. Some approaches to object design emphasize the idea of a 'facilitator': someone trained in group facilitation, who can ensure that everyone gets their say, that no ideas are rejected outright, that no-one dominates the group, and so forth. But object modelling is a design exercise, not a brainstorming exercise. It should be participatory design, certainly, so the lead object modeller does need reasonable interpersonal skills. But he or she can and should be willing to give immediate feedback on any suggestion: "Yes, that helps," "No, that's not an object" and so on.

A good rule of thumb is that the lead object modeller should be sufficiently competent and confident to do the whole object model alone. This does not imply that the team exercise is just a pretence. The team will undoubtedly make useful suggestions that the lead modeller might not have thought of. There are also certain modelling activities that the team will do better than an individual – some of which are described in the next chapter. Even in dynamic periods where the lead modeller is taking many of the design decisions directly, just forcing him or her to think aloud in front of the group and justify those decisions will probably improve the modelling, as well as the group's understanding. Finally, other members of the team can and will give instant feedback on some of those decisions by mentally applying them to their own needs and business scenarios. If handled correctly, each member of the team will feel that they have made a useful contribution and will have a strong sense of ownership of the resulting model, but they will not be under any illusions that design is a democratic process.

One more thing about the lead object modeller: in our opinion this person needs to have programming experience, and in an object-oriented language. This does not mean that lead object modellers write code themselves (although they may do so), but they need to be very familiar with object-oriented design patterns right down to the programming level. Naked objects bring out the synergy between object-oriented analysis and object-oriented programming in a way that few other approaches do. The programming experience does not even need to be in Java – the basic syntax of which is very easy to learn once you've programmed in another object-oriented language. It is our observation (and others') that many of the best object modellers learned their technique from programming in Smalltalk, not from any design methodology. If you learned Java well, that can be just as good, but unfortunately many institutions and authors still teach Java as though it was procedural language.

Other roles are also needed on the exploration team. Depending on the application, it may be appropriate to have someone who has a broad familiarity with existing systems to which the new system might be interfaced, particularly existing databases. The more you can make use of realistic data during the exploration phase, the more effective it will be. In the Safeway case study even the prototype had a simple form of persistence that allowed the exploration team to work with a large and realistic set of Product and Location objects. This was important, because the rationale for the project had to do with managing the complexity of large numbers of potentially conflicting price adjustments and/or special promotions. Using a very small data set would have made it hard to understand the issues.

The exploration team will have many responsibilities – documenting the model, capturing the test scenarios, designing icons, giving demonstrations – several of which are described in detail later. These responsibilities might or might not translate into specialized roles: different teams will evolve their own styles. You need to find the right balance between the power of collective ownership, as championed by Extreme Programming, and the efficiency of having specialized expertise available.

Advance preparation

Before the team starts to explore the chosen business domain, it is important that it establishes a common vision of what the resulting system will look like. For example, one of the principles of Extreme Programming (XP) is that of 'system metaphor': all members of the team should have in mind a common picture of the resulting system that can be used to inform design decisions. The metaphor of a spreadsheet is cited as an example in several XP books. Yet many XP practitioners report that they have had difficulty identifying a suitable metaphor, or that the metaphor has been of little value in resolving real design issues.

Naked objects are, in themselves, a very strong metaphor. Once someone has understood one system designed from naked objects, they have a very clear mental model that they can translate into a new domain. Thus we recommend that all members of the team should be introduced to examples of naked object systems before beginning to explore the new problem domain. Ideally this will include reading the case studies in this book and playing with the demonstrations that you can download from our website. If this is not practicable, then kick off the exploration phase with a set of demonstrations to the team as a whole.

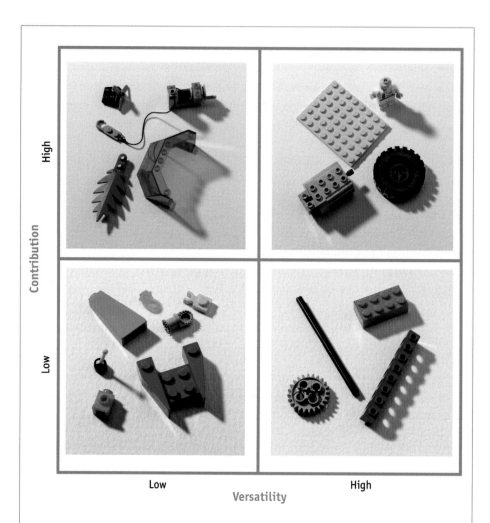

A useful preparation exercise is to get team members to classify a collection of Lego pieces according to their 'versatility' (i.e. the number of different models you could use them in) and 'contribution' (how much value the piece adds to the model on average). The same analogy can be applied to business objects. In a Naked Objects exploration exercise we are seeking to identify only the objects that belong in the top right hand corner: those that the user would deploy in solving a wide range of problems and yet which still yield a lot of value through their behaviour. Classical task-oriented systems design tends to focus on the top left quadrant, whilst classical object-oriented programming focuses on the lower quadrants.

It is possible to extend the generic naked object metaphor into a variety of more specific forms. Metaphors that we have used on several projects include the caseworker*, visual network management*, the workbench, and the parts catalogue.

*See page 28
*See page 214

The other area where we have found that preparation pays dividends is the physical environment. Exploration workshops are intense activities — poor lighting, ventilation, or ambient noise levels add to the stress and reduce your effectiveness. Try to use a room with natural light, preferably on two sides of the room*. Arrange the furniture so that all participants can see each other: an open U-shaped table is much better than a long thin boardroom-style table.

lexander
77

Plenty of whiteboards and/or places to stick up flipcharts are always useful, but make as much use as possible of electronic projection. You'll need it to do demonstrations of the evolving prototype, and it will enable multiple developers to view the evolving code structure. Where possible, we like to have two projectors and two screens, so that we can see both the developer and the user view of the system at the same time.

We also recommend that you try to capture the ideas arising from design sessions directly into electronic form. Unless the scribe has very neat writing, electronic capture improves legibility. It also means that the output can be instantly available to all participants as soon as the workshop is over. But the biggest reason is that electronic note capture with projection makes it easier to edit the notes, and particularly to restructure them as the discussion progresses. Our preference is to use a structured text outliner such as Word, although we have also seen a variety of the 'mind mapping' tools used this way. Either can be effective if the user is fluent with the tool.

169

Planning and scheduling

Exploration is an iterative exercise, with each iteration comprising three principal activities:

- Defining objects and their responsibilities.
- Building the objects into a prototype.
- Using the prototype to explore business scenarios.

It is possible, even desirable, to plan the exploration phase as a fixed set of formal iterations, perhaps four of five of them, and schedule the three activities within each iteration. But there may also be many informal iterations, where all three activities might be undertaken by a single individual in the course of a few minutes and where the boundaries between the activities is unclear and unimportant.

In ideal circumstances, during the exploration phase the whole team will be working full-time on the project and will be physically co-located. With such a set-up and with developers experienced in the Naked Objects approach, two weeks can be a realistic time-box for exploration. There is little need for formal planning as the team can decide its priorities and working style day by day.

Such ideal circumstances seldom arise. It is often hard to get user representatives to commit full-time to any systems project. In our experience it is far more important to get the right user representatives, who will be mentally engaged even if they can't apply themselves full-time, than it is to insist on a full-time user representative and end up with someone who 'won't be missed' by the business. But then there needs to be a slightly more formal plan: the whole team meets formally every three days for three hours, perhaps. The sessions start with a rehearsed demonstration of completed scenarios, a review of the whole object model and then a discussion of new avenues to pursue or problems to resolve. In between these meetings, individual user representatives and developers meet to work on a particular aspect of the model and prototype, or to specify and test new scenarios.

With such an approach, four weeks is more realistic for the time-box. And if it's your first go at designing systems this way or if there are many different stake-holders to be involved, then allow a little longer. Note, however, that none of the projects described in this book had an exploration phase of more than six weeks. Don't be misled by claims that the problem domain is especially complex. Naked objects thrive on apparently complex problems! (Some proposed business applications appear to be dauntingly complex precisely because they don't fit into the process-oriented paradigm that most development methodologies assume.)

We shall now look at each of the three elements of an iteration.

4.1.2 Defining objects and their responsibilities

Exploration starts by going straight for the objects. Don't attempt to capture use-cases before looking for the key objects. Our aim is always to get a first, crude, iteration of the complete business object model by the end of the very first day of exploration.

You don't need any formal preparation or documented input before you start, as you will rely on knowledge inherent within the team. Spend a couple of hours just talking about the selected business domain: what happens, what's difficult, how things are changing. This is informal, unstructured and undocumented. Its purpose it to get people warmed up, comfortable with each other, and familiar with the domain.

Initial identification of objects

Abbott 1983
Booch 1994 A long established technique for identifying candidate objects** is to write down a very informal description of the business domain and the desired contribution of the system, and then to underline all the noun phrases. Probably, during our informal discussion, we will have begun to do some mental underlining of noun phrases, but we have found it unnecessary to recognize this formally or to document any of the discussion.

So, after a couple of hours of discussion, the lead object modeller invites the whole team to start suggesting candidate objects, and captures these as a mind-map or structured text document. (If you decide to have a separate 'scribe', then that person and the lead object modeller should have pre-agreed the format, and carefully rehearsed the process of capturing and editing object ideas.) At this stage, the emphasis will be on getting lots of suggestions and maintaining a high level of energy. However, the lead object modeller should feel free to provide immediate feedback on suggestions, and add several of his or her own.

We have never yet seen a group that didn't enter into this initial task of suggesting objects with enthusiasm and effectiveness. One hour is usually quite sufficient to generate a good list of candidates – typically between 20 and 40.

Shortening the list

After a short break, start to refine this list. The clearly stated aim is to cut the list down to between five and ten 'core' business objects. One reason for this is the oft-quoted principle about the number of peer-level ideas that people can keep in their heads at one time. The Naked Objects framework encourages this stance because, at least for the prototype, all the core business object classes will appear in the classes window on the screen, and ten is about the visual limit before the screen looks overwhelmingly complex. The simple act of forcing the list to be cut down will also encourage more abstraction in the modelling.

To shorten the list, you can run through a series of simple tests, either casually or formally:

Is it an instantiable class? Does this candidate class represent a type of business entity of which there are several instances? The concreteness of naked objects can make this easier to see. Ask the team: Would there ever be two or more of this type of object shown on the screen at once? Would the user

This example, drawn from an exploration exercise undertaken by a North American electrical utility illustates how the object model may evolve rapidly in the first few hours.

The first cut of the object model featured a Network object connecting Generators to Households, Businesses and Industries. A separate demand-forecasting system balances the loads:

The team quickly realized that distributing responsibility for demand forecasting to each consumer – in the form of an active Power Profile object – would improve business agility. And by placing the responsibility for the delivery of electricity in a Contract object rather than the Network, the company could more easily sell electricity outside its principal territory.

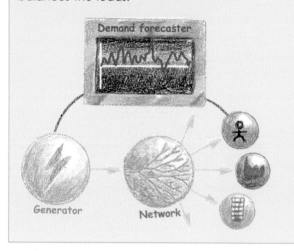

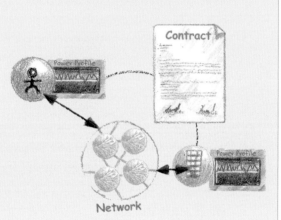

ever say (pointing at the screen): 'Not that one, that one!' If so then you have an instantiable entity class and it can move forward. Another test is simply to ask how each instance is uniquely identified: in Naked Objects terms, what is the object's title? If a candidate fails these tests, then you may have a function that should perhaps appear as a method on one of the other objects. A simple rule of thumb is that you should be cautious of any candidate object that ends in 'er' or 'or'. InterestRateCalculator is probably not an instantiable class, whereas InterestRate could be. (Like any rule of thumb, there are exceptions – Customer, for example!)

Can you think of an icon for it? We insist that for all object candidates taken forward from the very first modelling session, the team agrees on an icon that will represent an object of this class. Icons are needed for the prototype simply in order to distinguish the different types of object. Discussing icons from the outset also focuses the team on the concrete nature of objects. Disagreement over suggested icons sometimes reveals a fundamental difference in understanding of the object's definition. If the project progresses to the delivery phase then it is important to draw up a good set of icons that will be acceptable to a broad set of users. The icons must be both individually aesthetically pleasing, and together form a visually coherent set. But during exploration there is no need to be so rigorous, and it is often expedient to use icons from standard libraries. (The Naked Objects distribution includes a modest ee page 258 library of icons* suitable for use in exploration.)

There is a lot of talk about the need for icons to be 'intuitive'. They certainly need to be visually distinctive, so that no user would easily confuse one for another. And they need to be 'associative', so that once people have been told which icon stands for which type of business object they can easily memorize that association. But there is no need for users to be able to work out what an icon stands for without being told, and research shows that this goal is almost impossible to achieve anyway.

Are there any obvious synonyms? It is likely, given the way that the list was generated, that there will be candidates that are either identical or strongly overlapping. (Case and Claim were early examples in the DSFA exploration.) The differences may be subtle. The best strategy is to try to blend one into the other. Even when the two suggestions came from different members of the team, we have found that they are usually willing to accept the tentative merger, provided that a note is kept of the original distinction. Using an electronic outliner to drag notes around helps considerably here. It may subsequently prove necessary to split the composite object again, although more than likely you will find that the split occurs along different lines.

Do a group of candidates share common behaviours? Several candidates may not be synonyms, but they may share common behaviours. If so, you can make use of abstract types. CheckingAccount and SavingsAccount are both types of BankAccount, for example. To cut the list down you may focus initially on defining Bank Account, only later dealing with the more specific implementations of that type.

A note of caution: try to avoid getting caught in the tar pit of discussions on inheritance hierarchies. Java distinguishes between 'inheritance', where one class actually inherits the means to fulfil a responsibility from its super-class, and 'interface implementation' where one class merely has the same type, meaning the same external interface, as another. The latter is a powerful construct, and in the context of a business object modelling session, is actually more powerful than the concept of inheritance. Again Naked Objects makes this more obvious: if class A and class B implement the same abstract interface, that means

"Carve the problem at its natural joints" is the goal of most object modellers. The principle is hardly new: in Plato's Phaedrus Socrates advises that one should observe the natural articulation of a problem, "not mangling any of the parts like an unskillful butcher". But this is much easier said than done.

Consider the diagrams showing the different standards for jointing a carcass of beef in France, England and the United States. Why there should there be such differences in the three standards, when all have a common goal to maximize the total revenue from the carcass? One explanation is cuisine. Think of France and you think of casseroles; the English traditionally love their roasts; whilst Americans favour grilling. The three different standards reflect this preference somewhat.

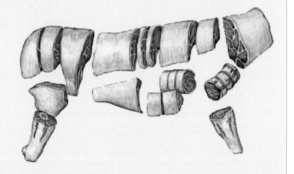

Cuisine is changing, however. Few British families regularly sit down to a traditional roast lunch, and even the French are becoming less willing to spend several hours a day cooking. Increased affluence has created demand for more 'exotic' cuts. A further complication is that the industry structure has changed: most of the actual carving has shifted from the local butcher's shop to central meat-processing facilities. This provides greater economies of scale but has tended to reduce flexibility: the customer must choose from a range of pre-packaged joints instead of being able to ask the butcher for a particular cut or weight.

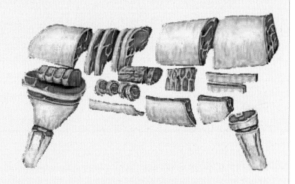

One major British supermarket chain has adopted an entirely new 'architecture' based on 10 larger constructs known as 'primals'. Carcasses are delivered to supermarkets already carved into the 10 primals, and the local meat manager decides how best to further sub-divide each primal. Thus, the new architecture not only addresses the fact that conditions have changed, but that they will continue to change. Can these supermarkets be said to have found the 'natural' joints? We doubt they would claim that the new system is perfect, but it is interesting to note that the primals follow the muscle groups of the carcass more closely than previous standards.

This is a good metaphor for business. The 'joints' of a business are reflected in its organizational boundaries (internal and external), product and service definitions, channel strategies and individual roles. Increasing competition and changing conditions of supply and demand have required new concepts that cut across those joints. Approaches such as business reengineering have left organizations better optimized to the conditions of the day, but no more able to respond to further changes.

In a Naked Objects project, the aim is the business objects should represent the 'primals' or muscle groups of the business, not the particular organising structure or product/service definitions of the day.

For example one reinsurance company that was implementing a new set of underwriting systems initially based its object representation on the industry-standard concepts of 'treaty' and 'facultative' business – the two main kinds of re-insurance underwriting, which were also reflected in its organizational structure. As the project progressed, the specification of the two elemental constructs was modified, and they were renamed as 'portfolio' and 'individual risk' – which that company saw as the more natural joints. These two new concepts could easily be mapped onto the treaty and facultative divisions in the business for the purpose of continuity, but the new representation opened up the possibility of constructing new hybrid insurance products in future. In other words, the criterion for judging the quality of the object representation was not the fitness for an immediate purpose, but the range of future situations that can be expressed using that representation.

There is no effective formula for finding the natural joints, despite the best efforts of many researchers to find one. The only way to achieve it is to keep merging related object candidates, then cleaving them along different lines to see what possibilities emerge. That most object representations fail to find the natural joints is largely because the designers do not believe in the value of the discipline.

that anywhere you can drop an instance of class A you can also, by default, drop an instance of class B. Thus we may initially think about an Order being associated with a Customer, and then realize that the Order might be from an Agent or a Distributor. All we need to do is define an abstract interface such as TradingParty and ensure that Customer, Agent and Distributor all implement that interface. They may well implement other common interfaces such as Communicable, meaning that we know we can call upon any of them to provide a communication address.

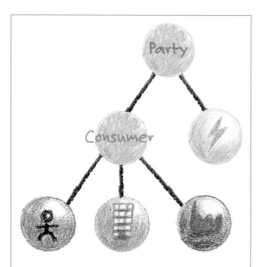

Households, Businesses and Industries are all consumers of electricity. Consumers and Generators are both forms of trading Party. However, it would probably be better to implement this commonality as shared interfaces than as an inheritance hierarchy.

This helps us to avoid getting stuck on questions such as whether Customer is a sub-class of Party, or of LegalEntity; and Employee a sub-class of Party, or of Resource? We make very little use of this highly abstract form of inheritance. Our rule of thumb is that we only use inheritance when the users themselves would whole-heartedly support the statement that 'X is a specialized form of Y'. If the user merely says 'X seems to share something in common with Y' then we use interfaces.

Is one candidate just a component of another? Something may be a clear candidate for an object (it is instantiable, has real responsibilities, and no overlap with other objects) but it solely exists within the context of another object. The technical term is 'aggregation'. A good example is the relationship between Order and OrderLine. There is good reason to make OrderLine an object: it has real responsibilities such as checking stock levels and applying VAT. Making it an instantiable class makes it easy to add a new OrderLine to an Order (again Naked Objects makes it easy to visualize this concept). But an OrderLine need never exist outside the context of an Order. OrderLine is an important object, but it is not one of our top-level objects.

Aggregation should not be confused with association. A Customer object may contain references to multiple Bookings, but those bookings are not aggregated into the Customer: they exist in their own right.

A simpler example of aggregation would be that a Product object might have a UPC (Universal Product Code). Good modellers will point out that it is better to model the UPC as an object than as, say, a text string, because that would allow the UPC to be able to print out a barcode, look itself up against a database and so forth. Good points all, but the UPC is very much a secondary object that can be addressed later on in the process: it should not make it onto

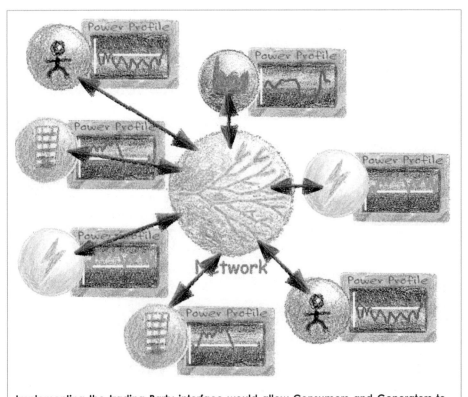

Implementing the trading Party interface would allow Consumers and Generators to be used interchangeable in certain contexts. By allowing the Power Profile to handle positive and negative demand, hybrid Generator/Consumers would become possible – something that electrical deregulation will encourage.

the list of five to ten core business objects. Just keep a note of it within the appropriate responsibility for the Product object.

Is this object a possible start point for a user activity? Objects that could form the start-point for a business scenario are more worthy of the term 'core' business object than those that don't. In our limousine-booking example we could certainly make the case that an operational business scenario might start with a new or existing Booking object, a Customer object, a City, or a specific Location. It would be much less likely to start with a CreditCard, but if we see CreditCard as implementing the more abstract type of PaymentMethod, which would also be extended to cover CompanyAccount, then PaymentMethod could easily form a start point of a scenario.

So, at the end of the first day of the exploration phase, you will aim to have a list of between five and ten core business object classes, each of which will be of key interest to the users and could potentially form the start point for some sort of business scenario. For some of these, specialized sub-classes may already have been identified. Some of them will also have what we call 'secondary' or 'aggregated' classes. You may also have identified some needs for common abstract interfaces that would allow different classes to be used interchangeably in certain contexts (i.e. you could drag either of them into the same field).

We usually find that during the first day we can make a useful start on defining and refining object responsibilities. In fact, doing so will typically either reinforce or challenge our initial choice of the core business objects. You may well find, for example, that two classes of objects appear to be sharing many of the same responsibilities and ought to be merged. Or you may find yourselves having to specify a responsibility for an object that doesn't seem to fit naturally with its name – a good indication that you should consider splitting that role into two.

Object responsibilities can conveniently be split into two categories: know-what and know-how-to.

Adding know-what responsibilities

Know-what responsibilities cover the attributes (simple values such as names, dates, and prices) and associations to other business objects.

Strictly speaking, we are referring only to those attributes and associations that are deliberately intended to be accessible from outside the object. Naked Objects helps to make this clear because anything with a public 'get' method is, by default, going to be displayed to the users when they open a view of that object. In fact, as Wirfs-Brock points out* these are attributes and associations that the object knows-how-to deliver to an external user, and/or allow the external user to specify or modify. So in fact all the responsibilities are really know-how-to's. The value of preserving the somewhat artificial distinction between the two types of responsibility is that it potentially encourages the modellers to push for richer behaviours.

*Wirfs-Brock 1989

In theory, it would be better to start by specifying those richer 'know-how-to' responsibilities: they are more in keeping with our goal of behavioural completeness. In practice, we have found that all but the most experienced object modellers find this hard to do. Allowing the team to give a candidate object a little more substance, in the form of some attributes and associations, can help to keep things moving along.

To identify the association responsibilities, ask the team: 'If you opened up one of these objects, what other objects would you expect to be able to get to directly from that object?' A common mistake by inexperienced object modellers is to include an attribute from another object instead of the object itself. Thus, they specify that an Order 'knows the name and address of the customer', when it should be 'knows the Customer' (which in turn, knows how to communicate). Encouraging the team to specify associations before simple attributes helps to avoid this mistake. It gets them used to thinking about navigating to things they can find out from an Order rather than being part of an Order.

For each association, ask also whether the association needs to be bi-directional or not. If a Booking needs to have an associated Customer, do you also want to be able to get directly to the Booking from the Customer object? Sometimes you won't see the need for this until you start walking through some business scenarios. If one object is aggregated into another then there is no need to do this: an OrderLine does not need to explicitly hold a reference to the Order it belongs to because it can never be accessed except through that Order. Bear in mind also that whilst it may be tempting to make all other associations navigable in both directions, it does incur some overhead in terms of both development effort and performance (because of database implications), so don't specify it without reason.

Turning to the simple data attributes, try to keep these to a minimum as long as possible. There is a great temptation to start listing lots of simple 'low-value' attributes, just because they are easy to think of: name, address, sex, date of birth, hair colour etc. These attributes seldom add much value, and they distract the team from concentrating on the higher-value responsibilities.

We recommend that, for the first iteration at least, you keep the basic attributes to the minimum necessary to identify the object uniquely and conveniently. A good rule of thumb for a Naked Objects implementation is this: add only those attributes that you need to use in the title method. Add other attributes as you need them to fulfil your operational test scenarios – but only after seriously questioning whether that attribute might not better be replaced by a know-how-to responsibility.

Adding know-how-to responsibilities

People find know-how-to responsibilities harder to conceive. You'll probably start with just a few simple ones, and then add some more as you consider business scenarios. One way to get started is to familiarize yourself with other ee page 37 examples. The DSFA's business object model* would be a good starting point.

A useful technique is to look at each of your know-what responsibilities (i.e. the associations and attributes) and ask yourself if it could be better stated as a know-how-to responsibility. Some examples are shown in the panel.

It can sometimes be valuable to take this principle to extremes. For example, on one occasion we challenged a public sector organization about why their Customer object definition included the date of birth as a know-what. The audience was incredulous. Date of birth was needed for lots of purposes, they said: for identification (have we got the right Fred Smith?), for authentication (is the person on the end of the phone who he says he is?), for determining if a client is an adult or not. We argued that each of those uses should have been modelled as explicit know-how-to responsibilities. It may be that the object uses a stored date of birth for these purposes, or it may not (the object might delegate the responsibility to an external agency). In fact, it is bad practice to base identification and authentication on the same data. Moreover, if they design the Customer object to be able to answer the question 'Is [the customer] over 18?' rather than 'What is [the customer's] date of birth?' then they are not leaving themselves vulnerable to charges of misuse of age information. (Anyone who thinks that is a spurious line of argument should read the European electronic privacy legislation.)

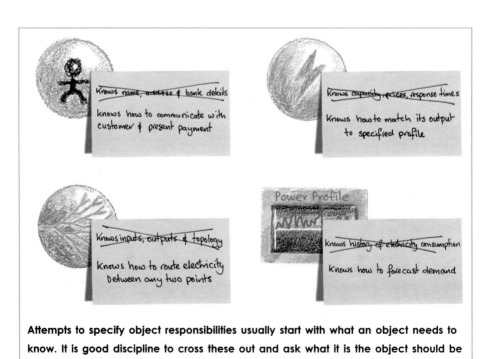

Attempts to specify object responsibilities usually start with what an object needs to know. It is good discipline to cross these out and ask what it is the object should be able to do with that knowledge.

Avoid the temptation to fill up the page with responsibilities that are automatically provided by the framework. There is no need, for example, to specify for each attribute and association a corresponding know-how-to responsibility for reading and/or writing it – that should be assumed. The only reason you should specify that the Booking object 'knows how to choose a Seat [on the Flight]' is if it is the Booking object itself that will do the selection rather than, say, the user.

Similarly there is no need to specify the responsibility for the object to make itself persistent, or to manage authorization and security, distribution or version control. These are generic capabilities provided by the infrastructure and are presumed to apply to all classes of business object.

You can also omit the generic class responsibilities. All naked object classes automatically provide the generic class responsibilities (unless the programmer suppresses them):

- Create a new instance of that class.

- Retrieve a particular instance by its unique reference.

- List all instances that match a set of criteria.

- List sub-classes.

You can add class responsibilities specific to a business class – for example to create a particular kind of report on instances of that class – but the need for these is more likely to emerge later in the exploration phase.

Dealing with the concept of process

We have already made clear that we do not agree with the practice of translating use-cases into objects in their own right, nor of the split in roles between Entity or Model objects, and Controller objects. Using Naked Objects, only the former category of objects is permitted. To put it another way, all classes of business object should be thought of as persistent classes.

Wirfs-Brock
'Characterizing
our objects'
Coad 1999

That said, it is quite legitimate to think about different broad categories, or stereotypes** of business object. In particular, we often draw the distinction between purposeful and non-purposeful objects. Non-purposeful objects are things like Product, Customer, Employee, and Location. The state of those objects will change over time, and that state will be made persistent, but the changes don't go in any particular direction. They can be thought of as random.

The state of a purposeful object generally changes in a pre-ordained direction. Thus, an Order may go from the status of an Enquiry, to Committed, to Shipped, to Invoiced. The status may occasionally backtrack, or the Order may be terminated prematurely; but there is a clear intended direction. In general, whereas the state of a non-purposeful object is just the agglomeration of its various attributes and associations, a purposeful object is more likely to have an explicit state, represented by a single field that can take one of a finite set of pre-determined values. It is also often appropriate to model the behaviour of purposeful objects using state-transition diagrams, which specify the conditions under which the object will move from one of those pre-determined states to another. Indeed some people describe such objects as 'stateful' rather than purposeful.

So isn't a purposeful object just a process object, or a Controller, by another name? There is an important difference. In our approach both non-purposeful and purposeful objects are Entity objects. They are all made persistent by default. They continue to exist as objects even when they have reached their intended end-state. This is not a unique idea. We have had many conversations with experienced object modellers and well known authors who have reached the same conclusion: that Transfer, Withdrawal, and Deposit (in a banking application) are not use-cases or Controller objects, but persistent Entities in their own right. But that is not the way that the bulk of the object literature treats them.

Naked objects make the advantage of this way of thinking clearer. In most approaches to object modelling, once a transaction, process or use-case is completed, there is no way of referring to it explicitly. In an application developed using Naked Objects, these activities show up as icons in their own right: you can open them and inspect them, and invoke whatever valid actions remain available. Thus, even after a (bank) Transfer has been made, you could examine it, decide to reverse it, charge a fee for it, or notify the customer of its successful completion – all potential action methods.

Any business activity where the verb describing the activity can easily be mutated into a noun is a prime candidate for a purposeful object. Thus the users might have a requirement to adjust (verb) the prices. But they will also talk readily about 'making price adjustments'. This is a cue for thinking about PriceAdjustment as an instantiable entity object, rendered as an icon on the screen by the Naked Objects' viewing mechanism. Another good clue, as others have pointed out, is that verbs that can easily be modified into nouns are often embodied in paper forms in a manual system.

4.1.3 Building the objects into a prototype

The second of the three core activities during exploration is building the objects into a prototype. Your aim should be to get your object ideas implemented in the Naked Objects framework as quickly as possible, to help the team to visualize the attributes, associations and (most importantly) the behaviours of the objects.

For each of the business objects that you have identified, you will need to:

- Define a NakedObject class.
- Add one or more value fields that can be used to identify each instance of that class (e.g. a name or reference field).
- Specify the most obvious associations between the new business object and any other types of business objects already specified.
- Write a title method that will identify an object instance to the user.
- Add the new class to the set of classes in a test application.
- Specify two icons (one large and one small) to be associated with that class.

Once this is done for each of the identified classes then you can start the framework and use the application. This will provide immediate feedback, allowing you to confirm or question your design decisions, and indicating further possibilities. The next step is to enrich the application, for example by:

- Adding further fields containing value objects or associated business objects.
- Considering whether each field should be read-only or allow updates and deletes.
- Adding object methods and perhaps additional class methods.
- Adding about methods to control access to individual, classes, fields and methods based on business rules or user authorisation level.

Sometimes the prototyping takes place 'off-line'. Translating the initial list of candidate objects (produced on the first day) into a working prototype may take several hours of programming. The same may apply when, in subsequent iterations, new business object classes or responsibilities are identified, or there is a significant re-factoring of the object model, or reassignment of responsibilities.

However, many changes suggested by the team – a new sub-type, attribute, association or simple method – can be programmed in minutes, and Naked

Objects makes these changes instantly visible to the user. It follows that it makes sense to try to make as many of these changes as possible in real time. Often we have observed programmers saying to the users: 'This will probably take a few minutes: you can come back later if you like', only to hear a user respond: 'I'll stay – I'm enjoying this!' The net result is that it is often possible to get through ten or twenty iterations with the users in a single day.

One of the reasons for prototyping in real time is that it encourages the team as a whole to explore more than one approach to a business issue. Object modelling exercises can often get bogged down in debates about two different ways to represent a problem domain*. With Naked Objects, much of this debate can be eliminated simply by offering to prototype both approaches and then showing them to users on the screen. When confronted with the two models as tangible icons that can be dragged and dropped, right-clicked and opened to view their contents, it is surprising how quickly the superior modelling solution – if there is one – becomes obvious.

*Riel 1996

4.1.4 Using the prototype to explore business scenarios

The third core activity of exploration is using the prototype to explore business scenarios. During each iteration, formal or informal, the evolving prototype should be tested against business scenarios. There are two main types of scenario, operational and what-if.

Operational scenarios

Operational scenarios are specific envisaged uses of the system. They cover both frequently-occurring tasks and one-off usages, such as: 'Mary Cahill has three children under 16 of which the younger two are twins, but one is living with Mary's mother. Work out how much Child Benefit is owing' or 'We have a 15% discount on all beer, wines and spirits in our hypermarket stores, and a "£1.00 off" promotional offer on Australian wines in all stores. Resolve any arising conflict in prices.' Applying a range of these ad hoc scenarios is a much better way to test the power of the emerging object model than just emphasizing the oft-repeated tasks.

Operational scenarios should always be specified in concrete terms. This prevents the users from asking for impossible functionality. For example, consider a user requirement or story along the lines of 'the system should be able to identify and resolve conflicting price adjustments that arise from different sources.' The criteria for identifying conflicts may be straightforward (e.g. two adjustments for different amounts applied to the same product with overlapping time periods), but resolving that conflict may not be. Forcing the user to write one or more concrete test cases each giving an example of a conflict and specifying exactly how that particular conflict is to be resolved will either clarify the algorithm or persuade the user that the conflict can only be resolved by a human.

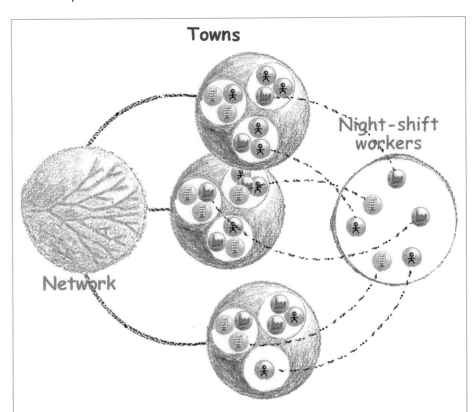

By envisioning the core business objects at the user interface, the electrical utility saw the possibility for creating new communities of Consumers that had common (or complementary) Power Profiles – literally by dragging and dropping icons on the screen. These communities could be offered special billing rates, or be sold to other power companies.

An operational scenario may well highlight the need for new object classes, sub-classes, or new methods and associations. Some of these will be proto-typed during exploration – others may simply be flagged for consideration in the Specification phase. In such cases it is often appropriate to add, say, new method names to an object, so that they will show up as actions on the user's pop-up menu, but without necessarily writing any of the code necessary to implement that method.

Operational scenarios should be documented, because they will form a useful set of prompts during the specification phase. Those that are carried forward into the specification of a particular phase will be codified more formally as one or more executable user acceptance tests (explained in the Delivery section). Once you become fluent with the Naked Objects approach you may decide to capture the operational scenarios in this form right from the beginning – but it is not essential.

Demonstrations

Operational scenarios are useful as demonstration scripts. Throughout exploration, the rule is to demonstrate early and demonstrate often. These demonstrations may be within the team, to bring everyone up to speed on the latest version of the business objects model; or they may be outside the exploration team to test a particular idea or to help build political support. Because systems built from naked objects 'feel' very different from conventional systems, we have found that the first such project in an organization gains a lot of attention, with frequent demands for demonstrations even from those not involved in that business domain. You need to be ready to demonstrate the evolving prototype at the drop of a hat, and we have often charged a particular member of the team with being the demonstration specialist (though this can be combined with other roles or responsibilities). In some cases we have even dedicated a single machine for demonstrations, updating the demonstration at the end of every day when all the various modifications have been integrated.

You need to devise a 'general tour' demonstration that shows roughly what each of the objects knows and knows how to do. The rest of the demonstrations will typically be based on the operational test scenarios. Here again, the concrete nature of the scenarios helps. It saves the demonstrator from having to think up realistic example data on the fly. (Using unrealistic data in a demonstration is far more confusing to the observers than most people realize – most non-programmers don't naturally identify with customers or products called Foo and Bar!)

Paradoxically, although one of the motivations for providing the users with access to the naked objects is to provide them with more choice in how to tackle a particular problem, we recommend that demonstrations are very tightly scripted. Continually interrupting a demonstration of a test case with comments such as 'of course, I could have done that last bit this way, instead' is very confusing. Only do this if your observer asks about the possibility, or suggests that the way you just did something is counter-intuitive to him, or suboptimal in some way. Another approach is to select a range of demonstration scripts to show problems being tackled in a variety of different ways, or from different start points.

What-if scenarios

What-if scenarios test the object model against future changes to the business. Such changes might arise from new technological capabilities such as smart cards, new generation mobile phones, or digital signatures. They might be driven by new government legislation, industry regulations, or internal rules and policies. Or they might reflect changes in the relationship with suppliers and partners, and in particular with customers. The panel shows a few real-life examples of such scenarios.

What if...

...we shifted to some kind of value-based pricing?

What if...

... we wanted to offer a limousine service to the airport, with check-in at the point of collection?

What if...

... we wanted customers to be able to specify their own product configuration?

What if...

... our customers demand that we manage their stock for them, but the stock is still off our books?

Some example what-if scenarios generated during exploration sessions:

The idea is not to ensure that the object model can cope with all these hypothetical what-if scenarios without modification, but to ensure that the required modifications would be easy to identify and are localized to one or perhaps two object classes, instead of being scattered across the whole system.

To be more specific, the aim of what-if scenario testing is not to ensure that you have specified all the responsibilities that will ever be needed of an object: new responsibilities will be added throughout the life of the system. The aim of what-if scenario testing is to ensure that you have got the boundaries between the objects right. In other words, that you have carved the problem at its natural joints*.

See page 174

187

4.1.5   The outputs from exploration

The primary deliverable from the exploration phase is the working prototype. Because Naked Objects renders the core business objects and their principal behaviours visible and accessible to the users, the prototype is itself the best documentation of the business object model. The one-to-one correspondence between what the user sees on the screen and the underlying Java class definitions eliminates the need for much of the documentation generated by conventional approaches. This is one reason why participants find exploration so enjoyable and rewarding. By contrast, most of the documentation produced in the early phases of conventional approaches is actually counter-productive: it is difficult to write, unrewarding to read, and very hard to keep in synchronization as the project evolves.

As well as the prototype, you must document the high-level responsibilities of the business object classes. Whilst some of these responsibilities will translate directly into visible attributes, associations and action methods, some do not translate so directly. Some responsibilities will have been identified but not simulated on the prototype. And some responsibilities are there to guide future development direction (a typical example is the required responsibility on a Customer object of 'being able to communicate [with the customer] using their preferred channel' – even though the prototype, and perhaps the first delivered implementation, will handle only post and telephone).

These responsibilities should be captured in a form that is easily readable. The DSFA's business object model* provides a good example of such documentation. Another approach is to use XML to document the objects and their responsibilities, with specific tags for Class names, Methods and so forth. This would aid the subsequent production of an electronically navigable document.

*See page 37

The challenge is to keep this documentation in synchronization with the system itself as it evolves. There are sophisticated and expensive tools available for this purpose, but our preferred approach is to use the Java code as its own documentation. Write the high level responsibilities in the form of comment statements at the top of the code file for each class definition. If a responsibility is completely and obviously fulfilled by a specific method (such as the responsibility for the Customer object to know the Bookings made by that customer) then the description of the responsibility can be deleted – it is redundant. If a responsibility has not been implemented in code, or spans multiple methods, or is more abstract than the current implementation (as in our communications channel example above) then the responsibility definition should be kept in as a plain text comment.

Embedding these responsibility definitions in the code does not guarantee that they are consistent with the code, but makes it much more likely. Furthermore, you can use a tool such as JavaDoc to auto-generate some well-formatted and electronically-navigable documentation direct from the code, including both the high-level responsibility statements and the existing business-level methods. This is a very effective solution.

What about UML?

Readers may ask why we appear to make so little use of the Unified Modeling Language (www.uml.org) (UML) in this book, when its notation is now accepted as the standard way to document an object model.

Capturing your business object model directly as naked object definitions renders much of the object relationships immediately visible to the users: open any object and you can see the types of objects that it relates to. We have found this to be far more accessible to users than a UML class diagram. And of course the naked object representation is executable.

Admittedly, UML is much richer than the Naked Objects framework in its ability to specify different forms and constraints on relationships. UML also provides the ability to view sequence diagrams, state transition diagrams and many other useful forms. But many people do not make use of all these representations, and unless you have a sophisticated tool set, keeping them all in synchronization can be a nightmare.

A further argument for using UML, and the related Object Constraint Language (www.omg.org) (OCL) is that they are programming language-neutral. Naked Objects is written in Java 1.1. It is upwards compatible with Java 1.2, 1.3 or 1.4 – but it doesn't use any of the new features. This is a conscious choice. Using the latest features would have made our task of writing the framework easier. But Java 1.1 is highly portable: there are implementations for a huge range of hardware platforms from Palm Pilots to mainframes. Moreover, Java 1.1 is to all intents and purposes now a public standard: there are open source compilers available and even open-source Java Virtual Machines. In other words, the Java used to specify a Naked Objects application is just about as open as UML.

Specifying business rules, relationships and constraints directly into a well established, simple, and open-standard programming language, instead of some form of pseudo-code, has other advantages. It encourages a closer correspondence between object modelling and object-oriented programming,

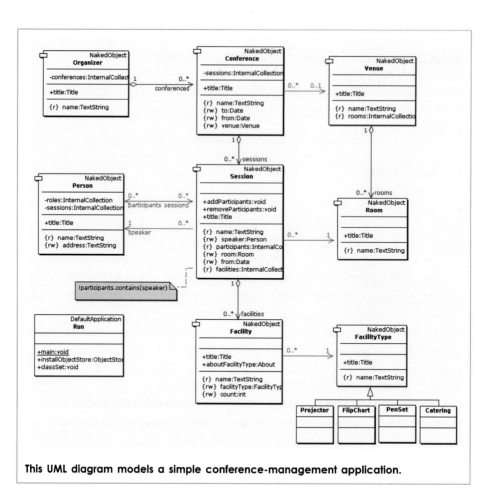

This UML diagram models a simple conference-management application.

which we believe to be a good thing. For example, we have found that many of the object-oriented patterns widely considered to be good practice by experienced programmers (for example*) are highly applicable at the level of business object modelling. See for example the use of the Strategy pattern in the 'Case study: Arrears and collections'* – this pattern in the business object model corresponds directly to the same pattern in the code.

*Gamma 1995

*See page 201

One thing that may change our view on UML is the recent emergence of tools (such as TogetherJ (www.togethersoft.com)) that can translate UML diagrams automatically into Java code structures and back again. This not only saves time, but more importantly ensures that the two remain in synchronization.

At the OT2002 conference, we ran a workshop in which delegates had just two and a half hours to design an object model for a conference administration system and then build it into a working Naked Objects prototype. All four

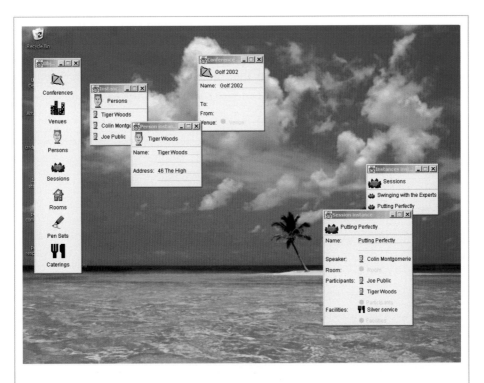

Using the TogetherJ tool the UML shown opposite was automatically converted into this Naked Objects prototype. (Thanks to Dan Haywood for supplying the screen captures.)

of the four-person teams were successful, and everyone was surprised by what they had achieved. One team chose to start by drawing UML diagrams on a flip chart, but their resulting prototype was poorer than the two teams who had represented their ideas directly into Naked Objects. The fourth team drew UML diagrams on TogetherJ and auto-generated the initial Java class definitions from these, ready for use by our framework. Many of the subsequent enhancements were made directly in the code, but the UML diagram was kept up to date by the tool. Theirs was in fact the most impressive of the prototypes, and is shown in the screenshots on this page.

Such tools change the nature of UML. In effect, the UML now becomes an alternative view of the code – one that hides complexity and renders things like relationships more visible. We like that idea. Don't think about modelling and programming as two distinct activities: they are two different views of the same thing. Another useful move in this direction is the recent research work on UML virtual machines. As this idea progresses we see potentially more synergy between UML and Naked Objects.

Indeed, we have already made it clear that the user screenshots shown throughout this book are the output from just one of many possible viewing mechanisms. It is conceivable that another such viewing mechanism would be a UML diagram. Perhaps someone will be inspired to write one . . .

4.2 The specification phase

During specification, the business requirements are formally specified and prioritized, releases planned, costs estimated, and infrastructural implications identified. It is also worth pointing out that it is not until the specification phase that the commitment is made to develop a system – the initial commitment is only to undertaking the exploration phase.

The specification stage starts with getting agreement on the business functionality required either for the complete system, or for the first of a series of planned releases. This will be followed by estimating the resources required to develop and test the new functionality, to integrate it with any existing systems, to provide whatever new infrastructure may be needed, to train the users, and so forth. Much of this sort of planning is conventional, if something of a black art, and we suggest that you use the planning methodology that works for you. However some practitioners have pointed out that Naked Objects does make estimation slightly easier – particularly once you have a couple of such projects under your belt – because all the development effort is focused on the business objects themselves. A sensible approach is to grade the various methods that need to be written in terms of the estimated effort involved, using feedback to translate this into the resources required. (This technique has much in common with 'the planning game' aspect of Extreme Programming).

You will find that the exploration phase eases the initial task of specifying the requirements. Business sponsors will have a much clearer idea of what they require. Some of it will have been simulated in the prototype, some just envisaged and recorded in textual form. And even at the high-level planning stage, it is possible to agree with the customer the capabilities required in terms of objects and responsibilities on those objects. This structure will help, if only a little, in the difficult task of estimating the development effort required.

4.2.1 Writing XP-style user stories

If you are keen on Extreme Programming (XP) then our specification stage can be run according to the principles of the XP 'planning game', wherein the business requirements are now captured as one- or two-sentence stories on index cards and then prioritized into releases. With the object-oriented prototype to hand it is quite straightforward for the users, with a little help from the modeller, to specify each of these stories in terms of specific operations on specific objects. Some examples are shown in the figure.

I want to be able to create a new Booking, entering all the details from scratch but in any order that suits the customer, check for availability at any point that there is sufficient data, and confirm the booking when it is complete. The only pre-existing objects will be the Cities where we provide service.

1

At any stage during the creation of a Booking I want to be able to create a return-journey Booking. All relevant details will be copied across into the return Booking, with the pick-up and drop-off locations reversed.

2

I want any Payment Method, and Telephone created in a Booking to be associated directly with the Customer, so I can re-use them in a future booking. Where there are multiple Payment Methods and Telephones, I want the customer to be able to specify which is the preferred one.

3

I want to be able to create a new Booking from within the Customer object, where the Customer, and the preferred Payment Method and Telephone are copied in automatically.

4

I want the Customer object to be able to store Locations used by that customer and to give them 'nicknames', with the most frequently used Locations at the top of the list.

5

I want a City object to hold a list of common locations (e.g. Airports, Theatres).

6

I want to be able to create a new Booking by dropping a Location directly onto another Location, indicating pick-up and drop-off. This should work whether I am doing it from a Customer's list of frequent locations, or a City's list, or both.

7

These XP-style stories were generated for the Executive Car Services system.

We have arranged this group of seven stories so that they build (approximately) upon each other in terms of functionality and/or complexity. We have found that encouraging users to specify their requirements (for any given release) in order of increasing complexity helps them to avoid getting bogged down in the most complex exceptions early on. In fact it is useful to encourage the users to express their stories in this fashion from the outset: start with the simplest possible case, and then gradually add more complexity. (The stories won't typically follow a single thread of complexity – there might be several quite different such threads in a release.)

The official XP concept is that customers should prioritize the stories for any release, without any interference from developers. We think this is a case where a little guidance from the lead modeller will produce a better result for both parties. The progressive build-up in functionality, combined with the fact that all the stories are specified in terms of operations on an object model that has been tested against multiple scenarios during exploration, gives developers much more confidence to adopt the program-one-story-at-a-time discipline of XP. Refactoring between stories will then typically be at the level of methods, not at the boundaries between objects, which is much better news for the database administrators.

4.3 The delivery phase

In the delivery phase, the system is developed, integrated, tested and released.

No code is carried forwards from the exploration phase. The style of coding adopted during exploration will have been fast and loose. There was absolutely no emphasis on rigorous design and/or testing; nor even on input validation, rule enforcement, or error prevention. Exploration assumes either that the prototype will only be used by an expert user, or that errors don't matter. To let any of this code be carried forward is to invite future problems.

The object model, and the high level definitions of responsibilities that evolved during exploration, are carried forwards. You may even want to retain the method signatures, especially where they are a direct reflection of certain responsibilities, but all the code inside those methods must be wiped clean.

We have found that allowing developers to preserve these class definitions and method signatures in the development environment helps to reduce the temptation to carry forwards some of the code. They provide a useful model of the overall design, and psychologically this helps developers to overcome the sense that they are starting all over again with a blank sheet of paper. Many actually welcome the chance to write the code again from scratch in a more disciplined fashion.

If you use an environment that can maintain a UML representation in synchronization with the code itself, bi-directionally, then you can think of the UML as what is passed from exploration to delivery – provided that you also adopt some convention for recording the higher level statements of object responsibilities. Unless you have such a tool, then we think you are better off not using UML but rather recording the responsibilities in the form of textual comments at the top of each Java class file.

During delivery, writing business functionality might involve creating some specific new sub-classes not explicitly modelled but at least foreseen during exploration. It may also involve writing some new aggregated classes that sit entirely within one of the business objects. But in the main, coding activity in the delivery phase will consist of writing methods on business objects.

4.3.1 Test-first coding

When writing those methods we strongly advocate adopting the discipline of test-first coding: before you start writing the method you write one or more

executable unit tests that will check whether the method is correctly implemented. These tests should continue to be run throughout the development
cycle to ensure that new errors haven't crept into the system. Using the Junit
(www.junit.org) framework, it is possible to invoke these tests at the touch of
a button. Converts to this approach often run their unit tests every few minutes
during development. We have made a number of extensions to Junit to make
it easier to apply within the context of the Naked Objects framework.

Extreme Programming (XP) seeks to apply this principle of writing up-front executable tests not only to unit testing but also to acceptance testing. In XP, when
a particular story (or requirement) is to be implemented, the short description
is fleshed out through direct discussion between developer and user. They also
jointly write one or more executable acceptance tests for that story. By writing
them in executable form, the developers can run these tests frequently during the development of the story, to get an indication of progress, and can
run them as regression tests after subsequent refactoring*. The primary role of
acceptance tests in XP, however, is as a measure of value delivered: when all
the acceptance tests run, that story is deemed to be implemented and the play-
ers move on to the next one.

Fowler 2000

Naked Objects makes it easier to adopt this particular XP practice. Writing executable acceptance tests for systems with graphical user interfaces (GUIs) is generally recognized as being very difficult*. There are many tools that can capture
and replay the keyboard and mouse events of an actual user operation, but this
approach to testing has many problems*. Any change to the layout or style of
the user interface will require these tests to be re-recorded, as, in many cases,
will porting the application onto a machine other than the one where the test
was recorded. Worse, from the XP viewpoint, is that these record-and-playback
tests can only be captured after the system has been developed. Some of the
tools provide a high-level GUI scripting language that, in theory, would allow
the test scripts to be written in advance. However, with conventional systems
design this still leaves the problem that it is very difficult for the user to imagine
a yet-to-be-implemented user interface in sufficient detail to be able to write a
detailed test script.

*Kaner 1997

*Groder 1999

197

4.3.2 Writing executable acceptance tests

*Finsterwalder
2001

The Naked Objects framework utilises tests written in terms of higher level
user actions*. When the users come to flesh out a story during delivery, they
can use the exploratory prototype. Because the user interactions take a standard form, users can specify the implementation of any story in terms of direct

operations upon business objects (instances or classes) that they have become used to manipulating on the prototype. The prototype is far from complete, so some stories will entail attributes, methods and associations that do not exist on the prototype, but we have found that the users have little difficulty in imagining extensions to the concrete objects that are in front of them. This is much less true if the prototype takes the standard 'scripted' form.

So, when a new story is to be started, a user and a programmer sit down together and write out the task in a formal language consisting of noun-verb style operations on the business objects and classes. (Note that this is merely a definition of a set of actions that a user may choose to follow. It is not a definition for an executable procedure that will eventually form a part of the system.)

Our original idea was to define a specialized constrained-English language for writing these acceptance test scripts, using XML. This language could then be simply converted into a Java executable test. However it soon became clear that this constrained-English was so close to Java that we might as well work the other way around. In theory, the user could write the constrained-English version alone. In practice, we found that whatever the language, a user and programmer working together were more effective and ultimately faster. So switching to a simple Java framework did not impede the process.

The programmer captures the detailed storyline, live, as a sequence of methods on specialized test classes provided as part of the Naked Objects test framework. These test classes simulate the interaction between the framework's viewing mechanism and the business objects.

When the acceptance tests for a story are completed, the programmer(s) can then start designing and coding the necessary functionality, and writing unit tests for each of the methods to be created or altered. The acceptance tests are run in a manner very similar to unit tests under Junit. Just as with the Junit approach to unit testing, we have found that some programmers use the executable acceptance tests to guide the work: in other words they address the errors thrown up by the tests in sequential order. This is a matter of personal choice.

4.3.3 Auto-generating the user training manual

Once you have a generic framework for writing executable acceptance tests, something else becomes possible: those test classes can be given the ability to translate themselves into a set of plain English step-by-step user instructions for performing the same task manually. This tells the user how to undertake the same acceptance test manually if they wished to. An example of this automated output is shown on this page.

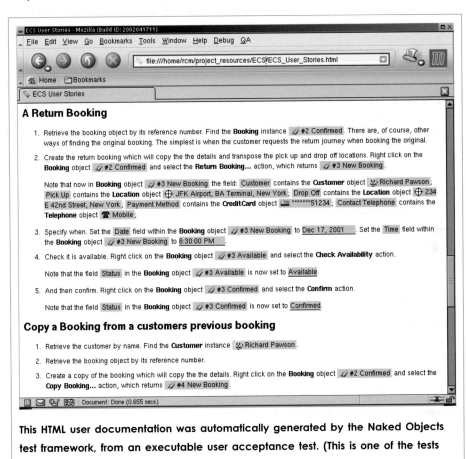

This HTML user documentation was automatically generated by the Naked Objects test framework, from an executable user acceptance test. (This is one of the tests associated with Story 2* from the ECS system).

*See page 194

More significantly, perhaps, these auto-generated English-language user instructions represent a significant proportion of the user training manual for the system under development. After all, unlike unit tests (which are concerned primarily with technical correctness) the user acceptance tests were all defined in terms of delivering value to the user. These acceptance tests represent scenarios that the users can expect to encounter, some of them routine and some of them exceptional; and a training manual would have explicit instructions on how to cope with such scenarios on the system.

Some people have queried whether this use of scripts is not at odds with treating the user as a problem solver rather than a process follower. It is important to understand that these scripts are simulations of what a user does. They are not executed within the application itself, but within the testing framework that sits outside the application. And even when used to generate pages of a training manual, these scripts don't say 'you have to fulfil this story this way', but 'here is a way that you can fulfil this story'. There may be several alternative scripts for the same story, and there may be many ways to fulfil the same story that are not written as formal acceptance tests. Some may object that this implies that the testing is not comprehensive. That is necessarily true of any event-driven system, which effectively means anything with a GUI. But the ease with which you can now write executable acceptance tests is in practice likely to lead to more thorough testing than is typically the case for most commercial systems development.

The training manual would need other things as well, including a conceptual introduction to the application, and an explanation of the various business objects and their methods. In addition there must be some generic explanations of the user environment, equivalent to the generic instructions for any Windows-based, or for a web-browser-based, application. (We'll be providing an updated version of this generic introduction on our website).

Apart from saving on work, auto-generating the user training documentation from the executable acceptance tests guarantees that it is consistent with the operation of the system. It is as though when users are fleshing out a particular story, they are writing the page of the training manual for that story, and we are using an executable version of that page as our acceptance test.

Case study: Arrears and collections

This case study is based upon a short exploratory project undertaken by a large UK-based bank. As for any large bank, 'Arrears and Collections' is a core business activity. At any given time it will have tens of thousands, perhaps hundreds of thousands, of products in arrears, ranging from a current account that has exceeded its agreed overdraft limit, to a mortgage where whole payments have been missed. Many of these situations are not serious: they may have arisen from a simple oversight or misunderstanding on the part of the customer, or possibly a clerical error by the bank itself, and will rectify themselves within a few days. At the other end of the spectrum, the arrears and collections department must deal with serious default, bankruptcies and fraud.

Business background

The sheer volume of the minor infringements dictates that they be handled initially by an automated system. This bank has a sophisticated system for generating a series of automated letters, of rising severity. The wording of these letters is a science: the system constantly tracks the effectiveness of each letter template, and tests new 'contenders' against the 'champion' letter for any given arrears status.

If the letters fail to correct the situation then at a certain point the case will come to the attention of an arrears and collections officer. The threshold for that transfer may be based on fixed criteria such as the amount and duration of arrears, or upon an assessed risk profile for the customer. The officer will then decide what new course of action to initiate. This may involve seeking to negotiate an agreement for the gradual repayment of the arrears, restructuring the debt, repossessing the goods (for a secured loan), or pursuing the debt through the courts. It may even involve the discovery that the borrower is deceased and the initiation of a claim against the estate.

Whilst the generation of automated letters is a model of technical sophistication, IT support for the interventions of an officer is minimal – little more than a spreadsheet and word processor. Ideally, an arrears and collections system should seamlessly integrate the automated early stages of a case with the intensely manual later stages. Such integration would make it easier to track a single case from end to end, and to monitor the relationship between early tactics and later ones. It would also allow the officers to intervene earlier in some cases, and place others back into 'auto-pilot' for a period.

Approach

We worked with a small team of business and IT managers to explore a possible design for such a system using Naked Objects. The team had no difficulty identifying certain core business objects that would feature in the system, including Customer, Officer, Account, Transaction, and Case.

At any given time, each arrears case will be subject to a particular 'strategy', though this strategy will change according to how the case progresses. At the start of the exercise, the business managers referred to 'thousands' of such strategies. However, within a couple of weeks the team had abstracted them to just 13 core strategies, each of which has branches and variations:

- Identify cause and try to identify non-arrears situations (e.g. technical errors).

- Extend facilities (e.g. extend overdraft, offer new loan product).

- Generate automatic letters of increasing severity.

- Accept the customer's verbal promise to remedy by a specified date.

- Make direct contact with the customer and establish circumstances.

- Make and monitor an arrangement to repay (over a period).

- Trace a customer who has gone missing.

- Recover securities.

- Take legal action.

- Write off the debt.

- Outsource the debt.

- Claim against (the deceased's) estate.

- Monitor account closely after rehabilitation.

One of the main challenges we faced was that both the IT and business manager involved had a very strongly process-oriented view of the world. They assumed that these strategies would be implemented using a workflow engine or some other form of high-level scripting mechanism, and would draw data, and perhaps even some limited forms of behaviour, from the core business objects. However, since part of the purpose of this exercise was to evaluate the potential of the Naked Objects approach, the team somewhat reluctantly agreed to think of these strategies as objects in their own right. (In fact the 13 strategies would all be sub-classes of a generic Strategy class.) Unlike, say, the Customer object, these Strategy objects have a sense of direction: they would be designed to follow a sequence of known states, even if that sequence might sometimes backtrack. It can be useful in object modelling to draw a simple distinction between 'purposeful' objects and 'non-purposeful' objects: the former can be thought of as vestigial processes, but it is important to understand that they do not 'sit on top of' the other objects in the way that processes are usually conceived. In fact, it is just as valid to envisage them as 'sitting inside' the non-purposeful objects.

Prototyping the system using the Naked Objects framework not only helped the team to envisage this concept, but also to see the benefits of this way of thinking. Now, instead of thinking of the strategies as verbs on a top-level menu, they saw them as nouns – represented as icons. Changing the strategy being applied to a particular arrears case could be envisioned, both metaphorically and literally, as dragging a new Strategy object into the Case object. Moreover, when an officer reviews a case, she can immediately see the history of the case summarized as a list of icons representing the Strategies previously attempted. Double-clicking on any of these icons would permit inspection of how that Strategy actually progressed and was terminated. It is very hard to get this kind of view from a workflow system. Each Strategy object is capable of executing a sequence of actions and responding to events such as new Transaction on the Account that is in arrears. Additionally, each Strategy will have its own exit conditions, which may include simply the passage of sufficient time. Upon exit, a given Strategy may replace itself with a different one or it may bring the Case to the attention of an Officer to make the decision.

In fact, experienced object-oriented programmers will recognise that this is a standard programming design pattern, coincidentally named 'Strategy'*. Such patterns seldom seem to be known by business analysts, however. This brings out another general point about Naked Objects: they make it easier to apply the rich, expressive power of a language like Java or SmallTalk to solving business problems. Most methodologies insist that the analysis be independent of any programming language. This would be a laudable aim except that the net effect is that resulting designs fail to take advantage of these powerful object patterns.

Gamma 1995

203

Evaluation

Two things surprised the team. The first was that it was possible to design a sophisticated system purely in terms of behaviourally rich objects, without ever having to draw a set of process diagrams. The second was that accepting the constraints of the Naked Objects approach quickly yielded some insights into the nature and structure of the arrears and collections activity that no-one had previously seen (specifically, the abstractions that existed within the notion of strategies). Given the very limited amount of time that the business representatives could devote to the exercise, they were very surprised at the amount of useful work that actually got done. One comment was that: "In the time that we would normally have spent just discussing how to get started on gathering the requirements, we had actually built a simple working model of the business domain that yielded some new and useful insights into how our business actually operates."

A brief description of the responsibilities of four of the naked object classes follows.

Class: Account

 Sub-classed for different types of account including: mortgage, credit card, unsecured loan, bank account etc. The object acts as a wrapper onto the account management system, which will perform the transactional and management reporting responsibilities. Specific responsibilities include:

- Identify if it is in arrears and be able to advise the amount and age of arrears.

- When the account first goes into arrears, either create a new Case, or if a Case already exists for that Customer, then add this Account to that Case.

- Display a zoomable, visual history of the account for a specified period, showing planned and actual balances.

- Calculate the impact of one or more hypothetical transactions upon the account (mostly used when making an arrangement – this ideally should be done like a spreadsheet).

- Alert the Case either to a significant change to the arrears situation (in amount or age) or to any transaction.

- Report arrears to credit agency if appropriate.

- Freeze or make temporary restrictions.

Class: Asset

Most commonly these will exist because they are securities on a loan (e.g. a mortgaged property) or because they form part of the loan contract (e.g. a car). Asset can also be used to model any known physical asset in cases of recovery. The most common assets will be modelled as specialized sub-classes of Asset so that they can record their own specific details. Specific responsibilities include:

- Initiate physical recovery.

- Realize value (initiate a sale of the asset).

- Assess net worth (e.g. apply depreciation).

Class: ArrearsCase

Responsible for managing the workload of the arrears and collections process, and for producing management information. The majority of arrears cases, however, will not involve the intervention of an officer. Specific responsibilities include:

- Split, merge, or subsume other Cases.

- Be brought back to the attention of an officer.

- Be forwarded to another officer.

- Choose initial Strategy upon creation.

- Alert Strategy to changing events.

- Provide management reporting on current status.

Class: Strategy

Some Strategies will operate automatically – others will involve an Officer. Each strategy has a desired outcome, which may be fixed or may be determined by the officer. Strategy is an active object – it is not merely an attribute. Strategy is a means to achieving an outcome, not a sequence of actions. Specific responsibilities include:

- Select the version to be used (most Strategies have 'champion' and 'challenger' versions). This is done by the system, not by the user.

- Take next action – when and what.

- Generate the standard Communications appropriate to that Strategy.

- Instruct the Account (e.g. freeze withdrawals).

- Respond to events such as a transaction, communication from customer, increase in debt, or the passage of time.

- Terminate itself (or be terminated manually by an Officer) and pick the next strategy (including referral to a officer to decide manually).

- Benchmark itself – whether it worked or not, including by version.

Section 5:
Extending Naked Objects

Naked Objects is still in its infancy. There are many ways in which we plan to extend the framework. And because it is open source we expect that the framework will also be extended by other developers in ways that we haven't planned or foreseen. In this section we shall look briefly at some of those possibilities.

Naked Objects is a work in progress. We've included in this book only those aspects of the framework that we believe to be reasonably stable. Future releases of the framework may render some of the details in this edition of the book incorrect, but the basic principles we expect to remain the same. If you find something that doesn't seem to work then please check first on our website, where you will find the most up-to-date version of the various documents that make up this book.

5.1 Additional documentation available on our website.

The website (www.nakedobjects.org) is the primary repository for information about the Naked Objects framework and techniques for using it. Already on the website you will be able to find additional documentation for:

- The complete Application Programming Interface (API) for the framework. (This is automatically included with the distribution of the framework itself.)

- Coding examples for various aspects of using the framework.

- Tutorials on using Naked Objects.

- How to customize the existing viewing mechanism including: altering the appearance (fonts, window colours etc); changing the default icons (used when no icon is specified for a particular naked class); and using the debug mode, which shows each object's unique ID number in grey next to the object's title.

- How to customize the server and clients, including: specifying alternative protocols by which the client application makes requests of the server, or changes to objects are updated to the viewing mechanism; specifying an alternative operator console for the server; specifying the level of logging (via the Log4J framework) for use in debugging.

- How to extend the framework, including: creating new value objects; building new object viewers; constructing other viewing mechanisms; developing and customizing object stores.

5.2 Some ways in which Naked Objects could be extended

The website is also the forum through which we will manage the ongoing extension of the framework. Naked Objects is fully open source. That means that you can copy and use it freely, and have access to the source code if you wish to extend it. The core of the framework has been written entirely by Robert Matthews, although with input and suggestions from a number of interested developers. Some of those have already started to write their own extensions, such as Dave Slaughter's EJB Object Store. We expect that with the launch of this book, a substantial development community will grow around the framework. We need your help if Naked Objects is to realize its full potential. On the website you will be able to find more details of extensions that are currently being developed, planned or just considered. In brief though, there follows a list of some of the principal directions in which we see that extension taking place.

New value objects and extensions

Many of the NakedValue types could be provided with additional behaviours both for use in adding business functionality and/or to be made available to the user via a suitable viewing mechanism. For example, a Date value object should allow date arithmetic, and a Money value object should support currency conversion.

There is also a need for many new types of generic NakedValue including a form of TextString that can be limited to a fixed number of characters (to fit existing database schemas), and another type that could support rich text formatting using XML.

Additional Views

The initial viewing mechanism is extensible and allows for new views to be added to it. New views could be written for many of the existing value objects (as well as for new ones) to better display them and to assist in the entry of data. One example is for a simple pop-up calendar for date values allowing a user to select a date with a single click.

Naked objects can be displayed in a number of ways, e.g. all business objects can be viewed as an icon or as a form. Other views can easily be added so, for example, some type of summary view could be provided that takes up less screen space. In addition, the table view, as an alternative to the list view, needs to be improved. Views specific to generic supertypes and interfaces are also possible.

To date we have done very little with graphics. There is huge scope here. Numerical type value objects could be viewable in chart form, for both input and output (in much the same way that modern spreadsheets allow you to draw the graph and then compute the numbers from it - a feature that shows remarkable insight into how sales projections are done!) Maps, schematics, networks and other spatial layouts should all be possible. The case study on Norsk Hydro* shows one example of how such capabilities could be added, *See page 214 without violating the core philosophy of Naked Objects (that the object-oriented user interface should be derived 100% automatically from the business object definitions).

Related to the graphical views is the need for an image viewer along with an image object type.

Additional viewing mechanisms

The graphical drag and drop user interface is just one of many possible viewing mechanisms. Other mechanisms could be written to replace this particular interface. The benefit that the framework offers is that a specific viewing mechanism can be used to suit a user's current requirement, e.g. if the system needs to be accessed from a browser over a slow modem link then an HTML viewing mechanism could be employed instead of the current graphical interface. Different viewers can all be used at the same time to view the same objects providing they are being run on different clients i.e. within different JVMs.

New object stores

Naked Objects is an object-oriented system and is least complicated when used with some form of object based persistence mechanism. We would like to see simple object persistence mechanisms being used to store objects for small and medium sized projects as well as interfaces to the current OO databases.

However, a good proportion of the applications that Naked Objects will be used for will be based on existing databases and these need to be accommodated. Alongside the generic SQL and EJB based object stores that are available at the moment, other object stores are needed to support specific or demanding applications and to handle proprietary systems.

Infrastructural services

As already mentioned we have not implemented any security mechanism other than the About objects. This needs to be explored and a suitable authorization and authentication interface needs to be built into the framework.

Re-usable patterns for business objects.

Just reading through the five case studies in this book you will see that there are a lot of common patterns, even common business object classes: Customer, Case, Communication and so forth. The idea of a library of business object classes is not new — there are several public as well as proprietary libraries available. We have not yet evaluated any of these libraries to see if they could be used, or adapted, to form a set of standard naked business object patterns, but that would be a useful exercise. Our main concern is the extent to which the modellers have pursued the idea of behavioural completeness. We may, in parallel, start making our own collection of re-usable naked object patterns.

5.3   Will naked object systems scale?

One of the questions we get asked most frequently is: "Will naked object systems scale up to large numbers of users?" Right now, the only honest answer is "We don't know for sure." We haven't yet seen any systems implemented using Naked Objects that service a large number of simultaneous users, although we have already seen applications that involve large amounts of data and must deliver the performance equivalent of mainframe transactional systems (for example at Safeway*).

*See page 155

As we've made clear in this section, we've designed the basic architecture of the naked objects with the intention that it will scale up to very large applications. But we haven't developed all the pieces yet. We're quite sure that as bigger systems are built, new problems will emerge that we haven't explicitly foreseen and that we will need to address with new extensions or modifications.

The fact that we haven't yet seen very large systems developed in Naked Objects is hardly surprising. Any significant new technology involves a learning curve: it is right and proper that organizations will want to start by applying it to smaller problems, where there are fewer variables. (In fact many first applications of Naked Objects are in areas where traditional systems approaches have failed badly, and there is arguably nothing to lose by trying a radical approach).

So we welcome the question, provided that it represents a genuine desire to understand whether the architecture has the capability to scale up with increasing demand – fuelled by increasing experience. We have no interest in responding to those who use such questions merely as an excuse to maintain the status quo. We recall that the pioneers of the relational database, client-server architecture, peer-to-peer networks, asynchronous messaging, and, of course, object-orient techniques in general have faced similar scepticism.

Much of our confidence lies in the fact that Naked Objects is open source. As the development community grows we will get offers of help from people who have very substantial expertise in this area. In fact it's already started to happen. Many people have told us that they regard Naked Objects as fundamentally 'the right way to design software' and have offered their support. We find that very motivating. One thing is true of software development in general and community-based open source development in particular: where there is a will, there is almost always a way.

The most encouraging thing is that people who have a great deal of experience of scaleability of distributed objects have been very supportive. We're delighted to give the last word in this book to Oliver Sims, author of 'Business Objects'*, co-author of 'Building Business Objects'* and 'Business Component Factory'*, and a widely-respected authority in the field of large-scale distributed-object and componentized business systems:

Sims 1994

Eeles 1998

Herzum 2000

"I think that Naked Objects is both exciting and important. Although there are some technical concerns about scalability that will need to be addressed, I can see nothing in the fundamental concepts behind Naked Objects that would pre-vent it from scaling up to very large numbers of users. And most importantly I believe that it will be possible to address these issues in a way that does not compromise the fundamental philosophy of Naked Objects."

Case study: Energy Trading

Norsk Hydro is a large multi-national conglomerate, headquartered in Norway. The company's origins lie in hydro-electric power generation, but it is now also a major producer of oil and gas, and has other core businesses in aluminium and fertilizer production – all of which are energy-intensive businesses. Over the years Norsk Hydro has had to build expertise in buying and selling energy within the many national markets where it has plants.

Business background

In 2000 the European electricity market was deregulated, allowing large-scale producers or consumers of electricity to source or supply across national borders – expanding the trend that has been happening inside many national borders. (A similar trend is happening in the European natural gas industry.)

The combination of its expertise, scale, and geographic coverage in both supply and consumption allowed Norsk Hydro to gain an early lead in European energy trading. (Note: Although the collapse of Enron towards the end of 2001 generated some public cynicism about energy trading, it is now generally accepted that that disaster was caused by financial irregularities rather than by the nature of the business itself. Energy trading remains a strong, and indeed very important, business.)

Opportunity

Given the newness of the opportunity, no packaged IT solutions existed to support this activity. Trading is typically conducted on the telephone, backed up with faxes, and with large spreadsheets for analysis. This was effective for the start-up phase but clearly would not cope with the forecast growth in both the volume and complexity of the business. At some point, a purpose-designed system would be needed. The system would need to be very agile: capable of extending into new geographic areas, and accommodating finer-grained territories within individual countries. It should ideally be capable of being extended into the trading of other energy forms, especially gas. This suggested an object-oriented solution. (Object-orientation was invented in Norway in the mid-1960s, and there is still a higher awareness of the value of objects in that country than elsewhere).

A small group in the IT Strategy department became aware of the concept of Naked Objects. Apart from the obvious commitment to object-orientation, they saw two other advantages. One was the ability to use rapid prototyping to explore the requirements of a very new and rapidly-changing business domain. The other advantage was the potential to build a system that was very 'expressive' – capable of supporting the traders in their daily task of balancing their network 'positions'. The energy traders manage a large number of long-term contracts to buy electricity from producers, sell it to industrial consumers, and to transport it via power lines from one to the other. The parties that it trades with include subsidiaries of Norsk Hydro and third-party energy companies. These long-term contracts are intended to balance supply and demand. However, many contracts allow the consumers to specify their actual requirement, within specified limits, only the day before it is required. On a daily basis, therefore, the traders have to balance these variations with additional short-term contracts to buy, sell and transport, including trades on the 'spot markets' in various key centres such as Amsterdam and Leipzig. If there is a significant difference between the spot price in two of those exchanges, and the traders have access to surplus transmission capacity, then they may want to move as much as they can from one location to another.

Thus, energy trading is inherently a problem solving activity. Even when the network is simple, involving just half a dozen nodes representing the Northern European countries, say, it is difficult to understand the actual trading position without some kind of visual representation. An IT strategy group at Norsk Hydro perceived that with Naked Objects it would not only be possible to produce a visual (map) representation of the position, but that it would be possible to execute all the balancing activities through this map.

Approach

Just two weeks were allocated for a team to undertake an exploratory project that had to include all the following activities:

- Train some of their own Java developers to use the Naked Objects framework

- Identify the core business objects that modelled the energy trading business

- Build a simple proof-of-concept showing how a trader would engage with these objects, through a map representation, to undertake some typical daily activities including balancing a network position.

In addition it was necessary to write an extension to the Naked Objects framework that would support the desired visual map interface. It would be easy to write a customized user interface that invoked responsibilities from the underlying objects. But we wanted to try to find another approach, one that was more in keeping with the philosophy of Naked Objects. In the end the solution was quite elegant. We defined a new interface, Spatial. In order to conform to this interface a business object must be capable of yielding a pair of coordinates, representing latitude and longitude. Then we extended the viewing mechanism so that any collection of objects that implemented the Spatial interface could be viewed by the user in the form of a map, with the individual objects showing up as icons positioned on that map. The map backgrounds were provided as image files and specified through a configuration file. The result is that the entire application could still be written without the business objects knowing anything about the user interface, and without having to write any application-specific user interface code. We have some more work to do in refining this concept, but such a capability will be released in a future version of the framework.

Evaluation

The exercise was considered to be very successful. In addition to the Java developers, the team included IT strategists representing both the electricity and gas trading businesses. The latter reported that they found the experience of taking part in the design process to be enjoyable and rewarding. In the interests of speed, a great deal of the development and debugging was done live in front of these user representatives even though they were not programmers.

The proof-of-concept has now been taken to the energy businesses for evaluation. If successful it is hoped that this will lead to a full-scale implementation.

Here is a brief explanation of each of the business classes together with an illustrative responsibility. (Each object has many more responsibilities).

Trading Party

 May be a Norsk Hydro subsidiary or third party. Knows how to create a new Contract using default values for this party.

Exchange

(Sub-class of Trading Party.) Knows how to quote a spot price for a given period.

Contract

Knows the Trading Party, Period and type of contract (buy, sell, transmission, short-term, long-term, etc). Knows the Power Requirement.

Power Requirement (volume)

In its simplest form this is just a standard value object – a number and a unit of measurement (Megawatts), with the ability to perform standard arithmetic operations. Modelling it as a business object allows for more sophisticated power requirements e.g. variable limits, or profiles that vary throughout the day.

Network

Knows the Locations and Links that make up this Network, and how to generate a Network Position for a given period (usually a day). Treating the network as a business object in its own right will allow the traders to handle multiple networks, which are either geographically distinct, or which handle different forms of energy (e.g. gas). Knows how to add new Locations and Links.

Location

Models a node in the Network. Knows the Trading Parties that operate in this Location, and how to buy or sell on the local Exchange if there is one. Knows how to create a Location Position for a given period.

Link

Models a transmission line between two Locations. Knows how to buy or sell capacity from appropriate Trading Parties.

Network Position

This is position in the sense of trading (e.g. long, short, balanced) not geography. The Network Position is made up from the individual Location Positions and Link Positions for the same period. Knows how to calculate the profitability of the Position.

Location Position

Knows how to find and summarize Contracts active at this Location in the specified period.

Link Position

Knows how to calculate how much of the available capacity is being used. Knows how to create a 'movement' (an operational instruction to transmit a specified amount of power).

A typical energy trading scenario

The day's Network Position shows that we are 60 Megawatts (MW) 'long' in the Tennet location and 60 MW short in the RWE location:

Right-clicking on the Link Position for the Link between the two, we select 'Buy More Capacity', which creates a new 'short-term' Contract with the owner of that Link, for which we specify a flat Power Profile of 60MW:

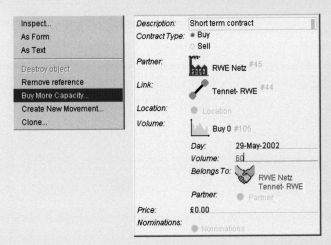

We now have transmission capacity to move power from where we are long to where we are short (this might take several trades at different prices). Right clicking on that link position again we can now create a Movement instructing the line operator to 'transport' 60 MW:

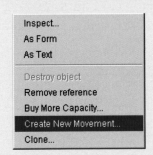
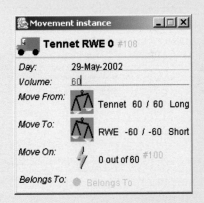

The green Location Position icons (scales) show that we are now balanced in Tennet and RWE, but still have the Eltra Location to balance:

As the business grows, new Locations, Links and whole Networks can be added just by creating new object instances:

The newly-added location and links are immediately available for trading:

Appendix A: Getting started

This section aims to get you up and running using Naked Objects, using a very simple application as an example. Although this section will be of particular interest to Java programmers it has been written with enough detail that developers proficient in other languages and other software professionals can make sense of it. We will discuss what software is required, where to obtain it, and then look at how to code a simple application.

For this example we will work with basic command-line tools rather than with an IDE (Integrated Development Environment). This enables us to see the exact steps needed to write, compile and run the application, which you can then apply to your specific IDE.

Requirements

To run Naked Objects you must be able to compile and run Java programs; the framework works with Java version 1.1 and higher, but for this example we will be using version 1.2. In addition the framework uses the Log4J* logging framework to log its activities. To develop applications some form of development environment is required; either an IDE or the JDK* and a text editor. An icon editor can also prove useful, although we will not be using one during this tutorial as all the icons that we will use are included with the framework distribution.

*Available from Apache (jakarta.apach as part of the Jakarta projec

*Available from Sun (java.sun.com)

Getting the framework

The framework can be downloaded as a zip file from the 'downloads' page on the Naked Objects (www.nakedobjects.org) web site.

Once the zip file has been downloaded, its contents should be extracted into a convenient location so the various files that we will need later can be accessed easily. Make a note of the extracted directory name as it includes a version number and, therefore, will be different from the directory we are using. For this example we will use version 0.8.0 and extract the files into our root directory. This will give us the following paths: C:\nakedobjects0.8.0 in Windows and /nakedobjects0.8.0 in Unix.

Project preparation

Before we start you should create a working directory where you can place your files. For this example we will use a directory called project created off the root of our file systems: C:\Project in Windows and /project in Unix.

Writing an Application

To understand the principles of coding Naked Object applications we will now look at a very simple, but complete, application. The requirement is for a system that allows us to quickly organize employees into teams so they can work on specific projects. When a project is set up, distinct skills are identified, and individuals are assigned to the project based on those requirements.

This will require three classes whose objects will represent the projects, the employees and the roles (a role being a combined set of skills). These classes will need to relate to each other: a project identifying its required roles and each role identifying the individual who is to join the team.

The classes we will define for this application, therefore, are: Employee, Role and Project. Each Project object will hold a collection of Role objects and each Role will hold a reference to an Employee object.

We start by defining the classes for the three types of object. For each class we need to create a .java file and within it declare the class as an extension to the AbstractNakedObject class.

Start the three classes as follows:-

Project.java

```java
import org.nakedobjects.object.AbstractNakedObject;

public class Project extends AbstractNakedObject {
}
```

Role.java

```java
import org.nakedobjects.object.AbstractNakedObject;

public class Role extends AbstractNakedObject {
}
```

Employee.java

```java
import org.nakedobjects.object.AbstractNakedObject;

public class Employee extends AbstractNakedObject {
}
```

Now we consider what fields each object should have. First we add fields that allow the user to identify the different objects (e.g. so we can see that one object represents Dave and the other represents John). Next we add fields that describe any relationships between the objects (e.g. every role is performed by an employee so a Role object will need a field to reference an Employee object).

Employee Objects

Taking the simplest object first, an Employee need only have a name as this should be enough to distinguish it. To store this name we add a private final variable, of the type TextString, called name to the Employee class. A TextString value object stores simple textual information. The variable is marked as final as it is a composite part of the Employee and should never be replaced. As it is final we initialize it as soon as it is declared (alternatively, this could be done within the constructor). To make this field available to other objects, and to the framework so it can be displayed, we add an accessor method that will return the reference to the value object.

Employee.java

```
import org.nakedobjects.object.AbstractNakedObject;
import org.nakedobjects.object.value.TextString;

public class Employee extends AbstractNakedObject {
  private final TextString name = new TextString();

  public TextString getName() {
    return name;
  }
}
```

Role Objects

Next, we do a similar thing for the Role class as this also requires a name. In addition to this basic data we also need to hold a reference to the Employee object that this role is being performed by. To do this we declare a private field of the type that we want to keep a reference to; in this example it needs to be an instance of the Employee class. Like the value object, we also need to make this field available so we define a standard pair of accessor methods (getEmployee and setEmployee).

Inside these two methods you will see two necessary calls that keep the object current in the object store (our link to a persistence mechanism) and in any other views of the same object (on both the local and any remote clients). In the set... methods for any reference objects (as opposed to the value objects we saw earlier) the objectChanged method should be invoked. This notifies the object store that this object needs to be stored away again and also notifies any other views showing this object so they can refresh themselves.

Within get... methods, resolve should be called to ensure that the object that is being requested has been completely loaded from the object store. This is required as each object is stored independently using soft references rather than as one large object graph.

Role.java

```
import org.nakedobjects.object.AbstractNakedObject;
import org.nakedobjects.object.value.TextString;

public class Role extends AbstractNakedObject {
  private final TextString name = new TextString();
  private Employee employee;

  public TextString getName() {
    return name;
  }

  public Employee getEmployee() {
    resolve(employee);
    return employee;
  }

  public void setEmployee(Employee employee) {
    this.employee = employee;
    objectChanged();
  }
}
```

Project Objects

Project is more complex in what it contains, but is actually simpler to code. As a project involves many roles the Project object will need to store a number of Role references in some kind of collection. To create a collection field that is a composite part of the object, we make use of the InternalCollection class provided by the framework and declare it as private and final. To initialize the collection we create a new object, specifying the type of objects it is allowed to hold (Role objects) and a reference to the object that it belongs to (this project). As with the composite TextString, this field only requires a get method (in fact, as it is marked final a set method would not compile).

As for the two previous classes the Project should also have a name field and this is added as before.

Project.java

```
import java.util.Enumeration;
import org.nakedobjects.object.AbstractNakedObject;
import org.nakedobjects.object.collection.InternalCollection;
import org.nakedobjects.object.control.About;
import org.nakedobjects.object.control.ActionAbout;
import org.nakedobjects.object.value.Case;
import org.nakedobjects.object.value.TextString;

public class Project extends AbstractNakedObject {
  private final TextString name = new TextString();
  private final InternalCollection roles = new InternalCollection(Role.class, this);

  public TextString getName() {
    return name;
  }

  public InternalCollection getRoles() {
    return roles;
  }
}
```

In addition to the two fields that this object offers we will add the following method, which will be made available to the user from the object's pop-up menu. This method is simple: it creates a new Role object; sets the name field using a text value; and then adds the new role to the project's roles field. It ends by returning the new role object, which, when invoked thought the graphical interface, will result in the new object being displayed. (Admittedly, this method is somewhat superfluous, but it does demonstrate how easy it is to offer object behaviour to the user.)

```
public Role actionAddProjectLeader() {
    Role projectLeader = (Role)createInstance(Role.class);
    projectLeader.getName().setValue("Project Leader");
    roles.add(projectLeader);
    return projectLeader;
}
```

The above method, however, is only suitable when no project leader has been assigned already (as will be the case before the method is first invoked). Methods like this can be controlled by a corresponding about... method. An about... method must return an About object, which can be queried later to determine whether the menu item for the action method should be disabled or not.

The method below is matched to the actionAddProjectLeader method by its similar name. When invoked, the collection held in the roles field is iterated through. If one of its Role objects has the name 'project leader' then an About object – hardwired to disable the option – is returned. If none of the roles match, then an About object – hardwired to enable the option – is returned instead. Both of these objects are retrieved from the ActionAbout class.

```
public About aboutActionAddProjectLeader(){
    Enumeration e = getRoles().elements();
    while(e.hasMoreElements()){
        Role role = (Role)e.nextElement();
        if(role.getName().contains("project leader", Case.INSENSITIVE)){
            return ActionAbout.DISABLE;
        }
    }
    return ActionAbout.ENABLE;
}
```

Titles

Before we can compile and run the application we have to implement the title method for each class. Then when the objects are displayed they will each have a distinct title allowing the user to distinguish each object from the others. Each of the objects we have just defined has a name field which we will use as the title for each object by adding the following code to each of the three classes. To implement the title method we must return a Title object, and the easiest way to get a suitable Title object is to ask another Naked object for one. We do this here by asking the name field for its Title object.

```
public Title title() {
  return name.title();
}
```

The Title class is part of the main package and needs to be imported.

```
import org.nakedobjects.object.Title;
```

The Complete Code

The resultant three classes are as follows, and should be saved in the project directory:

Project.java

```java
import java.util.Enumeration;
import org.nakedobjects.object.collection.InternalCollection;
import org.nakedobjects.object.AbstractNakedObject;
import org.nakedobjects.object.Title;
import org.nakedobjects.object.control.About;
import org.nakedobjects.object.control.ActionAbout;
import org.nakedobjects.object.value.Case;
import org.nakedobjects.object.value.TextString;

public class Project extends AbstractNakedObject {
  private final TextString name = new TextString();
  private final InternalCollection roles = new InternalCollection(Role.class, this);

  public TextString getName() {
    return name;
  }

  public InternalCollection getRoles() {
    return roles;
  }

  public Role actionAddProjectLeader() {
    Role projectLeader = (Role)createInstance(Role.class);
    projectLeader.getName().setValue("Project Leader");
    roles.add(projectLeader);
    return projectLeader;
  }

  public About aboutActionAddProjectLeader(){
    Enumeration e = getRoles().elements();
    while(e.hasMoreElements()){
      Role role = (Role)e.nextElement();
      if(role.getName().contains("project leader", Case.INSENSITIVE)){
        return ActionAbout.DISABLE;
      }
    }
  }
```

```
        return ActionAbout.ENABLE;
    }

    public Title title() {
        return name.title();
    }
}
```

Role.java

```
import org.nakedobjects.object.AbstractNakedObject;
import org.nakedobjects.object.Title;
import org.nakedobjects.object.value.TextString;

public class Role extends AbstractNakedObject {
    private final TextString name = new TextString();
    private Employee employee;

    public TextString getName() {
        return name;
    }

    public Employee getEmployee() {
        resolve(employee);
        return employee;
    }

    public void setEmployee(Employee employee) {
        this.employee = employee;
        objectChanged();
    }

    public Title title() {
        return name.title();
    }
}
```

Employee.java

```
import org.nakedobjects.object.AbstractNakedObject;
import org.nakedobjects.object.Title;
import org.nakedobjects.object.value.TextString;
```

```
public class Employee extends AbstractNakedObject {
  private final TextString name = new TextString();

  public TextString getName() {
    return name;
  }

  public Title title() {
    return name.title();
  }
}
```

Running an application

Having defined our business objects we should set up some icons and write a simple class that will make these classes available to the user. The icons are used to represent our objects on-screen and are just images, stored in files, that the framework can display. Each image file name is based on the name of the class and the file itself must be located in a directory called images and should have an extension of .gif.

Configuration

To set up the icon images for this application, create a directory in the project directory called images. Then copy six suitable images, from the icon-library directory in the nakedobjects0.8.0 directory, into the new images directory and rename them. The filenames given, must correspond to the names of the classes with an image size appended (16 or 32 pixels).

The suggested images are HouseUnderConstruction, Hammer, and Man. These should be renamed as Project, Role, and Employee respectively. For example Hammer16.gif will become Role16.gif and Hammer32.gif will become Role32.gif.

The window below shows the new directory with the six new image files within it.

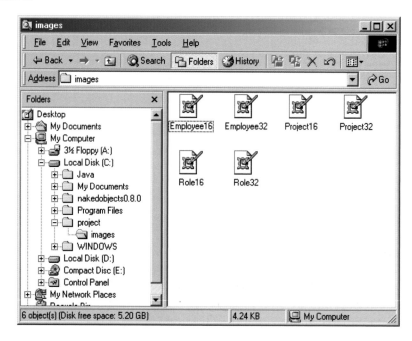

In Unix the cp command can be used to copy and rename each image file, as shown below:

```
mkdir images
cd /nakedobjects0.8.0/icon-library
cp HouseUnderConstruction16.gif /project/images/Project16.gif
cp HouseUnderConstruction32.gif /project/images/Project32.gif
cp Hammer16.gif /project/images/Role16.gif
cp Hammer32.gif /project/images/Role32.gif
cp Man16.gif /project/images/Employee16.gif
cp Man32.gif /project/images/Employee32.gif
```

The test application

To show these classes in a test environment we need to write a simple class that will load the framework, set it up, and then make the classes available to the user. Please note that this class is used only to test our application; when we make the application available to the end user it is setup differently.

The following class is used to load our three classes into the framework, which will then make them available to the user.

Run.java

```java
import org.nakedobjects.Exploration;
import org.nakedobjects.object.NakedClassList;

public class Run extends Exploration {
    public static void main(String args[]){
        new Run();
    }

    public void classSet(NakedClassList classes){
        classes.addClass(Project.class);
        classes.addClass(Role.class);
        classes.addClass(Employee.class);
    }
}
```

Compilation

To compile both the business object classes and the Run class we need to invoke the Java compiler, specifying the framework library (nakedobjects.jar) in the classpath. (Remember that the directory name used, due to the version, could be different.) To do this under Windows, start an MS-DOS window and enter the commands as shown below.

After this the project directory should contain the .java and .class files and the images directory as shown below.

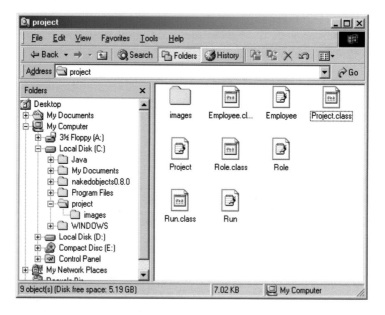

In Unix the command is very similar:

javac -classpath /nakedobjects0.8.0/lib/nakedobjects.jar:. *.java

Listing the files shows the same set as in Windows:

Employee.class
Employee.java

Project.class
Project.java
Role.class
Role.java
Run.class
Run.java
images

Starting the application

To run the application (the Run class) invoke the Java Virtual Machine (JVM) from within the project directory. The classpath must refer to the framework, the Apache Log4j library and the current directory where your class files resides. For Windows:

java -classpath
c:\nakedobjects0.8.0\lib\nakedobjects.jar;c:\nakedobjects0.8.0\lib\log4j.jar;.
Run

(This command should all be on a single line.)

And in Unix:

java -classpath
/nakedobjects0.8.0/lib/nakedobjects.jar:/nakedobjects0.8.0/lib/log4j.jar:.
Run

(This command should all be on a single line.)

A small window will appear with the three classes showing. The following screenshots show these classes in use.

1. The classes window pops up showing the three classes we specified:

2. Right-clicking the Employees class and selecting New Employee... creates a new employee object:

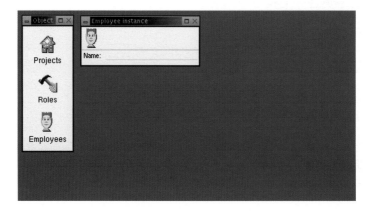

3. Entering a name into the Name field gives the object a title. The title, as defined by the title() method returns the value of the Name field:

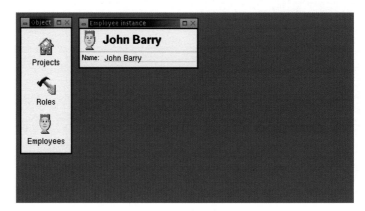

4. Similarly, right-clicking the Roles class and selecting New Role... creates a new role object:

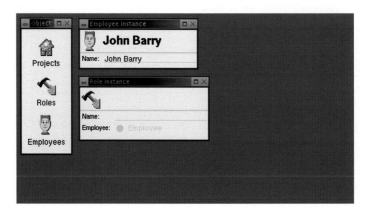

5. Entering a name into the **Name** field also gives the **Role** object a title:

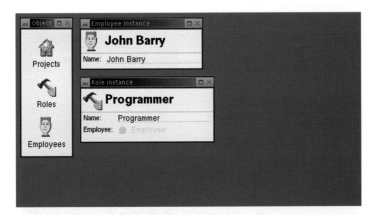

6. Now dragging the employee **John Barry** onto the **Employee** field sets up a relationship between the two objects: the role knows the employee:

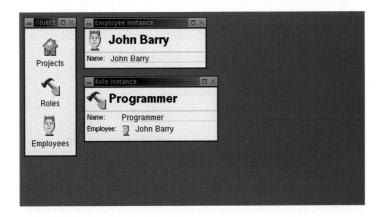

7. As discussed a project is the normal starting point and here one has been created and a name assigned:

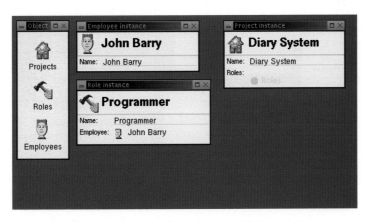

8. Dragging the Programmer role onto the Roles field adds our programmer to the project:

9. Right-clicking on the Project object shows the action we added: Add Project Leader...:

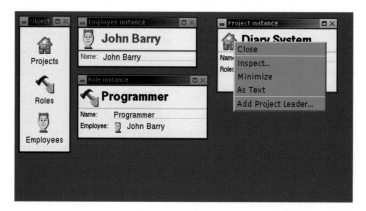

10. Selecting that option creates a new Role object, labels it 'Project Leader' and adds it to the Roles field:

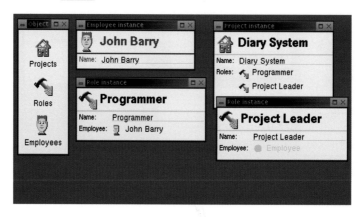

11. The same pop-up menu now shows the option as disabled as the about method found a role containing 'project leader':

12. The final state of the project once all the roles have been added:

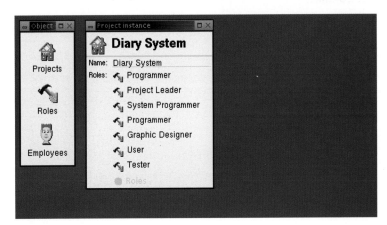

Appendix B: Code example

The following is the complete code for the Booking class as defined for the ECS application. The complete code for the application can be downloaded from our website (www.nakedobjects.org/downloads.html). This example shows how a naked object is defined within the framework and demonstrates most of the techniques covered in this book.

Booking.Java

```
package ecs.delivery;

import org.nakedobjects.object.AbstractNakedObject;
import org.nakedobjects.object.Title;
import org.nakedobjects.object.control.About;
import org.nakedobjects.object.control.ActionAbout;
import org.nakedobjects.object.control.FieldAbout;
import org.nakedobjects.object.control.ProgrammableAbout;
import org.nakedobjects.object.value.Date;
import org.nakedobjects.object.value.TextString;
import org.nakedobjects.object.value.Time;


/* Every business object is created by subclassing AbstractNakedObject
* and implementing the title method */
public class Booking extends AbstractNakedObject {
    /* The version number is required for serialization, used when
    * passing objects between the client and server. */
    private static final long serialVersionUID = 1L;

    /* The values we want the user to be able to change, via the
     * keyboard, are declared as NakedValue objects. */
    private final TextString reference;
    private final TextString status;
    private final Date date;
    private final Time time;

    /* All the associations between the booking and the other objects
     * are declared as other NakedObject objects. */
```

```
    private City city;
    private Customer customer;
    private Telephone contactTelephone;
    private Location pickUp;
    private Location dropOff;
    private PaymentMethod paymentMethod;

    /* The constructor is commonly used to set up the object, specifically
     * so all the value field objects are immediately available. */
    public Booking() {
        /* Each value object is created via its default constructor. */
        reference = new TextString();
        /* The reference field is made read-only by assigning this FieldAbout. */
        reference.setAbout(FieldAbout.READ_ONLY);
        status = new TextString();
        status.setAbout(FieldAbout.READ_ONLY);
        date = new Date();
        time = new Time();
    }

    /* An aboutAction... methods control the action... method that matches it's
     * name. */
    public About aboutActionCheckAvailability() {
        /* A ProgrammableAbout can be used to check a number of conditions. */
        ProgrammableAbout c = new ProgrammableAbout();

        /* Checks conditions and adjusts the About accordingly: if the
         * argument is false then the About is altered so that a call
         * to canUse returns a Veto. */
        c.makeAvailableOnCondition(!getStatus().isSameAs("Available"));
        c.makeAvailableOnCondition(!getDate().isEmpty());

        return c;
    }

    public About aboutActionConfirm() {
        ProgrammableAbout c = new ProgrammableAbout();

        /* This version of the makeAvailableOnCondition method also adds a
         * message to the Veto. */
        c.makeAvailableOnCondition(getStatus().isSameAs("Available"),
                        "Status must be 'Available'");
```

```
        return c;
    }

    public About aboutActionCopyBooking() {
        int sets = 0;

        sets += ((getCustomer() != null) ? 1 : 0);
        sets += ((getPickUp() != null) ? 1 : 0);
        sets += ((getDropOff() != null) ? 1 : 0);
        sets += ((getPaymentMethod() != null) ? 1 : 0);
        sets += ((getContactTelephone() != null) ? 1 : 0);

        /* An About can be conditionally created: if the argument is true then
         * the returned About enables the action; if false, it disables it. */
        return ActionAbout.enable(sets > = 3);
    }

    public About aboutActionReturnBooking() {
        ProgrammableAbout c = new ProgrammableAbout();

        /* A description can be added to the About to tell the user what
         * the action will do. */
        c.setDescription(
                "Creates a new Booking based on the current booking.  The new
booking has the pick up and drop off locations reversed.");
        c.makeAvailableOnCondition(getStatus().isSameAs("Confirmed"),
                                "Can only create a return based on a confirmed
booking");

        /* If the About is still allowing the action then the action's
         * name will be changed. */
        c.changeNameIfAvailable("Return booking to " + getPickUp());

        return c;
    }

    public About aboutPickUp(Location newPickup) {
        ProgrammableAbout c = new ProgrammableAbout();

        c.setDescription("The location to pick up the customer from.");

        if ((newPickup != null) && (getCity() != null)) {
            if (newPickup.equals(getDropOff())) {
                c.makeUnavailable(
```

245

```
                              "Pick up must differ from the drop off location");
                } else {
                    boolean sameCity = getCity().equals(newPickup.getCity());

                    c.makeAvailableOnCondition(sameCity,
                                        "Location must be in " +
                                        getCity().title());
                }
            }

            return c;
}

/* Zero-parametered action methods are made available to the user via
 * the object's pop up menu. */
public void actionCheckAvailability() {
    /* The value field is accessed and its value changed. */
    getStatus().setValue("Available");
    objectChanged();
}

public void actionConfirm() {
    getStatus().setValue("Confirmed");

    /* The locations used are added to the customer's Locations field.
     * Note that the accessor methods are used to ensure that the objects
     * are loaded first. */
    getCustomer().associateLocations(getPickUp());
    getCustomer().associateLocations(getDropOff());

    if (getCustomer().getPreferredPaymentMethod() == null) {
        getCustomer().setPreferredPaymentMethod(getPaymentMethod());
    }
}

public Booking actionCopyBooking() {
    /* A new instance is created by calling the createInstance method. This
     * ensures that the created method is always called and that the object
     * is made persistent. */
    Booking copiedBooking = (Booking) createInstance(Booking.class);

    copiedBooking.associateCustomer(getCustomer());
    copiedBooking.setPickUp(getPickUp());
    copiedBooking.setDropOff(getDropOff());
```

```
    copiedBooking.setPaymentMethod(getPaymentMethod());
    copiedBooking.setContactTelephone(getContactTelephone());

    /* By returning the object we ensure that the user gets it: it is
     * displayed to the user in a new window. */
    return copiedBooking;
}

/* One-parametered action methods are also available to the user and are
 * invoked via drag and drop.
 *
 * When an action method is marked as static then it works for the
 * class rather than the object.  To invoke this method the user must
 * drop a customer onto the Booking class icon. */
public static Booking actionNewBooking(Customer customer) {
    Booking newBooking = (Booking) createInstance(Booking.class);

    newBooking.setCustomer(customer);
    newBooking.setPaymentMethod(customer.getPreferredPaymentMethod());

    return newBooking;
}
```

```
/* The recommended ordering for the action methods can be specified
 * with the actionOrder method.   This will affect the order of the
 * menu items for this object. */
public static String actionOrder() {
    return "Check Availability, Confirm, Copy Booking, Return Booking";
}

public Booking actionReturnBooking() {
    Booking returnBooking = (Booking) createInstance(Booking.class);

    returnBooking.associateCustomer(getCustomer());
    returnBooking.setPickUp(getDropOff());
    returnBooking.setDropOff(getPickUp());
    returnBooking.setPaymentMethod(getPaymentMethod());
    returnBooking.setContactTelephone(getContactTelephone());

    return returnBooking;
}

/* The associate method overrides the get/set and is called by the
 * framework instead of the ordinary accessor methods.  They are used
```

```
* to set up complex or bidirectional associations.  This method delegates,
* to the other class, the work to set up a bidirectional link. */
public void associateCustomer(Customer customer) {
    customer.associateBookings(this);
}

public void associateDropOff(Location newDropOff) {
    setDropOff(newDropOff);
    setCity(newDropOff.getCity());
}

public void associatePickUp(Location newPickUp) {
    setPickUp(newPickUp);
    setCity(newPickUp.getCity());
}

private long createBookingRef() {
    try {
        /* The object store provides the ability to create and maintain
        * numbered sequences, which are unique. */
        return getObjectStore().serialNumber("booking ref");
    } catch (org.nakedobjects.object.ObjectStoreException e) {
        return 0;
    }
}

/* The created method is called when the logical object is created,
* i.e. it is not called when an object is recreated from its persisted
* data. */
public void created() {
    status.setValue("New Booking");
    reference.setValue("#" + createBookingRef());
}

/* The dissociate method mirrors the associate method and is called
* when the user tries to remove a reference. */
public void dissociateCustomer(Customer customer) {
    customer.dissociateBookings(this);
}

/* The recommended order for the fields to be presented to the user
* can be specified by the fieldOrder method. */
public static String fieldOrder() {
```

```java
        return "reference, status, customer, date, time, pick up, drop off, payment
method";
    }

    /* Each association within an object requires a get and a set method.
     * The get method simply returns the associated object's reference after
     * it has ensured that the object has been loaded into memory. */
    public City getCity() {
        resolve(city);

        return city;
    }

    public Telephone getContactTelephone() {
        resolve(contactTelephone);

        return contactTelephone;
    }

    public Customer getCustomer() {
        resolve(customer);

        return customer;
    }

    /* Each value field only has a get method, which returns the value's
     * reference.  No set is required as the value objects must be a integral
     * part of the naked object. */
    public final Date getDate() {
        return date;
    }

    public Location getDropOff() {
        resolve(dropOff);

        return dropOff;
    }

    public PaymentMethod getPaymentMethod() {
        resolve(paymentMethod);

        return paymentMethod;
    }
```

```
public Location getPickUp() {
    resolve(pickUp);

    return pickUp;
}

public final TextString getReference() {
    return reference;
}

public final TextString getStatus() {
    return status;
}

public final Time getTime() {
    return time;
}

/* The association has a set method so a reference can be passed to
 * the object to set up the association.  As the object has now changed
 * it also must be notified. */
public void setCity(City newCity) {
    city = newCity;
    objectChanged();
}

public void setContactTelephone(Telephone newContactTelephone) {
    contactTelephone = newContactTelephone;
    objectChanged();
}

public void setCustomer(Customer newCustomer) {
    customer = newCustomer;
    objectChanged();
}

public void setDropOff(Location newDropOff) {
    dropOff = newDropOff;
    objectChanged();
}
```

```
public void setPaymentMethod(PaymentMethod newPaymentMethod) {
    paymentMethod = newPaymentMethod;
    objectChanged();
}

public void setPickUp(Location newPickUp) {
    pickUp = newPickUp;
    objectChanged();
}

/* The title method generates a title string for the object that will
 * be used when the object is displayed.  This title should identify the
 * object to the user. */
public Title title() {
    /* A Title object is normally retrieved from one of the object's
     * field (all Naked objects can return a Title).  All of the title's
     * methods return the same Title object. */
    return reference.title().append(status);
}
}
```

Appendix C: Cliché code

Developing software by cutting and pasting code from other programs incurs some risk, but when you are learning about a system it is a pragmatic, and often effective, approach. We provide here some examples of 'cliché code' often used in in Naked Objects programs.

Exploration class

To explore a set of classes that you have developed, create an extension of Exploration and add your classes to the ClassSet in the classSet method.

```java
import org.nakedobjects.Exploration;
import org.nakedobjects.object.NakedClassList;

public class MyExploration extends Exploration  {
    public void classSet(NakedClassList classes)  {
        /* Add to the list all classes that are to made available to
         * to the user in the classes window*/
        classes.addClass(NakedObjectClass1.class);
        classes.addClass(NakedObjectClass2.class);
        classes.addClass(NakedObjectClass3.class);
         :
    }

    public void initObjects()  {
        NakedObjectClass newObject;
        /* create instances via the class and initialize them */
        newObject = (NakedObjectClass) createInstance(NakedObjectClass.class);
        newObject.getValueObject().setValue(value);
        newObject.setAssociation(object);
    }

    public static void main(String[] args)  {
        new MyExploration();
    }
```

Naked Object

The following template shows the declaration of a business object. Only the zero-parameter constructor and the title method is required.

```
import org.nakedobject.object.NakedObject;
import org.nakedobject.object.Title;
import org.nakedobject.object.value.ValueType;
:
:
public class ClassName extends AbstractNakedObject {

    /* Makes the class uninstantiable: no new objects can be created */
    public static About aboutClassName()  {
        return ClassAbout.UNINSTANTIABLE;
    }

    /* Gives the class a name */
     public static String singularName()  {
        return "Singular Name";
    }

    /* Gives the class a plural name */
    public static String pluralName()  {
        return "Plural Name";
    }

    public Object()  {
        /* Set a value's about so the value is uneditable */
        value.setAbout(FieldAbout.READ_ONLY);
    }

    /* This method is only called when the logical object is created.
     * The constructor will be called every time the object is
     * recreated (by the persistence mechanism). */
    public void created() {}

    /* Titles can be generated directly from both value and one-to-one
     * association objects, but not from one-to-many associations.  See
     * below for details of the Title class. */
    public Title title()  {
        return value/object.title();
    }
```

```java
/* Makes the object read-only */
public About about() {
    return ObjectAbout.READ_ONLY;
}

/* Value fields: TextString, Date, Time, DateTime, WholeNumber,
 * FloatingPointNumber, Percentage, Money, Option, URLString and Label.
 * Should be marked as final and not have a set... method. */
private final ValueType value = new ValueType();

public ValueType getVariable() {
    return value;
}

/* Association fields: any other class based on AbstractNakedObject.*/
private ClassName object;

public ClassName getObject() {
    resolve(object);
    return object;
}

public void setObject(ClassName object) {
    this.object = object;
    objectChanged();
}

/* The associate... and dissociate... method can override
 * the set... method and, hence, used to set up associations. */
public void associateObject(ClassName object) {
    setObject(object);
}

public void dissociateObject(ClassName object) {
    setObject(null);
}

/* The About object returned by this method field determines
 * if the field can be changed. */
public About aboutObject(ClassName object) {
    return FieldAbout.READ_ONLY;
}
```

```
/* One-to-many association.  The collection object must be instantiated
 * with the element type and a reference to its parent, the owner.
 * This should be marked as final and only a set... method provided. */
private final InternalCollection objects = new InternalCollection(ClassName.class,
this);

    public InternalCollection getObjects() {
        return objects;
    }

    /* The associate... and dissociate... method
     * can override the get... method and, hence, are used
     * to set up associations.  The collection's add and
     * remove methods are used to change the collection. */
    public void associateObjects((Object object) {
        objects.add(object);
    }

    public void dissociateObjects((Object object) {
        objects.remove(null);
    }

    /* The About object returned by this method determines if
     * objects can be added and removed from this field. */
    public About aboutObjects() {
     return FieldAbout.READ_ONLY;
    }

    /* action methods */

    /* Zero-parameter methods are show in the object's pop-up menu.  If the
     * method returns an object then this will be shown.*/
    public void/Object actionOptionName() {
        :
        return object;
    }

    /* The about method determines whether the option will disabled or not. */
    public About aboutActionOptionName() {
        return ActionAbout.enable();
    }

    /* One-parameter methods are made available through drag and drop.
     * If the method returns an object then this will be shown. */
```

```
public void/Object actionOptionName(Object object)  {
    :
    return object;
}

/* The about method determines whether the option will disabled or not. */
public About aboutActionOptionName(Object object)(Object object)  {
    return ActionAbout.enable();
}
}
```

Title

There are three basic ways to create Title objects.

value.title()
association.title()
new Title("**text**")

Titles can be appended to, which adds necessary spacing, or have details concatenated.

value.title().append("**text**");
association.title().append(**value**)
new Title("**text**").append(**association**)

value.title().concat("**text**");
association.title().concat(**value**)
new Title("**text**").concat(**association**)

Appendix D: Icon library

These icons are included with the current distribution of the Naked Objects framework, in both small (16 × 16 pixel) and large (32 × 32) format. They are suitable for use during the exploration phase of a project. For a delivered system we recommend that you use a purpose-designed set that is visually consistent.

 Aircraft32.gif

 Car32.gif

 Factory32.gif

 Audiotape32.gif

 Cheque32.gif

 Fax32.gif

 Bargraph.gif

 ChessPiece32.gif

 Folder32.gif

 Basket32.gif

 City32.gif

 Globe32.gif

 Bed32.gif

 Coins32.gif

 Hammer32.gif

 CallCentreAgent32.eps

 CreditCard32.gif

 Handshake32.gif

 Can32.gif

 Crosshairs32.gif

 HouseUnderConstruction32.gif

KnifeFork32.gif

 Network32.gif

 Scales32.gif

 Letter32.gif

 Pen32.gif

 Smiley32.gif

 LightningFlash32.gif

 Phone32.gif

 SpeechBubble32.gif

 Man32.gif

 PiggyBank32.gif

 SteeringWheel32.gif

 Map32.gif

 Question Mark32.gif

 Taxi32.gif

 MissedTarget32.gif

 RadialPlot32.gif

 Truck32.gif

 Missile32.gif

 RoundTable32.gif

 Woman32.gif

 MobilePhone32.gif

Bibliography

Abbott, R. J. (1983). 'Program design by informal English descriptions.' *Communications of the ACM* **26(11)**: 882–894.

Alexander, C., S. Ishikawa, et al. (1977). *A Pattern Language*. New York, Oxford University Press.

Beck, K. (1999). *EXtreme Programming EXplained.*, Addison-Wesley.

Beck, K. and W. Cunningham (1989). *A Laboratory for Teaching Object-Oriented Thinking* OOPLSA '89, Association of Computing Machinery.

Booch, G. (1986). 'Object-Oriented Development.' *IEEE Transactions on Software Engineering* **12(2)**: 211–221.

Booch, G. (1994). *Object-Oriented Analysis and Design: with Applications*. Addison-Wesley.

Brown, J. S. and P. Duguid (2000). *The Social Life of Information*. Boston, MA, Harvard Business School Press.

Bruner, J. (1966). *Toward a Theory of Instruction*. Cambridge, MA, Belknap Press/Harvard University Press.

Clement, A. (1996). 'Computing at work: Empowering Action by Low-Level Users.' in *Computerization and Controversy – Value Conflicts and Social Choices*. R. Kling Ed. San Diego, CA, Academic Press.

Coad, P. and E. Lefebvre (1999). *Modeling in Color*. Software Development. March 1999.

Collins, D. (1995). *Designing Object-oriented User interfaces*. Redwood City, CA, Benjamin/Cummings.

Dahl, O. J. and K. Nygaard (1966). 'Simula – an Algol-based simulation language.' *CACM* **(9)**: 671–678.

Deligiannis, I., M. Shepperd, *et al.* (2002). *A Controlled Experiment Investigation of an Object-Oriented Design Heuristic for Maintainability.* Bournemouth University, ESERG,.

Dietel, H. and D. P (1999). *Java: How to Program.* Third Edition, Prentice Hall.

Eeles, P. and O. Sims (1998). *Building Business Objects.* New York, John Wiley.

Finsterwalder, M. (2001). *Automating Acceptance Tests for GUI Applications.* XP2001, Cagliari.

Firesmith, D. (1996). 'Use Cases: The Pros and Cons.' in *Wisdom of the Gurus.* R. Wiener. New York, SIGS books.

Fowler, M. (2000). *Refactoring.* Addison-Wesley.

Gamma, E., R. Helm, *et al.* (1995). *Design Patterns – Elements of Reusable Object Oriented Software.* Reading, MA, Addison-Wesley.

Garson, B. (1988). *The Electronic Sweatshop – How Computers are Transforming the Office of the Future into the Factory of the Past.* New York, Simon and Schuster.

Groder, C. (1999). 'Building Maintainable GUI Tests.' in *Software Test Automation.* M. Fewster and D. Graham, Eds., ACM Press / Addison-Wesley.

Hammer, M. and J. Champy (1993). *Reengineering the Corporation: A Manifesto for Business Revolution.* Harper Collins.

Herzum, P. and O. Sims (2000). *Business Component Factory.* Wiley.

Hiltzik, M. (1999). *Dealers of Lightning – Xerox PARC and the Dawn of the Computer Age.* New York, HarperCollins.

Holub, A. (1999). 'Building User Interfaces for Object-Oriented Systems.' *Java World.* July 1999.

Hunt, A. and D. Thomas (2000). *The Pragmatic Programmer.* Addison-Wesley.

Hutchins, E., J. Hollan, *et al.* (1986). 'Direct Manipulation Interfaces.' in *User Centered System Design: New Perspectives on Human-Computer Interaction.* D. Norman and S. Draper, Eds. Hillsdale, NJ, Lawrence Erlbaum.

IBM (1991). *CUA-91 Manual: Common User Access-Advanced Interface Design Reference*. IBM.

Ingalls, D., T. Kaehler, *et al.* (1997). *Back to the Future: The story of Squeak.* OOPSLA'97, Association of Computing Machinery.

Jacobson, I., M. Christersson, *et al.* (1992). *Object-oriented Software Engineering: A Use Case Driven Approach.* Reading, MA, Addison-Wesley.

Jacobson, I., M. Ericsson, *et al.* (1995). *The Object Advantage – Business Process Reengineering with Object Technology.* Reading, MA, Addison-Wesley.

Jacobson, I., J. Rumbaugh, *et al.* (1999). *The Unified Software Development Process.* Addison-Wesley.

Kaner, C. (1997). 'Pitfalls and Strategies in Automated Testing.' *IEEE Computer* **30(4)**: 114–116.

Kanigel, R. (1997). *The One Best Way – Frederick Winslow Taylor and the Enigma of Efficiency.* London, Little, Brown and company.

Kay, A. (1990). 'User Interface: A Personal View.' in *The Art of Human-Computer Interface Design.* B. Laurel. Reading, MA, Addison-Wesley: 191–207.

Kay, A. (1996). 'The early history of SmallTalk.' in *History of Programming Languages.* T. Bergin and R. Gibson. Reading, MA, Addison-Wesley / ACM Press: 511–589.

Krasner, G. and S. Pope (1988). 'A cookbook for using the Model-View-Controller user interface paradigm in Smalltalk-80.' *Journal of Object Oriented Programming* **1(3)**: 26–49.

Laurel, B. (1991). *Computers as Theatre.* Reading, MA, Addison-Wesley.

Levy, S. (1994). *Insanely Great.* New York, Penguin Books.

Maloney, J. and R. Smith (1995). *Directness and Liveness in the Morphic User Interface Construction Environment.* UIST, Pittsburgh, ACM.

Meyer, B. (1988). *Object-oriented Software Construction.* Prentice-Hall.

Pawson, R., J.-L. Bravard, *et al.* (1995). 'The Case for Expressive Systems.' *Sloan Management Review* **Winter 1995**: 41–48.

Porter, M. (1985). *Competitive Advantage: Creating an Sustaining Superior Performance*. New York, Free Press.

Raskin, J. (2000). *The Humane Interface*. Reading, MA, Addison-Wesley / ACM Press.

Riel, A. (1996). *Object-Oriented Design Heuristics*. Addison-Wesley.

Roberts, D., D. Berry, *et al.* (1998). *Designing for the User with OVID*. IndianApolis, Macmillan Technical Publishing / IBM.

Rosson, M. B. and E. Gold (1989). *Problem-Solution Mapping in Object-Oriented Design*. OOPSLA '89, New York, ACM.

Rurnbaugh, J., M. Blaha, *et al.* (1991). *Object-Oriented Modeling and Design*. Englewood Cliffs, NJ, Prentice-Hall.

Rumbaugh, J., I. Jacobson, *et al.* (1999). *The Unified Modeling Language Reference Guide*. Reading, MA, Addison Wesley

Sharble, R. and S. Cohen (1993). 'The object-oriented brewery: a comparison of two object-oriented development methods.' *SIGSOFT Software Engineering Notes* **18(2)**.

Sharp, A. (1997). *Smalltalk By Example*. McGraw-Hill.

Shlaer, S. and S. J. Mellor (1988). *Object-Oriented Systems Analysis – Modelling the World in Data*. Yourdon Press.

Shneiderman, B. (1982). 'The Future of Interactive Systems, and the Emergence of Direct Manipulation.' *Behaviour and Information Technology* **1**: 237–256.

Shneiderman, B., Ed. (1998). *Designing the User Interface*. Reading, MA, Addison-Wesley.

Sims, O. (1994). *Business Objects: Ease of Programming for Client-Server*. McGraw-Hill.

Smith, R., J. Maloney, et al. (1995). *The Self-4.0 User Interface: Manifesting a System-wide Vision of Concreteness, Uniformity, and Flexibility.* OOPSLA '95, Association of Computing Machinery.

Stabell, C. and O, Fjeldstad (1998). 'Configuring Value for Competitive Advantage: On Chains, Shops and Networks.' *Strategic Management Journal* **19**: 413–437.

Sutherland, I. (1963). *Sketchpad: A Man-Machine Graphical Communication System.* Spring Joint Computer Conference.

Taylor, F. (1911). *The Principles of Scientific Management.* New York, W.W. Norton and Co.

Wirfs-Brock, R. 'Characterizing Your Objects.' *SmallTalk Report* **2(5)**.

Wirfs-Brock, R. 'How Designs Differ.' *Report on Object Analysis and Design* **1(4)**.

Wirfs-Brock, R. and B. Wilkerson (1989). *Object-oriented Design: A Responsibility-Driven Approach.* OOPSLA, New Orleans.

Index